What Earl Scruggs Heard

ALSO BY BOB CARLIN
AND FROM MCFARLAND

*The Birth of the Banjo: Joel Walker Sweeney
and Early Minstrelsy* (2007)

String Bands in the North Carolina Piedmont (2004)

What Earl Scruggs Heard

String Music Along the North Carolina–South Carolina Border

BOB CARLIN

McFarland & Company, Inc., Publishers
Jefferson, North Carolina

LIBRARY OF CONGRESS CATALOGUING-IN-PUBLICATION DATA

Names: Carlin, Bob, author.
Title: What Earl Scruggs heard : string music along the North Carolina–South Carolina border / Bob Carlin.
Description: Jefferson, North Carolina : McFarland & Company, Inc., Publishers, 2022. | Includes bibliographical references and index.
Identifiers: LCCN 2022008725 | ISBN 9781476686677 (paperback : acid free paper) ∞
ISBN 9781476644240 (ebook)
Subjects: LCSH: Old-time music—North Carolina—History and criticism. | Old-time music—South Carolina—History and criticism. | String band music—North Carolina—History and criticism. | String band music—South Carolina—History and criticism. | Country musicians—North Carolina. | Country musicians—South Carolina. | Fiddlers—North Carolina. | Fiddlers—South Carolina. | Scruggs, Earl. | BISAC: MUSIC / Genres & Styles / Country & Bluegrass
Classification: LCC ML3553.7.C3 C37 2022 | DDC 781.62/00975—dc23/eng/20220304
LC record available at https://lccn.loc.gov/2022008725

BRITISH LIBRARY CATALOGUING DATA ARE AVAILABLE

**ISBN (print) 978-1-4766-8667-7
ISBN (ebook) 978-1-4766-4424-0**

© 2022 Bob Carlin. All rights reserved

No part of this book may be reproduced or transmitted in any form or by any means, electronic or mechanical, including photocopying or recording, or by any information storage and retrieval system, without permission in writing from the publisher.

Front cover: Smith Hammett band, *front, left to right*: Will Grady, Jim Grady and Coley Fisher; *standing, back*: Bernard "Big Mac" McDaniel, Dewey McDaniel, Rex Brooks and Smith Hammett (courtesy Eula Bridges); *background photograph* Shutterstock/Marin de Espinosa

Printed in the United States of America

*McFarland & Company, Inc., Publishers
Box 611, Jefferson, North Carolina 28640
www.mcfarlandpub.com*

Acknowledgments

Thanks to McFarland for taking on a third book based on my research and presenting it in the best possible light. Special thanks to my wife, Rachel Smith, for love and support. And, as always, thanks to my younger (and better looking!) brother, Richard, who offered helpful suggestions in the shaping of the manuscript.

Table of Contents

Acknowledgments	v
Preface: Why Earl?	1
One. Pre-History "B.E." (Before Earl)	5
Two. The Greatest Musical Tournament in Western North Carolina	18
Three. John W. Ross, Charlie Parker and Mack Woolbright Part One	33
Four. Mack Woolbright: Parts Two and Three	53
Five. What Earl Scruggs Heard	65
Six. Crazy Crystals and Aristocratic Pigs: The Fisher Hendley Story	75
Seven. WBT-Charlotte	87
Eight. Crazy Water and Crazy Bands	105
Nine. Aristocratically Yours, Fisher Hendley	129
Conclusion: Post-History "A.E." (After Earl)	162
Discography	165
Chapter Notes	171
Bibliography	195
Index	201

Preface: Why Earl?

"Gastonia to Boiling Springs,
From Flint Hill back to Charlotte,
Still trying to find the place of birth,
Still talking about who played it first,
Of the boys from North Carolina."—John Hartford[1]

On March 28, 2012, banjoist Earl Scruggs passed away at the age of eighty-eight. His illustrious career included stints with Bill Monroe's

Flatt & Scruggs (pictured minus Lester Flatt). Left to right: Curly Seckler/mandolin, Paul Warren/fiddle, Uncle Josh Graves/resophonic guitar and Earl Scruggs/banjo, onstage in Charlotte, North Carolina, circa 1960, (author's collection).

Preface: Why Earl?

legendary group that codified bluegrass music as well as the band Scruggs co-led with Lester Flatt, which was responsible for introducing bluegrass to the wider public. In their role as musical disseminators, Flatt & Scruggs provided soundtracks for *The Beverly Hillbillies* television program and the film *Bonnie and Clyde* as well as performed for non-country audiences throughout the United States. After separating from Lester Flatt, the Earl Scruggs Revue, featuring the three Scruggs offspring, further her expanded Earl's musical reach into rock, pop and beyond. During his lifetime, Earl Scruggs was honored with, among other numerous prizes and recognitions, a Lifetime Achievement Award from the Grammy organization and a National Medal of the Arts as well as a star in the Hollywood Walk of Fame.[2]

For the entirety of his sixty-seven-year career as a professional musician, Scruggs, aided and abetted by his manager, booking agent, press proxy and spouse, Louise, spun a creation myth around his playing. According to Earl and Louise, Scruggs was the sole proprietor and perpetuator of a three-finger up-picking banjo style that he and only he had invented out of whole cloth. Like Athena emerging fully formed from the skull of Zeus, so had the banjo playing of Earl Scruggs sprung from Earl's mind and fingers. Other banjoists had played in the area around the Scruggs home in the Flint Hill community of Cleveland County, North Carolina. But only Earl had made the quantum leap to this new method that, uniquely for bluegrass music, came to bear his name.

To anyone attempting to make a living in the music business, this single-minded promotion of Scruggs as the progenitor of a style should come as no surprise. When Earl began in country music, even the most successful performers made only a nominal income. So, in his attempts at a successful career, it was not unusual for Scruggs to assert himself as the originator of his approach. After all, Ralph Rinzler, during the short period he had "managed" the unmanageable Bill Monroe, as a marketing tool labeled the mandolinist, truthfully or not, the "Father" of bluegrass music. Similar promotional campaigns were regularly utilized in any business, let alone music, to sell products and personalities.

My work is in response to the public story of Earl Scruggs. I have elected to utilize the information that is available in an attempt to tell a different facet of the Earl Scruggs account. What this narrative endeavors to accomplish is, using deep research, to reconstruct the musical world that surrounded the settlement where banjoist Scruggs spent his formative years. I hope to show that, rather than emerge with a style

Preface: Why Earl?

totally apart from any influences, Earl Scruggs' playing was formed by a rich musical milieu.

There were many unknown and semi-famous regional players that laid the groundwork for the young musician, bridging and bringing forward string band styles of the past through their own performances. Some were just average musicians, creating music in their youth to entertain family and friends as well as pass the time between their labors. Others aspired, as did Scruggs, to utilize string music as an avenue out of the drudgery of farm, mill and factory labor.

This book, in detailing my "journey into the past," includes those players that directly launched Earl Scruggs on his lifelong career with the banjo. Beginning with the scantest of details provided in interviews by Earl and another well-known area banjoist, Dewitt "Snuffy" Jenkins, I've used the Internet, local newspapers and libraries to help locate family members of those legendary musicians to whom Earl gave the credit of starting him on the instrument.

More than ninety years have passed since the events of Scruggs' youth, and since that time, many trails have grown cold. The informants that fueled my research, some of them participants in the events chronicled within these pages, or friends and relatives of the musicians profiled here, have all passed on. Therefore, my research over the last three or four years has shifted away from living persons to the paper trail of documents, newspapers and other artifacts in online archives that these players have left behind.

I've spent the last thirty-plus years researching string band music within North and South Carolina, with a specific focus on this project for about half of that time. Many individuals and institutions were invaluable in providing information and guidance for this latest journey. These include (in no particular order) Tommy Forney, Larry Hammett, Genealogical Society of Old Tryon County, Nell Ramsey Brooks, Johnny L. Williams, James Bollman, Ronald Hammett, Jesse Hammett, Tommy Thirston Hammett family, Tommy Ramsey, Bob McKee, Jenna Withrow, Danielle Withrow, Patricia Wilkie Camp, Jannette Deaton, Lois Smith, Cary Melton, Judy Latham, Ellen Brooks, Cherokee County Public Library, Hellen Permar Hendley, Gail Gillespie, Jim Mills, Alvin Wall, George Stahlberg, Matt Neiburger, Katherine Berger, Elmo Hatley, Rachel Wiles, Dr. William H. Boyce, Pat Ahrens-Striblin, Aileen Morris, Bill Furr, Mildred Wheless, Gibson and Buck Wheless, Jack Harrington, Blake Hildreth, Jr., Kirk Sutphin, Marc Howell, Nancy Ezell Suggs, Evangeline Sparks Small, Anson County Library, Stanly County

Preface: Why Earl?

Library, Anson County Historical Society, Duke University Archives, UNC–Chapel Hill Libraries, Mecklenburg Public Library, Rowan County Library, Greenville (South Carolina) Public Library, Katie Harford-Hogue, Steve Terrill and Sarah Bryan. However, the ultimate responsibility for the contents of the pages that follow—the interpretation of the information and the conclusions drawn—is mine.

Readers will notice the lack of mentions for African American musicians within these pages. Because the white press ignored African American news except to repeat stereotypical tales, and Black musicians were denied the outlets for telling their own stories, newspaper searches turned up little of consequence. And the scant information that has emerged is fleeting and lacking in detail. Although there exist some tantalizing references to Black fiddlers, banjoists and "string bands," they are missing the exact instrumentation and members of those groups are few and far between. Even the major works on African American music and musicians of North and South Carolina, such as Bruce Bastin's two book-length studies of Piedmont blues,[3] contain only a few sentences on non-blues string band music. And the book-length study on black fiddler George "Trotting Sally" Mullins (props to the author for his attempt), because of the paucity of details about Mullins' life, adds little to our knowledge of the African American musical experience.[4]

I have also attempted to give voice to the female string musicians that participated in area music-making. As commented in the following pages, a few show up in period newspaper coverage and photographs. Those small numbers may reflect a cultural bias against the embracing of women players by fiddling contests and other community gatherings and/or against including them in the subsequent reportage. Regardless, I have related what rare players that I've found.

Therefore, what follows is my best attempt at giving the biographies of Earl's mentors and the musical atmosphere in which they developed their own "three-finger picking" style that so enchanted a young Earl Scruggs. I hope you find enjoyment and enlightenment within these stories.

One

Pre-History "B.E." (Before Earl)

Hicks' Farewell

Cleveland, Rutherford and Gaston counties in southwestern North Carolina and Union and Cherokee counties in northwestern South Carolina are areas typical of the rural upland south. At the turn of the 19th into the 20th century, land covered with cotton was punctuated with towns that arose around the mills turning that cotton into yarn and cloth. The cotton mills recruited workers off area farms, many of whom could handle a fiddle, banjo or guitar. With so many musicians in an abnormally close proximity to each other, it was inevitable that some would form string bands.

The original 19th-century African American banjo method was to hit down on the strings in a manner labeled alternately down-picking, frailing or (later) clawhammer. In the period when Earl Scruggs learned to play, area banjoists had left this style behind, instead utilizing a right-hand system of up-picking, drawing elements from African music and a late 19th- and early 20th-century approach known as "classic" banjo.

Even before the birth of Earl Scruggs, traditional string music was widespread in the upstate of South Carolina and just over the border in North Carolina. Fiddles (and later, banjos, guitars, mandolins and the like) were used to accompany singing and provide the rhythm for square, line and step dancing. The repertoire of songs, rooted in hymn books and ballads brought from the old world, was expanded with the addition of popular songs of the day. Dance tunes from Scotland, Ireland and England were transported to the new world as well. The blackface minstrel ditties of the mid–19th century, sentimental lyrics from after the Civil War and the novelty ragtime, blues and jazz of the early 20th century all found their place in the Southern repertoire.

What Earl Scruggs Heard

Zeno Hicks house (Bill Fitzpatrick, Wikipedia).

Outside of Chesnee, South Carolina, in rural northern Cherokee County, sits the homestead of Dr. Zeno Hicks. Near the North Carolina state line, the original section of the two-story frame farmhouse was constructed in 1886. The home was eventually expanded into today's structure, which is included in the National Register of Historic Places.[1] Four generations of the musical Hicks family were to make a major impression on area music throughout the 19th and into the first part of the 20th centuries.

The Hicks relations trace their musical talents back to the Rev. Berryman Theodore Hicks. Descendants seem at odds about the birthplace of the Reverend Hicks, probably because the family maintained outposts in both Rutherford County, North Carolina, and what became Cherokee County, South Carolina, then part of Spartanburg County.[2]

It appears from the best evidence that Berryman Hicks was born in Rutherford County on July 1, 1778, to William R. and Mary Edith Cates Hicks.[3] In 1799, Hicks married Elizabeth Durham (January 30, 1779– April 24, 1846),[4] settling in 1807 with what eventually became his large family on a land grant of forty-four acres abutting the Sandy River. By March of 1833, Berryman Hicks was farming across the state line near Buck Creek in Spartanburg County, South Carolina. He was appointed postmaster, a profession followed by at least three generations of his descendants. Berryman's commanding presence was aided by his size,

One. Pre-History "B.E." (Before Earl)

as Hicks weighed in at over three hundred pounds.[5] Berryman Hicks passed away at Little Buck Creek June 11, 1839.[6]

Sometime around 1800, Hicks joined the State Line Baptist Church, eventually preaching in that house of worship.[7] Along with Drury Dobbins, Berryman Hicks went on to originate many of the Baptist churches in that part of North and South Carolina,[8] including, in 1816, Mt. Ruhama Baptist.[9] Berryman has been described as having a wonderful singing voice, which he accompanied with the fiddle, an instrument the reverend had learned in his youth.[10] Berryman Hicks was also a talented writer of hymns and spiritual songs, which he utilized to great effect at religious revivals.[11]

It should come as no surprise that, as a hotbed of religious activity, the upstate of South Carolina was also an incubator for hymn singing and songwriting. During that period, sacred compositions were taught to congregations with limited musical literacy through systems utilizing different shapes to indicate pitches. This practice, known eventually as "shape note singing," greatly simplified the instruction and learning of congregational and choral music for thousands of parishioners.

Another area resident, William "Singing Billy" Walker (May 6, 1809–September 24, 1875), was a pioneer in the dissemination for this method. Walker first introduced a songbook utilizing four shapes, titled *Southern Harmony*, in 1835. Included in *Southern Harmony* was the earliest appearance in print of Berryman's song "Hicks' Farewell." This song-poem had been composed and sent to his wife while Hicks was ill on a missionary trip to East Tennessee.[12]

"Hicks' Farewell" is in the vein of a Celtic lament, a first-person narrative addressed to the loved ones left behind. With an underpinning of religious advice, the lyrics tell the thoughts and feelings of an individual facing certain death.

The *Southern Harmony*, which also contained the first printed appearance in the form we know it today of "Amazing Grace," sold north of 600,000 copies. The volume's popularity propelled "Hicks' Farewell" into the public consciousness. The composition has been recorded by artists such as the late Doc Watson, who utilized a fiddle accompaniment that conjures up the one possibly played by Berryman Hicks.[13] And the continuing use of the songbook into the present time ensures that the Hicks' influence will live on for future generations.[14]

The teaching of singing from books, such as the ones published by

What Earl Scruggs Heard

Walker, was accomplished through "singing schools" led by "song leaders" that traveled from church to church. The tradition of teaching shape notes through "schools" continued in upstate South Carolina well into the first half of the 20th century.

One of the many children from the union of Berryman and Elizabeth Hicks was Richard Henry Hicks.[15] Born October 27, 1815,[16] Richard was a sickly child, with a variety of medical issues, including a life-long heart condition, that kept him out of the Confederate military. Richard Hicks became a teacher in the local school, eventually marrying one of his students, Myra Lewis Simmons (April 9, 1820–May 25, 1892),[17] on November 5, 1844.[18]

According to Hicks family historian Helen Hicks Ezell, Richard built a home for his family on the Broad River that reflected the level of wealth and comfort attained by Richard Hicks:

> It was constructed in the traditional style of many southern farm homes, two stories high, [with] the kitchen separated from the house by a breezeway. Hand-wrought hinges, white paint, green shutters, and an imported fanlight above the front door entrance contributed to the elegance of this stately home. Two chimneys of brick which had been imported from England still stand, and boxwoods marked the driveway. Myra also apparently had imported Wedgewood china which some descendants are said to still have.[19]

In the September 1850 Census, Richard is listed as a "merchant." The 1850 and 1860 slave schedules and Hicks' will list his ownership of between two and ten slaves. Following his father's lead, Richard Hicks served as the postmaster of Islandford/Hicksville, North Carolina, until his untimely death[20] on January 29, 1864.[21] Richard Henry Hicks left behind his wife to raise the seven remaining children aged from two to fifteen years of age at the time of his passing.[22]

Before his death, Richard Henry Hicks passed onto his offspring Berryman's love of music. Richard Hicks was an accomplished player of the flute, and seven of his eight children took up musical instruments. Most specialized in the violin/fiddle of their grandfather. As each child learned to play, they were added to the family band.[23]

The oldest of Richard Henry and Myra Hicks' children was named Romeo. Evidently, the influence from Richard's study of classical literature affected the christening of his children.[24] Romeo Hicks was born August 5, 1845.[25] Unlike his father, although underage, he was in good enough health to join the Confederate calvary.[26]

After the war, Romeo studied medicine. While maintaining a residence in Rutherford County,[27] Romeo Hicks practiced for fifty-three

One. Pre-History "B.E." (Before Earl)

rear FRANK, OLA, JAMES & LEO HICKS. front ERNESTINE HICKS ERWIN w/ELLEN, VOLNEY HICKS, ABI HICKS, EDNA HICKS

Volney Hicks family, circa 1895. Back row, left to right: Franklin, Viola, James and Leolya. Front row, left to right: Ernestein Hicks Erwin holding her daughter Ellen, Volney, wife Abia and possibly Ernestein's daughter, identified as "Edna," but maybe named "Annie" (courtesy Hicks family).

years, over thirty in Spartanburg County and twenty years in Henrietta, just to the north of Cliffside, North Carolina.[28] Dr. Hicks passed away after an extended heart illness on February 3, 1930.[29]

Like his older brother Romeo, Volney Hicks lived his entire life in Rutherford County. And, as with his older sibling, V.C. was underage when he enlisted in the Confederate army.[30] Born January 8, 1848, Volney Charles Hicks survived the conflict, eventually co-owning the mercantile business of Cowen & Hicks.[31] Volney Hicks passed away from pneumonia January 13, 1910.[32]

Duke Wellington Hicks (September 14, 1850–May 12, 1913)[33] was to lead a peripatetic work life. Like his brother Volney, as early as 1882, D.W. began in the mercantile business,[34] running a store in Hicksville, North Carolina.[35] Duke Hicks married the former Jesse Grist (January 25, 1872–March 21, 1946) on May 14, 1891, moving in March of 1897 to Jesse's hometown of Yorkville, South Carolina.[36] There, D.W. went to work for her family's mercantile business, Grist Cousins.[37] For the remainder of his life, Duke Hicks worked in either the grocery business, as a cotton buyer, or an insurance salesman.[38]

What Earl Scruggs Heard

Born in Rutherford County, Richard Hicks (December 24, 1854–December 30, 1916)[39] worked as a lumberman, then as a grocer and, finally, as a clerk for P.E. Brown.[40] The 1900 Census has Richard in Spartanburg proper, where Hicks was to stay until his death.

Zeno Hicks family, circa 1905. Back row, left to right: Grace, Helen and Will. Front row, left to right: Zeno, Estelle and wife Nancy McKinney (courtesy Hicks family).

Probably the best-known of the Hicks family siblings for his music making was "Dr." Henry Zeno Hicks. Zeno Hicks was born in Rutherford County on November 6, 1856.[41] Around 1886, Zeno married Nancy Elizabeth McKinney (June 30, 1866–January 13, 1935)[42] and built the home previously mentioned for his new wife and family on a farm just over the border in the upstate of South Carolina.[43] A "self-taught" dispenser of medical advice,[44] H.Z. Hicks died suddenly, not surprisingly, of the heart disease that ran in the family,[45] on March 27, 1922. Hicks had just mailed his notification for the Hicks Orchestra to participate in the upcoming Spartanburg fiddlers' convention April 15 when he passed.[46]

The youngest Hicks sibling was christened Berriman Theodore (June 10, 1862–December 12, 1935).[47] Named for his grandfather, Theo married twice, the first time around 1896, to Leila Myra Jane McKinney (April 27, 1869–March 31, 1911), the sister of his brother Zeno's spouse.[48] Leila and Theodore had relocated to Cherokee County, South Carolina, in time for the 1910 Census. After her death, Theodore Hicks married Carrie McKinney Crawford.[49]

Hicks Orchestra

According to local newspaper coverage and family stories, the beginnings for the Hicks ensemble date to 1875. This grouping would have probably started out playing a combination of traditional dance tunes and period songs. The melodies were rendered either in unison or, at the most, in harmony within the fiddles. Singing was backed by chording, with (again) the instruments stating the melody between the verses. The Hicks' family band would have provided entertainments at local homes, including for small house dances.

This extremely informal, original unit, based at one of their Rutherford County homes around Hicksville, would have included all of Richard and Elizabeth's offspring but one. Moses Junius Hicks (July 26, 1852–December 2, 1928), known as June,[50] instead would dance to his family's harmonious offerings.[51] It's unlikely that the full seven-strong grouping lasted very long, as, by the turn of the century, the majority of the siblings had married and were raising families in South Carolina.

It's hard to get a firm handle on the group's early appearances because their informality resulted in a lack of mentions by the local press. Two short articles, from 1895 and 1906, record the "Hicks Band" in Gaffney, South Carolina, and a third, from Rutherfordton, North Carolina, in 1905, specifically featured Zeno Hicks and his son William.[52]

Fiddler Volney Hicks has yet to emerge in listings for the family's public music making before his death in 1910. Nor does either the oldest sibling Romeo or brother Richard, who passed in 1916 between the deaths of Volney and Zeno, make it into the reportage as members of the Hicks ensemble.

Duke Wellington Hicks, whose nomadic work life took him around the area before his untimely death in 1913, was twice mentioned in print. In June of 1910, D.W. was joined by his son Duke and Dr. S.H. Griffith in entertaining at a private gathering.[53] A year later, Hicks competed as a soloist at the Henrietta, North Carolina, fiddlers' convention.[54] Obviously, on neither of these occasions did Duke appear with his siblings.

What the media, the Hicks descendants and surviving photographs indicate is that, by the end of the first decade of the 20th century, when

What Earl Scruggs Heard

fiddlers' conventions had become the main gathering place for area string band musicians, only two of the Hicks brethren were still performing. Zeno Hicks played banjo and Theo Hicks was the primary fiddler with what was named the Hicks Orchestra. A surviving photograph indicates that Zeno and Theo were joined by Zeno's son, Dr. W.R. Hicks, on guitar, along with Ed Crawford on banjo, Robert Crawford on fiddle and D.P.L. Martin on drum.

Hicks Orchestra, circa 1915. Left to right: Zeno Hicks/banjo, Dr. W.R. Hicks/guitar, Ed Crawford/banjo, Robert Crawford/fiddle, Theo Hicks/fiddle, possibly Theo's daughter Mary Elizabeth/piano, Theo's wife Carrie, and D.P.L. Martin/drum. The two women behind Martin are unidentified (courtesy Nancy Ezell-Suggs).

The use of the bass drum within a string band might seem unusual to modern audiences and musicians. Actually, one hundred years ago, many rural string ensembles were called upon to provide the marching music that accompanied graduation exercises at small, one- or two-room country schoolhouses. It was an added bonus that drummer D.P.L. Martin possessed a strong voice when, eventually, the Hicks Orchestra was hired to entertain on area stages.

Dillard Perry Lemon Martin was born on a farm in Martinsville, Spartanburg County, South Carolina, June 5, 1855.[55] Martin was known

One. Pre-History "B.E." (Before Earl)

either by his initials, D.P.L., or by the nickname "Dude" or "Dood."[56] By 1898, Martin was dealing in lumber,[57] moving his business and home into Spartanburg around 1900.[58] While living in the city, D.P.L. Martin served at least two terms as a township commissioner[59] and one stint with Zeno Hicks as a school trustee for the Cherokee District.[60] By the summer of 1914, Martin had relocated to Chesnee, South Carolina.[61] D.P.L. Martin died at the advanced age of one hundred one years on March 6, 1957.[62]

D.P.L. taught singing using William Walker's 1866/1867 book *Christian Harmony* in the same Baptist association where Berryman Hicks had been a member a half a century prior. Unlike *Southern Harmony*, this later work utilized a seven-shape notation.[63] The earliest reference I've found to Martin's activities as a song leader dates to 1897, when he participated in a "singing school" at Broad River Baptist Church.[64] D.P.L.'s song leading continued at least into the 1930s.[65]

D.P.L. Martin, circa 1890 (courtesy Ancestry Family Tree).

By 1921, the Hicks Orchestra had expanded to contain as many as ten instrumentalists. Besides the six musicians listed above, Zeno's wife Nancy Elizabeth and William's wife Lola would sing and recite. Lola also played violin and mandolin, and sister Nora Hicks (September 1, 1858–June 28, 1929),[66] along with Theo's daughter Mary Elizabeth (born December 8, 1902[67]), the piano.[68] This expansion helped the Hicks to make the adjustment from spot appearances at area fiddlers' conventions to full evenings of entertainment.

On October 30, 1921, in Chesnee, South Carolina, the Hicks Orchestra played in benefit of the local basketball team. Their program, reprinted

What Earl Scruggs Heard

Hicks Orchestra, circa 1920. Left to right: Ed Crawford/banjo, Zeno Hicks/banjo, Dr. W.R. Hicks/guitar, unknown, Robert Crawford/fiddle, Theo Hicks/fiddle, possibly Mrs. W.R. Hicks/mandolin and unknown/piano. Standing, left to right: Mrs. and Mr. D.P.L. Martin and unknown (courtesy Nancy Ezell-Suggs).

by an area newspaper,[69] illustrated a melding of the old pieces—fiddle tunes and 19th-century minstrel songs—rendered by Zeno and Theo Hicks with those (increasingly) introduced by Dr. William Hicks and his contemporaries. This mixed repertoire, probably learned from sheet music or recordings, was not unusual. For Piedmont string music as a whole, the musicians of North and South Carolina's mid-sections had varied outside influences embracing popular trends.

Myra Leanora Hicks, circa 1895 (courtesy Hicks family).

One. Pre-History "B.E." (Before Earl)

The fiddle-led instrumental selections included "A Life on the Ocean Wave," a medley of "[The] Girl I Left Behind Me" with "Turkey in the Straw" and "[The] Italian Waltz." These widespread tunes originated not in Britain, Ireland and Scotland, but were based on melodies published in America. "Ocean Waves," attributed to Epes Sargent and Henry Russell, dates to the early 1800s[70]; "Girl"/"Turkey" were both derived from the 1830s minstrel song "Zip Coon";[71] and "[The] Italian Waltz" was another ditty whose origins came from Tin Pan Alley. Two other songs rendered by the entire group, probably as instrumentals, included Dan Emmett's minstrel walk-around turned Southern anthem from 1860, "Dixie,"[72] and John Howard Payne and Henry Bishop's 1831 sentimental standard, "Home Sweet Home."[73]

Other instrumentals, featuring Dr. and Mrs. Hicks on Hawaiian guitar and mandolin, comprised "Paragon Waltz," published by Mrs. G.W. Scott in 1868[74]; "Helter Skelter Galop" by Carl Faust[75]; and the banjo-led "Spread Eagle March," claimed by the English classic up-picking finger-style banjoist Joe Morley.[76]

Vocal pieces featured the mawkish compositions "Silver Threads Among the Gold" by Eben E. Rexford and Hart Pease Danks as well as "When You and I Were Young, Maggie," written by George W. Johnson and J.A. Butterfield and published in 1866.[77]

Recitations also played a role within the Hicks Orchestra, especially with the older generation. Three spoken pieces, mostly in the blackface vein, showcased the two Mrs. Hicks, Zeno Hicks and Dude Martin.

As one can deduce from the program analyzed above, Will Hicks favored Hawaiian selections and a more modern band sound over the older square dance pieces. With the death of Zeno Hicks in 1922 and the succession of his son as the Orchestra's driving force, the metamorphosis of the Hicks ensemble was completed.

William Richard Hicks was born May 12, 1889,[78] into a family of, if not exactly great wealth, abundant comfort. His father, Henry Zeno Hicks, and his father's siblings all owned rather than rented their houses and farms. Will's uncles were doctors, farmers and business proprietors rather than, like many other area musicians, sharecroppers and cotton mill workers.

As a teenager, William Hicks began playing with his father at home entertainments, backing Zeno's fiddling with guitar and banjo.[79] At the age of twenty-one, Will completed his dental studies and opened a practice in Spartanburg County.[80] He served in World War I, possibly in the medical corp.[81] After his discharge, around 1919, Dr. Hicks

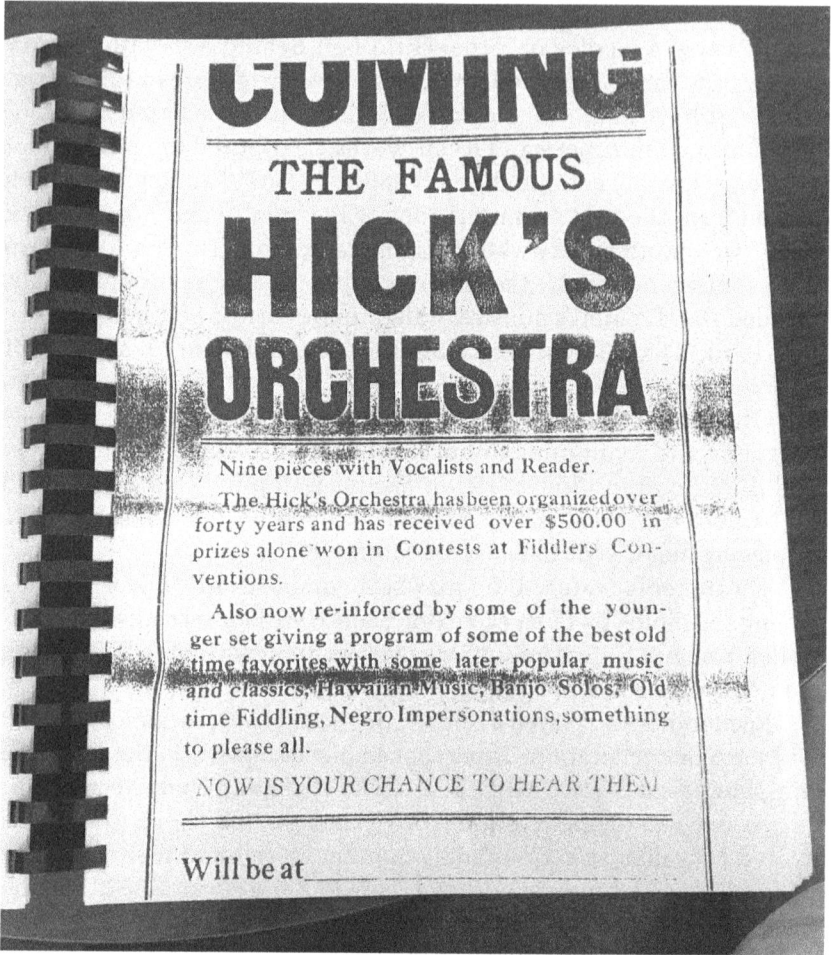

Flyer advertising Hick's [sic] Orchestra, no date (courtesy Nancy Ezell-Suggs).

married public school teacher Lola and bought a home in the Morgan community of Cherokee County, South Carolina, next door to his parents.[82]

Even while he continued to practice dentistry, Dr. William Hicks pursued a parallel career in music. At the beginning of 1922, Hicks founded the Aeolian Music and Dramatic Club in Chesnee, South Carolina, where he and Lola gave lessons on mandolin, classic finger-style banjo, Hawaiian guitar, "regular" guitar, ukulele, mandocello, tenor banjo and mandola. William's goal was to train and form a mandolin

One. Pre-History "B.E." (Before Earl)

The last generation of Hicks family musicians: Dr. W.R. Hicks/banjo, Ed Crawford and Robert Crawford, among others. Dated "1929" (courtesy Hicks family).

orchestra in order to present monthly concerts.[83] His efforts continued through the 1920s,[84] as did the Hicks' own performances.[85]

Dr. Hicks reentered the military for World War II, serving as a major in the dental service.[86] Following the war, William and Lola divorced. At the conclusion of a three-month illness, Dr. William Richard Hicks died on April 2, 1951.[87]

Although the Hicks family chose concertizing over fiddlers' conventions as their main performance venue, the siblings and their offspring did compete in a handful of contests. We'll next begin to explore how those events attracted and shaped string music in the area. Additionally, some other musical families will be profiled in the coming pages.

Two

The Greatest Musical Tournament in Western North Carolina

> Over one thousand heard the music, which was, according to performer, mild, weird, fast and furious or else awaking martial ardor or evoking....[1]
>
> An entertainment that does not bring a blush to the cheek yet is amusing and instructive.[2]

The Hicks family of musicians bridged a period where self-entertainment was the rule to public music making. As I've commented, late 19th-century string band music mostly occurred at home. However, by the end of the first decade of the 20th century, homespun entertainments began to be usurped by community fiddlers' conventions.

As researchers Wayne Martin and Gail Gillespie have noted:

> Detailed accounts of fiddle contests suddenly began to crop up in Southern newspapers of the 1890s. Suffused with nostalgia, these articles celebrated "olde tyme" fiddlers who played the tunes "our grandmothers danced to." Since the turn of the century was a time of disturbingly rapid change, pining for the good old days was probably quite natural. The year 1900 was a watershed in which for the first time American urban dwellers began to outnumber those in the country. In the growing cities of the South, new musical terms like ragtime, Dixieland and jazz were replacing older kinds of music. Aware of the rapid change, newspaper writers described "old time fiddle contests" in loving detail ... all the while emphasizing the quaint handlebar mustaches, mud-covered boots and old-fashioned rusticity of the fiddlers.[3]

By the middle of the century's first decade, two different fiddling events occurring in North Carolina dominated the public's imagination. Through the dual efforts of powerful, charismatic figures, musicians began to congregate at area fiddlers' conventions. Coverage flooded regional newspapers, placing old-style fiddling front and center.

Two. The Greatest Musical Tournament in Western North Carolina

One gathering was held in Raleigh, North Carolina's, state capitol. From 1905 through 1914, the contest occurred each Labor Day Monday on the grounds of the Agricultural and Mechanical School (which became North Carolina State University). The mastermind behind these conventions was William Johnston "Buck" Andrews (March 1, 1871–December 19, 1942[4]), the head of the Raleigh Electric Company, now part of Duke Energy Progress.[5]

The other promoter only held events at the end of 1907 and the beginning of 1908. However, his unrealized plans appear from a century later to have been much more ambitious than those of Buck Andrews. That organizer's name was Zack Whitaker.

Charles Zack Whitaker (February 9, 1876–November 3, 1950) was living in Oak Ridge, North Carolina, where Zack headed the music department of the local institute, when he staged his contests. Whitaker's goal was to use these events to organize a statewide fiddlers' association in order to preserve old time fiddling and tunes. Zack titled his gathering "Ye old tyme fiddlers' convention." In all, Zack Whitaker promoted fifteen contests and was affiliated with another eight. Whitaker located his events in North Carolina's cities such as Winston-Salem, Salisbury, Mount Airy, Raleigh, Greensboro, and Charlotte.[6]

There has not yet emerged any direct link between the "fiddling fever" in North Carolina and the contests held in Cleveland and Rutherford counties, North Carolina, and South Carolina's upstate. Generally, however, the same conditions that birthed Andrews' and Whitaker's events seemed to have existed in the areas being examined within these pages.

By scrutinizing area periodicals available online at newspapers.com and digitalnc.org/collections/newspapers/, the following picture was revealed.

Between the beginning of 1908, when coverage commenced, and the end of 1931, when in-depth articles cease, sixty-five fiddlers' conventions were held within our area of interest. Some years, none appear within the pages of the local newspapers (for example, World War I seems to have had an adverse effect on these events). The most documented per anum was seven. Unlike many of today's largest contests, these gatherings were held indoors, in either courthouse theaters located in county seats, or within the school auditoriums of smaller communities. Larger municipalities, such as Gaffney, South Carolina, might host multiple get-togethers within the same year. There does not appear to be a single, preferable fiddlers' convention "season" where all

Old Time Fiddlers Convention

BLACKSBURG, S. C.
Friday, Nov. 14th, 7:30 P. M.

OPERA HOUSE

Known as City Hall

The Following Cash Prizes Will Be Awarded:

Best Old Time Fiddler	$4.00
Second Best Old Time Fiddler	$2.00
Best Duet on Stringed Instruments	$3.00
Best Banjo	$3.00
Best Guitar	$3.00
Best Buck Dancer	$2.00
Best Old Time Dancer	$1.00

The convention will be under the management of a veteran musician, S. S. GAFFNEY. All Musicians wishing to take part please report to OPERA HOUSE, known as City Hall at 7:30 P. M. day of convention.

Admission 20 and 35 Cents

Advertisement for fiddlers' convention managed by S.S. Gaffney, at opera house/city hall, November 14, 1924. Take note of the prize awards (*Cherokee Times*, November 10, 1924).

the events were clustered. However, not surprisingly, due to the weather, the spring and the fall seem to have had the greatest concentration of contests.

Audiences of anywhere from one hundred to one thousand attendees (if coverage in the local rags is to be trusted) paid in the range of twenty-five to thirty-five cents each in order to hear their favorite musicians compete for prizes in fiddle, banjo, dance and various size ensembles. As few as ten and as many as thirty bow pullers, banjo twangers and guitar pickers contested at individual events for rewards ranging from $1.00 on up to $10.00. This was not a bad day's haul for a tenant farmer or mill worker in the nineteen-teens and twenties. When an event wasn't benefiting a local institution, as rapidly became the driving force behind fiddlers' gatherings, the promoter might evenly divide the profits among the combatants who finished out of the prize money.[7]

Just shy of one hundred individually named musicians appear in newspaper accounts publicizing fiddling events. It should come as no surprise that there was a preponderance of fiddlers among the contestants (after all, these were *fiddlers'* conventions). Ignoring that some pickers competed on more than one instrument, forty-nine played the fiddle/violin and half that number the banjo. There were fourteen guitarists and five other instrumentalists. A quantity of band names appear as well, many without their individual members or instruments identified. So there's a possibility of even more players who participated in fiddling events waiting to be discovered.

Not surprisingly, considering the morays of the time, the number of female contestants is limited to one fiddler, one banjoist and a handful of guitarists. The best I can tell, those musicians are either the spouses or off-spring of competing male musicians. There are no identifiable African Americans of either sex to be found.

The tunes and songs chosen by the musicians reflect at least a part of the repertoire for our area of study. However, we also must remember that the participants were competing for prizes and that some took winning seriously enough to choose pieces recognizable and beloved by judges and audiences alike. So, it should come as no surprise that fiddlers, banjoists and bands chose a selection of "greatest hits" including the fiddle tune "chestnuts" "Arkansas Traveler," "Billy in the Low Ground," "Black-Eyed Susie," "Downfall of Paris" (also known as "Mississippi Sawyer"), "Hell Broke Loose in Georgia," "Old Jimmy Sutton," "Old Molly Hare," "Sallie Goodin," "Sally Ann" and "Sugar in the Gourd" as well as Stephen Foster's "My Old Kentucky Home" and Dan Emmett's "Dixie."

Two fiddling conventions held in Gaffney several years apart reflect the range of music presented at these events. Dance tunes dominate the gatherings, while newer songs and song-melodies were also present.

The actual program for March 21, 1916, as reported in the pages of the *Gaffney* (South Carolina) *Ledger*, included ten "acts" performing six square dance tunes with their roots in the 1800s, two finger-picked classic banjo showpieces revealing a ragtime influence, two from popular sheet music or song books, as well as a Stephen Foster melody from before the Civil War.[8]

On March 1, 1918, the tentative program featured fourteen entities. This convention opened with the fiddling and singing of "America [the Beautiful]" and proceeded from there. The majority of the contestants performed at least one fiddle tune; only three exclusively rendered popular songs. The whole shooting match concluded with "an old-time cotillion ... by J.W. Reynolds' dancing pupils."[9]

DeStaffino Family

Even while the promoters of these musical events were attempting to perpetuate the older tunes and songs, some contestants and audiences showed their preferences for or against the "old familiar" pieces. Eventually, in an attempt at assuaging shifting tastes, those directing fiddlers' events began adding more modern, non-competing performers as "special" attractions.

In May of 1921, as the spring convention in Gaffney drew near, the *Ledger* announced that contest organizer John W. Ross would bring a distinctive feature to the upcoming fiddling contest. The crowd at the Strand Theater would be entertained by not only string band music, but, a group of singers known locally as the Fred DeStaffino family quartet.[10]

Frederick Lewis DeStaffino, born in upstate South Carolina October 2, 1880,[11] was the son of Frederick Graham Latham (born 1833)[12] and Rebecca Eleanor Ramsey (circa 1848–May 30, 1929).[13] When he was around the age of seven, Fred's Scottish father and American mother split up. Rebecca soon remarried, and Fred eventually adopted the DeStaffino surname from his Italian stepfather Joseph (born June 1851).[14]

It appears that Joe DeStaffino spent the years between 1888 and the early 1900s in Texas. Around the turn of the century, Fred and his older brother Pat (born 1878) joined Joseph, who was farming north

Two. The Greatest Musical Tournament in Western North Carolina

of Dallas–Fort Worth.[15] Upon his return to South Carolina, Fred DeStaffino established himself in Gaffney, eventually marrying Hattie Belle Floyd (born circa 1890),[16] with whom he had at least three children.[17] Fred worked as a barber[18] and, for a period, ran the Gaffney Café on Limestone Street.[19]

All documented appearances by the Fred DeStaffino family quartet, featuring Fred, Hattie and their young children, date to 1921.[20] A June 16 program at Cherokee Falls gives a good idea of their performing repertoire, which included the religious pieces "You've Got to Reap Just What You Sow" and "You've Got a Crown"; "Dreamy Moon," "a lullaby song and dance by Eugene DeStaffino, ... five years of age"; the novelty song from 1918, "JaDa JaDa, Jing, Jing, Jing"; "Whispering," a popular hit in 1920[21] "sung by [eleven-year-old daughter] Melrose DeStaffino"; as well as "Farewell Mother."[22]

Fred DeStaffino didn't live much longer. He contracted appendicitis and died June 29, 1922, at the age of forty.[23]

Usually, convention promoters and managers placed restrictions upon the competition. Several fiddling events were only for those contestants from within the host county. Most prohibited classical music, with a 1916 Gaffney convention warning, "No classic violinists will be permitted to take part in the convention."[24] There were some exceptions, as between 1918 and 1921, Gordon Westrope, the violin instructor from nearby Limestone College, participated or played a leading role in fiddling events held in Gaffney.[25] One promoter divided the competitors into "under fifty and over fifty" (years of age) categories.[26] Occasionally, attempts to "reform" the image of fiddling were the convention's stated goals, with wild behavior substituted by the playing of hymns and instrumental versions of songs with a religious content.[27]

Ultimately, as elsewhere, local presenters emphasized nostalgia. Adverts and articles promised Confederate veterans performing tunes from "before the [Civil] War," with a program that "will embrace good fiddling, old style banjo picking, plantation songs and dances."[28]

One prominent contest with a reputation for lucrative prizes was held from 1925 into the 1960s. It was founded by "The Merchant Prince" Julius Plato Durham (known by his initials J.P.D.) Withrow.

Born December 7, 1866, Withrow grew up on an area farm. After spending a few of his teen-aged years at the Shelby Military Institute, J.P.D. married in 1888.[29] Withrow made the switch from farming to retail sales in 1892. J.P.D. Withrow eventually ran two stores, one in Hollis, North Carolina, and another fifteen miles to the south in Ellenboro.[30]

What Earl Scruggs Heard

With his success in business, J.P.D. Withrow became the town's main benefactor. Labeled the "Patron Saint of Hollis" by the *Charlotte Observer*,[31] Withrow led the push to build a community center, donating the land and leading the fundraising to construct the rock structure. The building housed the Hollis school on the first floor, site of the fiddlers' convention, with space for civic organizations on the second level above.[32]

The predecessor to the convention were annual area picnics sponsored and organized by Withrow. The July 4 "Big Day" celebration, as named by J.P.D., was held at least as early as 1902[33]; the last on July 4, 1921, ended in a shooting death.[34] The Hollis fiddling contest on the Wednesday before Thanksgiving was begun as a memorial to Withrow's late spouse Laura Louella Hamrick, who had died on August 23, 1925.[35] When J.P.D. passed away on November 26, 1926, following the first contest,[36] his son Grady took up the reins. Inasmuch as the Withrow family was synonymous with Hollis, the contest was held to benefit the store and the community along with the school.

Marvin McDaniel remembers that the band led by his father Dewey

GORDON WESTROPE

Portrait of violinist Gordon Westrope from "Westrope Takes Part in Meeting," (*Gaffney Ledger***, June 15, 1920).**

Two. The Greatest Musical Tournament in Western North Carolina

WITHROW'S ENTERTAINMENT.

Will Be Held At ELLENBORO NEXT FRIDAY.

- And At - HOLLIS SATURDAY NEXT.

Instead of Lattimore. The people seem to appreciate them and at the above named places I will offer better premiums and the program will be complete. There will be Horse Races, Mule Races and a "Yankee Dance," more than has been on the program. Bring your fast Mules and Horses. If you win you will get a nice present. Several Clowns will be in the races and cut capers to please the children. Friday and Saturday will be days long to remembered and if you come expecting the

Biggest Time You Ever Saw,

You will not be disappointed. Good order will be observed. I have never had any trouble and do not anticipate any now. I will have plenty of clerks to wait on you and promise goods cheap and a good price for your Produce at Hollis. At 3 p. m. the exercises will close with an old fashioned "cake walk."

YOURS RESPECTFULLY,

J. P. D. WITHROW,

Advertisement, Withrow's Entertainment, (*Cleveland Star*, January 22, 1902).

every year aimed at winning the Hollis fiddlers' convention and that their main competitor was led by Dewey's former band mate, Smith Hammett. Local legend also has a young Earl Scruggs making his first public appearance at the Hollis contest, with his band coming away with the first prize.

What Earl Scruggs Heard

Additional musicians that might have competed at Hollis were numerous within this area and assembling a complete list would be impossible. Those better-known pickers included the McKee brothers, George William fiddle/banjo (November 17, 1881–October 19, 1974[37]) and Charlie Andrew fiddle/mandolin (January 1, 1884–June 21, 1968) of Polkville. George and Charlie were the offspring of farmer and miller Jacob Parham (August 19, 1851–February 8, 1934) and Rachel Amanda Goforth McKee (September 27, 1853–October 5, 1946).[38] After the brothers married, Charlie to Essie Novella Petty (October 21, 1885–May 18, 1956) November 9, 1911, and George to Oaksey Green (March 11, 1886–May 12, 1962) on August 8, 1909,[39] they both settled on or near their parents' farmstead.[40]

Other area string musicians included Polkville farmers "Big" George A. McKee/fiddle (May 1871–January 14, 1949) and Samuel Lee McKee/guitar (June 8, 1884–January 11, 1929),[41] George Greene/

Back row, left to right: "Big" George McKee/fiddle, George William McKee/fiddle, Landram Witt/harmonica and George Greene/fiddle. Front row, left to right: Luther Haynes/banjo, Sam McKee/guitar and Charlie Andrew McKee/mandolin (courtesy Janet Deaton).

Two. The Greatest Musical Tournament in Western North Carolina

fiddle, Johnny Whisnant/fiddle, Clete Newton/guitar, carpenter Solon Beam Butler/banjo (February 9, 1914–December 30, 1988) of Ellenboro,[42] Dennis Butler/fiddle, Porter Crotts/fiddle,[43] clawhammer banjoist Charles Melton, guitarist Claudius Melton and Ellenboro resident Grady McKinney/fiddle.[44]

Families of Musicians

A small number of musicians dominated the local fiddling events. Six of these families, residing in York County, South Carolina, were joined in matrimony as well as in music. Like the Hicks, they formed an interwoven band of musicians. However, instead of just being related through blood, these friends used unions with co-player's siblings to form further bonds. This is the story of the interrelated McDaniel, Strain, Comer, Blackwell, Robinson and Plexico families of upstate South Carolina.

The earliest documented version of this "string band" included H.B. McDaniel and V.C. Comer on "violin," Jimmy Strain playing the banjo, his brother Sam strumming the autoharp and Ethel Strain Blackwell plucking the guitar.[45] Sometimes, when Henry McDaniel would switch to the autoharp, Noble Blackwell was added on the fiddle, with Sam Strain or one of the McDaniel siblings bringing another guitar to the ensemble.[46]

Fiddler Henry Brooks McDaniel was born March 31, 1869.[47] His wife, Mildred Lenora (September 14, 1874–June 14, 1959), was the daughter of James Lyle Strain; three of her siblings were musicians.[48] Henry and Lenora married on March 15, 1893,[49] moving for the years of 1895–1896 to Cherokee County[50] and back to York County in 1897.[51] After that time, Henry and Nora McDaniel farmed in the community of Broad River,[52] where it appears they stayed for the remainder of Henry's life.[53] Henry Brooks McDaniel passed away on March 17, 1938.[54]

Four of the offspring from the McDaniel/Strain union took up the guitar and used the instrument to accompany the fiddling of their father. These included Olive Edna McDaniel (née Bennett; February 17, 1894–April 21, 1985),[55] who taught school,[56] at least until she married in 1913[57]; Martha Wilma McDaniel (née Carlton; October 27, 1895–September 9, 1977)[58]; Estelle Strain McDaniel (January 16, 1903–July 26, 2002) and their brother Otho "Otis" A. McDaniel (March 25, 1898–July 4, 1993).[59] Olive was the most active musician of the quartet and was the

> # MUSICAL CONCERT
> COURTHOUSE, YORK, S. C.—
> TUESDAY EVENING, MARCH 1,
> AT 8 P. M.
>
> ## "THE BETH-SHILOH SEVEN"
>
> Artists with Violin, Banjo, Guitar and Other Stringed Instruments. Programme to Consist of Old Time Musical Selections. — — — —
>
> Performance by—Mr. and Mrs. J. N. Strain and Miss Louise Strain, H. B. McDaniel, Miss Estelle McDaniel and O. A. McDaniel and Mr. J. J. J. Robinson.
>
> Part of the proceeds to go to Benefit of Beth-Shiloh School. An evening of wholesome entertainment. Remember the date—
>
> **TUESDAY EVENING, MARCH 1, 8 O'CLOCK**
>
> Admission: Children, 15 Cents; Adults, 25 Cents

Advertisement for Beth-Shiloh Seven, performing at the Courthouse in York, South Carolina, March 1, 1921, in benefit of the school (*Yorkville Enquirer*, February 22, 1921).

only of her siblings to consistently compete at area fiddlers' conventions with their parent.

The patriarch for the musical Strain siblings was "Colonel" James Lyle Strain (April 22, 1841–April 16, 1916).[60] Born in Chester County, South Carolina, Strain fought on the Confederate side during the Civil War, where he lost a leg from wounds incurred during the conflict.[61]

In 1870, J.L. Strain married the former Martha Keziah "Kate" Estes (April 25, 1848–January 13, 1915).[62] Three of their children took up musical instruments.

James Newton Butler "Jimmy" Strain (June 27, 1877–January 7, 1965) learned the banjo and the cornet.[63] In 1900, he chose to marry the

Two. The Greatest Musical Tournament in Western North Carolina

J.L. Strain family, circa 1905. Back row includes Jimmy, Sam, Mildred, and Ethel. Woman on far right is unknown. Front row: James Lyle Strain and his wife Kate (courtesy Ancestry Family Tree).

daughter of fiddler V.C. Comer, guitarist Mamie "Nora" Oceola Comer (December 3, 1881–November 21, 1954).[64] Their wedding celebration featured string band music as the entertainment.[65]

Younger brother Samuel Jefferson Strain (January 8, 1879–August 30, 1954)[66] went with the guitar. Originally, Sam planned to become a doctor. Unfortunately, a lack of funds directed Strain toward farming.[67] Eventually, Sam Strain also served as a local magistrate in Wilkinsville,[68] and, for the last twenty-seven years of his working life, was employed in textiles by Hamrick Mills and Limestone Manufacturing.[69]

Jimmy and Sam's sister Ethel Isabella (August 17, 1881–June 22, 1966)[70] learned to play guitar[71] and trained as a milliner.[72] On January 2, 1907, Ethel Strain married into the family of fiddler Noble Jackson Blackwell (November 11, 1877–January 9, 1948)[73] and Mattie Alexander Robina Estes (February 2, 1879–December 5, 1943).[74] Noble and Mattie had married around 1906, settling in the Gowdeysville community of Cherokee County.[75]

What Earl Scruggs Heard

Ethel took as her spouse Noble's brother Charlie Acey "Asa" Harris Blackwell (May 2, 1881–January 22, 1959).[76] N.J. and Asa were among the oldest of eight children born to farmers William and Catherine Blackwell of Cherokee County,[77] a profession that both brothers continued once married.[78] By the fall of 1918, Asa and Ethel had moved their family into Gaffney, where Blackwell worked as a "laborer" and "street overseer,"[79] eventually gaining employment in a textile mill.[80]

Sylvanus C. "Vaney" Comer (December 3, 1859–November 23, 1930)[81] lost his father as a toddler.[82] Around 1878, Comer married Edna Permelia "Amelia" Petty (August 1864–January 25, 1935)[83] and began farming in Cherokee County. In order to support his nine children,[84] it appears that Vaney Comer also traded horses, ferried people across a local river, and ran a neighborhood inn.

In the same vein as the Hicks family, the focus of the public music making for members of the six families discussed here was on community events. In June of 1900, a core group took the initiative to provide a more organized forum for their playing. As reported in the pages of the *Gaffney Ledger*, on June 6, "the young men of this section met at the Etta Jane academy and organized a 'string band' with the following officers": V.C. Comer/president, Samuel J. Strain/secretary and N.J. Blackwell/treasurer. "We hope ere long to have one of the best bands in this Piedmont belt."[85]

This grouping provided a structure for the informal sharing of music that was already occurring between these inter-related families. Of course, these events ensued almost ten years before organized public fiddlers' conventions were to sweep the area, which provided new outlets for their music.

From that point onward, until the fiddle contests started in earnest, this quintet plus or minus a musician or two was a familiar sight at community functions. This included area wedding parties and at other gatherings.[86] Members also played over the newly installed telephone lines.[87] Even after fiddlers' conventions took up the leisure time of these players, various combinations continued to meet neighborhood needs for music. These comprised school assemblies and graduations, wedding anniversary parties, home entertainments, prison camp programs (!), birthday celebrations, picnics and family reunions.[88]

When the McDaniel/Comer/Strain/Blackwell string band began attending fiddlers' conventions, they came into contact with J.J.J. Robinson. The most active musician in this grouping, fiddler John Joseph Jefferson Robinson (the oldest of all these players, born June 2, 1856)[89] was the son of William Alexander Robinson (May 27, 1827–January 18, 1906) and Julia A.C. Plexico (November 8, 1825–February 23, 1877).[90] On December 1, 1881,[91] Robinson married Martha Jane Elizabeth Mitchell (January 15, 1859–November 10, 1921), who was a Plexico through her maternal line (I am unclear about any direct relationship between Robinson's mother Julia, his wife Martha Jane and fiddler A.F. Plexico).[92]

J.J.J. was a lifetime farmer in York County,[93] and well-known throughout the county. According to his obituary, John Robinson was a "premier violinist of the old school.... He began playing when a small boy on a violin fashioned from a long neck gourd, with shoe laces for strings." Robinson was the most active and written about of the "old school" fiddlers from the area. From all appearances, J.J.J. Robinson loved the attention music and performing brought him. His violin, known as "Mary Ann," was a gift from United States Congressman D.E. Finley, who practiced law in York, South Carolina.[94]

One of Robinson's end of life highlights was a week spent entertaining at the 1929 Confederate Reunion held in Charlotte, North Carolina. During that event, "Three J" Robinson charmed the attendees with fiddle tunes such as "Turkey in the Straw," "Arkansas Traveler," "Soldier's Joy" and "Dixie."[95] Robinson passed away on May 7, 1933.[96]

Fiddler Alan Plexico was related to John Robinson through marriage. Born on May 3, 1859, Alan Feemster Plexico (died December 30, 1928) was married to Robinson's sister Nancy Frances Eugelia "Nannie" Robinson (May 19, 1861–April 20, 1905)[97] on December 1 of 1881.[98] After bearing Plexico six children, Nannie died, possibly from complications in the birth of their seventh child.[99] On November 13, 1908, A.F. Plexico remarried; his second wife was Mary Eudora "Dora" Love (November 9, 1872–October 19, 1947).[100]

Soon after his second union, Plexico opened a furniture store in the community of Sharon. A.F. Plexico was to run that business for the remainder of his life,[101] also serving as the town's mayor in 1913.[102]

Considering the popularity of fiddlers' conventions between 1908 and the end of the 1920s, fairly few from the McDaniel/Strain group chose to compete. Of the roughly ten players related by blood or marriage discussed above, only four are frequently mentioned in area newspapers as convention participants. Perhaps the demands of making a living and supporting a family diminished their musical activities.

Considering his outgoing personality, it should come of no surprise that John Robinson contended at fiddlers' conventions at least fifteen times. Within just one year, J.J.J. attended seven documented events.

Robinson garnered prizes at most conventions where he participated, including eight top honors.

H.B. McDaniel battled with J.J.J. Robinson for supreme fiddle honors a total of ten times. However, between 1911 and 1924, McDaniel only managed to best Robinson on one occasion. It took Robinson's absence for Henry to win his other first prize. Realizing the draw of their real or imagined rivalry, A.M. McGill invited the two bow wielders to a "Violin Contest" held in his store at Ramah Crossroads on August 7, 1915. Unfortunately, no surviving account reports on which musician was triumphant that day.[103]

Between 1908 and 1912, A.F. Plexico brought his fiddle to five conventions and Jimmy Strain played banjo nine times between 1911 and 1925. Plexico was only credited with one prize, while Strain had better luck. With the limited number of banjo contestants increasing his chances at victory, Jimmy Strain captured one second prize for a duet with fiddler John Robinson, as well as three firsts in solo banjo.

The man mostly responsible for these fiddlers' gatherings—the Buck Andrews and Zack Whitaker of the area, if you will—was fiddler John W. Ross. We'll next take a look at Ross's story and the events he promoted, along with his most famous musical cohorts.

Three

John W. Ross, Charlie Parker and Mack Woolbright
Part One

John W. Ross

The one individual most responsible for promoting fiddle contests along the North and South Carolina border was John W. Ross. Himself a bow puller, John Ross might have confined his involvement to the competition if not for an unforeseen accident that forced Ross into an early retirement from his day job.

John Wyles Ross, Jr., was born outside of Gaffney proper in Limestone Springs, South Carolina, on July 26, 1853. He was the son of farmer John Wyles Ross, Sr. (1823–September 19, 1897) and Dulcena B. Moore (January 12, 1821–June 17, 1899).[1] Ross lived on his parents' farm at least until the time of the 1880 census.[2] At the end of the 19th century, Ross Jr., was residing in Shelby, North Carolina. When his mother passed away,[3] John Ross returned to Cherokee County.[4]

As early as 1907, John W. Ross was employed by the Southern Railroad. Ross's job description was "car repairer" in the Blanding Street yards of Columbia, South Carolina. On September 1 of that year, as he was repairing a brake beam, John Ross was run over by a train. He was caught beneath one or more railway cars and severely harmed. The resulting injuries left Ross with a paralyzed right arm. This, along with the lawsuits that followed, effectively ended his career with the railroad.

After a series of three trials with verdicts favorable to Ross, the courts awarded him somewhere between $12,000.00 and $16,000.00. Once again, John Ross returned to Limestone.[5]

Already an accomplished fiddler before his accident, John W. Ross somehow managed to relearn how to manipulate the bow across the strings with a non-functioning right arm. When "Ye Olde Tyme Fiddlers

Convention" took over the Star Theatre in Gaffney the evenings of February 24 and 25, 1908, Ross was well-known enough for his fiddling prowess to be mentioned in the resulting publicity. Later conventions would play up his disability to attract spectators, labeling him the area's "only one-armed fiddler."[6]

These were still the early days for fiddling competitions and promoters were still tweaking their formulas to see what would draw a crowd. These adjustments resulted in some unusual aspects for the Gaffney convention of 1908. First off, the hall was booked for two nights, with the promoters assuming twice the financial risk (sooner after, contests were shortened to one session). Secondly, Charlotte-based classical musician Don Richardson had been contracted to demonstrate the difference between violinists and fiddlers (not that it wasn't already obvious to those in attendance). Still, twenty-odd fiddle players took to the stage for the contest. When the dust had cleared, even with his limited functionality, John Ross had captured the $10.00 first prize.[7]

JOHN W. ROSS

Photograph of John Ross with fiddle (*Gaffney Ledger*, May 12, 1921).

This may or may not have put the idea into Ross's head that he could run a fiddlers' convention as well or even better than Ed H. DeCamp had managed this one. Ten dollars was a pretty fair sum of money, but

Three: J. Ross, C. Parker and M. Woolbright Part One

> # HEAR YE. HEAR YE.
> ## AULDE TYME
> ## Fiddlers, Banjoists, Dancers and Singers.
> Come ye into convention at ye City of Gaffney
> # Dec. 29th, at 8 O'clock P. M.
> "Old Time Fiddlers' Convention," to be held under the auspices of the Hickory Grove Concert Band. Free Concert afternoon and evening.
>
> ### PRIZES.
> Best Fiddler, 1st Prize........................$4.00
> Best Fiddler, 2d Prize..........................2.00
> 1st Best Banjo Picker..........................2.00
> 2nd Best Banjo Picker..........................1.00
> 1st Best Dancer................................2.00
> 2nd Best Dancer................................1.00
> 1st Best Violin with Banjo or Guitar accompaniment............................2.00
> Best Vocal Quartett of any kind of music.......3.00
>
> **Admission: 35c., Children, 25c.**
> **Reserved Seats, 50c.**
> All contestants admitted free. All wishing to enter the contest will please send their names to   **GROVER W. BROWN,**
> **Sec. Hickory Grove Band,**
> Nov. 28 and Dec. 26-21   **HICKORY GROVE, S. C.**

Advertisement for the earliest contest won by fiddler John W. Ross documented in a newspaper ad (*Gaffney Ledger*, December 29, 1911).

possibly more could be made from promoting events. After all, now that he was forcibly retired, John W. Ross had nothing but time.

However, it would take eight years before Ross moved into staging his own contests. First, John Ross would have to make the acquaintance of the several musicians that would aid in his eventual enterprise.

John W. Ross finally took the plunge as a promoter, presenting his first fiddling challenge on his home turf of Gaffney. On Tuesday, March 21, 1916, Ross commandeered the Star Theatre for the afternoon and evening. In addition to himself, contestants included banjoists Charlie

Parker and his youngest brother Robert, as well as fiddler S.S. Gaffney,[8] whose family had provided the town with its name.

John Ross and Sam Gaffney were related by marriage (Ross's sister Amye was wedded to one of Gaffney's cousins),[9] and the two fiddlers often competed together with duets of standard fiddle pieces such as "The Downfall of Paris" or "Fisher's Hornpipe."[10] Following the style of the day, it is probable that one fiddler "seconded" the other by providing harmony and a rhythmical backup.

S.S. Gaffney

Fiddler Samuel Shelton Gaffney was born on a farm in Limestone Springs on June 28, 1856.[11] His grandfather, Robert Michael Gaffney, had come to the United States from Ireland and eventually purchased the land which became the future site for the town of Gaffney.[12]

On March 6, 1879, Sam Gaffney married Louisa Jane Harris (born May 10, 1860, in North Carolina),[13] eventually raising a large family on their farm.[14] By 1930, besides agriculture and fiddling, S.S. Gaffney was repairing and selling watches.[15] After fifty-nine years of marriage, Louisa Gaffney passed away on June 4, 1938.[16] Sam Gaffney followed on January 27, 1945.[17]

Between 1916 and his death in 1930, John W. Ross managed and promoted twenty-three fiddling contests. Ross partnered for three of them with S.S. Gaffney. Gaffney also presented another six contests on his own and one in conjunction with Charlie Parker. Parker helped Ross with two events and worked with Mack Woolbright on one. For many of these years, John Ross only presented one or two annual fiddlers' conventions. The return to peace in the year 1919 was the exception, as Ross, either on his own or with the help of others, held seven musical competitions.

Charlie and Robert Parker

One of the local banjoists of choice for both John W. Ross and S.S. Gaffney was Charlie Parker. Charlie was the third child of Jacob Gabriel Parker (May 1850–June 22, 1905), a farmer turned shoemaker, and Amanda Jane Ervin/Erwin (October 6, 1857–November 11, 1896) of southern Iredell County, North Carolina. Married in November of

OLD TIME Fiddler's Convention

Gaffney, South Carolina

Friday, December 19th, 7-30 P. M.

COURT HOUSE

THE FOLLOWING CASH PRIZES WILL BE AWARDED:

Best Old Time Fiddler	$4.00
Second Best Old Time Fiddler	$2.00
Best Duet on Stringed Instruments	$3.00
Best Banjo	$3.00
Best Guitar	$3.00
Best Duet on Handsaw and Violin	$3.00
Best Buck Dancer	$1.00
Best Old Time Dancer	$1.00

The Convention will be under the management of a veteran musician—S. S. GAFFNEY. All Musicians wishing to take part please report to Courthouse at 7:30 p. m. day of Convention.

Admission 20c and 35c

Don't forget the date and don't miss hearing these Old Timers pat their feet.

EVERYBODY INVITED TO ATTEND.

Advertisement for fiddlers' convention to be held Friday, December 19, 1924, at the Gaffney, South Carolina, courthouse, managed by S.S. Gaffney (*Gaffney Ledger*, December 13, 1924).

Old Fiddler's Convention

S. S. Gaffney, T. K. Thomason, Mr. Mitchel, H. B. McDaniel, J. C. Johnson, and a number of Contestants will compete for a number of valuable cash prizes, which will be awarded to the most proficient musicians at the Graded School Auditorium at Blacksburg Friday night April, 10th. at 8 p. m. A cash prize will also be given to the best buck & wing dancer. The public is invited to attend.

S. S. GAFFNEY
MANAGER

Advertisement for "Old Fiddler's Convention," managed by S.S. Gaffney, to be held in the grade school auditorium, Blacksburg, Friday, April 10, 1925 (*Cherokee Times*, April 6, 1925).

1877,[18] between 1878 and 1893, the couple had ten children. Charles Monroe Parker was born outside of Statesville on March 18, 1883.[19]

Amanda Jane died suddenly when Charlie was twelve or thirteen years old, leaving the eldest children to care for the younger ones. By his mid-teens, Charlie Parker had joined his older sister in the local cotton mill, where he gained employment in the spinning room as a speeder.[20]

Sometime between 1900 and 1908, Charlie Parker moved to the Gaffney, South Carolina, area, where he married Jessie Raymouth/Ramon Porter (1881–1924).[21] The couple produced two children.

Like Ross, Charlie Parker became a familiar sight at local entertainments and fiddling contests. Parker was definitely performing as early as 1910, when he accompanied John W. Ross at the Rehoboth School.[22]

The earliest newspaper reference for Charlie's appearance at a fiddling contest was in 1915. Although no prize was offered for banjo playing, Parker played as a part of the convention program at the Gaffney Court House on August 7.[23]

Charlie Parker with banjo, circa 1925 (courtesy Parker family).

Charlie's younger brother Robert Otto Parker was born May 29, 1893, as was Charlie, in Iredell County.[24] Bob Parker could have been living in the Gaffney area as early as 1916, when he attended Ross's fiddlers' convention in the company of his brother.[25] On Friday, March 17, Charlie proposed to perform "[The] Party [That] Wrote Home Sweet Home Never Was a Married Man," a song he was later to record with Mack Woolbright; as well as the fiddle tune "Cumberland Gap." Bob Parker was projected to render "Turkey in The Straw,"[26] a ragtime banjo showpiece previously recorded by classic finger picking banjo stars such as Vess L. Ossman and Fred Van Eps.[27] When the dust settled, the Parker brothers had captured both the first (Charlie) and second (Robert) banjo prizes.[28] A year later, at what appears to have become an annual event, the Parker brothers joined fiddler S.S. Gaffney and his son, guitarist Carl Leonard Gaffney (May 24, 1892–July 12, 1976),[29] to take first place string "orchestra." Charlie also won second prizes for backing fiddler Edgar

What Earl Scruggs Heard

Robert and Ollie Parker, circa 1918 (courtesy Parker family).

Three: J. Ross, C. Parker and M. Woolbright Part One

Lionel Stacy (January 4, 1885–October 14, 1949)[30] and in the banjo division, while both Parkers got a second-place award for backing John W. Ross.[31]

By June of 1917, Bob Parker had made the move from North Carolina to a farm in Thickety, southwest of Gaffney.[32] Several months later, on August 30, 1917, the youngest Parker brother married Ollie Eva Green.[33]

In March of 1918, the musical Parkers appeared at conventions in Gaffney as well as one held at Rock Hill high school.[34] For one contest, Charlie was slated to perform "Conscript Bill," which appears to reference the Civil War–time draft,[35] while Robert favored the topical novelty, "Get Out and Get Under."[36] This song, the full title being "He'll Have to Get Under, Get Out and Get Under (To Fix Up His Automobile)," was featured on Broadway and recorded in 1913 by both Billy Murray and Al Jolson.[37] The older Parker took the banjo prize.[38] On the 23rd of the month, Charlie and Robert entertained with John Ross at the school in White Plains.[39] However, within the year, Robert Parker was enlisted into the army, ending for the time being his local music-making.[40]

When Charlie Parker reported to the Draft Board in 1918, he was working at the Limestone Cotton Mill.[41] With his brother still away, Charlie continued his entertaining without Robert, attending the Cherokee County fiddlers' convention promoted by John W. Ross in 1919. On April 19, Parker took another first place for his banjo performance.[42]

In June of 1919, following his military service, Robert Parker rejoined Charlie on the fiddlers' convention circuit.[43] In Gaffney on June 14, the older sibling again grabbed the first prize for banjo.[44]

At the beginning of 1920, Robert and Ollie Parker were renting a house in the Limestone section of Gaffney, where Robert worked in a local cotton mill.[45] When Bob and Ollie Parker began having children, his public music making came to an end.[46] May 13, 1921, appears to have been Robert Parker's last fiddle contest.[47] Robert Otto Parker died in Gaffney, possibly from a heart attack, on August 8, 1930.[48]

Even while working full-time and with familial obligations, Charlie Parker aggressively pursued a musical career. In August of 1919, Parker traveled to Cleveland County, North Carolina, where John W. Ross was managing a fiddlers' gathering. Playing the hymn "[In The] Sweet Bye and Bye," "Conscript Bill," "The Man That Wrote Home Sweet Home Never Was a Married Man," "Me and my Gal" as well as "Cumberland Gap," Charlie was outgunned by local favorite Mack Crow. Crow won $3.00 for first place banjo, while Parker had to settle for the $2.00

> **THE NEW STAR THEATRE**
>
> **ONE NIGHT ONLY**
>
> **FRIDAY, MARCH 1st.**
>
> Second Annual Cherokee County
>
> **OLD FIDDLERS' CONVENTION**
>
> Under management of Cherokee's noted one arm fiddler; John W. Ross.
>
> **FIDDLING, SINGING AND DANCING**
>
> An entertainment that does not bring a blush to the cheek yet is amusing and instructive.
>
> **Admisson: 50c, 35c, 25c**

Advertisement for the Second Annual Cherokee County Old Fiddlers' Convention, New Star Theatre, Friday, March 1, 1918, managed by John W. Ross. The Parker brothers competed at this gathering (*Gaffney Ledger*, February 26, 1918).

second prize.[49] In the fall of the year, John Ross fiddled with Charlie on banjo for concerts at the schoolhouses in Butlers and White Plains, South Carolina.[50]

By the beginning of 1920, Charlie and Jessie Parker, along with their two children Beatrice and Oris B.,[51] were renting a farm in Gaffney's

STRAND TO-MORROW

YE OLE TYME

FIDDLERS' CONVENTION

Under Direction

JOHN W. ROSS

Cherokee's Famous "One Armed" Fiddler

Thirty musicians have volunteered to help in this entertainment.

It promises to be the best and most successful of old fidlers' conventions.

Fiddling, Banjo Playing, Singing and Dancing. A program of rare and unique entertainment.

ADMISSION - - - 25c, 35c, 50c

Seats now on Sale at the Box Office.

Advertisement for fiddlers' convention promoted by John W. Ross. This was the last documented appearance at a convention by Robert Parker (*Gaffney Ledger*, May 12, 1921.

Limestone neighborhood. It's possible that Charlie, as was a common practice, alternated agriculture with mill work, farming during the summer months and working in a textile mill during the winter.[52] Parker continued to perform with John Ross, returning to the Butlers school in March of 1920,[53] competing at Ross's convention on June 18 at the Strand Theatre in Gaffney (where the banjo prize went to Dr. William Hicks),[54] and again, a year later, with his two children, "who will sing and dance." Unlike the previous year, Charlie Parker took first prize.[55] For the last two weeks of May and the first week of June, John Ross and Charlie Parker played a string of engagements. The duo appeared in Blacksburg, South Carolina; in a benefit for the Sunday school at the Junior Order Hall in Cherokee Falls; and again in Blacksburg in benefit of the Junior Order United American Mechanics.[56]

Parker ended 1921 performing with Sam Gaffney for the Rotary Club at the Hotel Carroll. A local scribe noted, "That night, upon the conclusion of the excellent dinner, an enjoyable old-style dance was held in the hotel lobby."[57] Charlie also attended John Ross's October 1922 Gaffney convention.[58]

On January 19, 1923, John W. Ross and Charlie Parker performed at the Gaffney courthouse in benefit of the Confederate memorial fund. Along with Ross on fiddle and Parker on banjo that night was Mack Woolbright playing the guitar and mandolin.[59] Parker and Woolbright were later to join forces to record some memorable sides on 78 rpm records that influenced, among others, a young Earl Scruggs.

Mack Woolbright: Part One

George Mack Woolbright was born in Pinckney Township, Union County, South Carolina, on September 18, 1890. Mack was the son of farmer James (born January 1850) and Louise Woolbright (born August 1855). James had fought on the Confederate side in the Civil War.[60] Renting the farm where they were raising three children, two from a previous marriage, the Woolbrights had been married for eleven years.[61]

Partially sightless from birth, Mack was sent to the state school for the blind at Cedar Springs, South Carolina. Woolbright spent at least two school years at the institution, from the fall of 1900 through the spring of 1902.[62]

Mack's father died when he was seventeen years old.[63] Three years later, Mack Woolbright was living on a rented farm near Gowdeysville,

Three: J. Ross, C. Parker and M. Woolbright Part One

Cherokee County, South Carolina. Along with his widowed mother was Mack's only surviving sibling, younger brother James King Woolbright (born May 8, 1895).[64] His mother passed away from breast cancer twelve years later in 1919,[65] leaving Mack to a somewhat nomadic existence.

Although nothing is known of how Mack began playing, his earliest music-making, and/or his influences, it was not uncommon for vision-impaired Southerners to turn to music for their living. We know from his draft registration in June of 1917 that Woolbright was considered "unemployed" by the authorities,[66] and that no occupation other than "musician" was ever attributed to him.

John W. Ross and Charlie Parker were acquainted with Mack Woolbright at least by June of 1921, when Woolbright joined Ross associates the DeStaffino family for performances in Cherokee Falls and at the courthouse in Gaffney. As described by the *Ledger* newspaper, "Mr. Woolbright, although almost blind, is in a class by himself as a guitarist. He gives a remarkable performance of imitating other stringed instruments, such as the banjo, violin, harmonica, etc. He is a talented musician."[67] Their paths crossed again in the fall, when Parker and Woolbright (billed as "the blind guitarist") appeared separately at Ross's fiddlers' gathering in Gaffney.[68] By 1923, the trio's courthouse concert was followed by a Parker and Woolbright co-billing at Ross's October fiddlers' convention.[69]

For the initial appearances of Parker and Woolbright, Charlie played the banjo ("There is no better banjoist to be found than Charley [sic] Parker," bragged an unknown reporter in the local newspaper). Additionally, as related in the *Gaffney Ledger*, "Mr. Woolbright, although blind, plays five different musical instruments and also sings."[70]

As Mack Woolbright was establishing himself as a local performer, Parker's life went through an upheaval. At the end of 1924, Charlie lost his wife Jessie after a year-long illness. She was only forty-three years old and left Parker with their two small children to raise by himself.[71] So it came as no surprise when Charlie Parker quickly remarried. Within a year, Parker and Mary Maybelle/Mabel Yones (born circa 1905) had tied the knot.

Charlie rapidly returned to performing, appearing at the Holly Grove School on the South Carolina/North Carolina border with John W. Ross in June of 1925,[72] and with Woolbright at Ross's Gaffney courthouse convention October 16, 1926.[73] Mack also made a solo "visit" to Gastonia, North Carolina, at the end of August in 1926.[74]

It is opportune for banjo scholars that Parker and Woolbright were

> # Old Fiddlers Convention
> ## at the
> ## COURT HOUSE
> ### SATURDAY NIGHT
> ## OCTOBER 16th
>
> This promises to be the musical treat of the year. One of the features will be a 5 piece orchestra of banjos from North Carolina. Also there will be many other musicians from North Carolina. Anotheh headliner will be the two well known Gaffney musicians, Parker and Woolbright. Many dancers will take part, among them several young ladies who are Charleston artists.
>
> **CASH PRIZES AWARDED ALL WINNERS**
>
> ADMISSION 15c and 25c
>
> ## JOHN W. ROSS IN CHARGE

Advertisement for fiddlers' convention, courthouse, Saturday, October 16, 1926, promoted by John W. Ross. Parker and Woolbright would be featured, along with "a 5 piece orchestra of banjos from North Carolina" (*Gaffney Ledger*, October 12, 1926).

tapped to record for Columbia Records in the late 1920s. The ensuing coverage of the recording sessions opens a window into the lives of Mack and Charlie that would otherwise have been lost.

In 1927, Lawrence Eular Weaver, manager of the local Columbia Records distributor located in Gaffney, received an invitation to bring Woolbright and his performing partner Charlie Parker to Atlanta to

Three: J. Ross, C. Parker and M. Woolbright Part One

make "test" recordings (i.e., to audition). Weaver, born December 20, 1893, in Cleveland County, North Carolina, had farmed as a young man.[75] However, after serving in World War I, Lawrence Weaver married and moved to Gaffney to begin working in the retail music business. First, L.E. sold pianos,[76] later transferring over to the Gossett Music Company, where his wife Lillian also worked after he took over ownership of the store.[77] Gossett became somewhat proactive with the record labels, possibly initiating and carrying "personal" recordings (i.e., "vanity" records made for sale exclusively by the artists) manufactured by Gennett Records for the Parham Brothers Quartet.[78]

In early April, Weaver, Woolbright and Parker journeyed to Atlanta, where, according to the *Gaffney Ledger*, Mack and Charlie "made a number of test records and signed contracts as Columbia Phonograph Company artists, exclusively." On April 6, four sides were committed to wax. Two, "Where Shall I Be" and "While Eternal Ages Roll," were obviously in a religious vein and remained unissued. "Give That Ni**er Ham," with its roots in blackface performance, and "Rabbit Chase" both featured Parker's old-style banjo down-picking and lead singing. The duo was issued on Columbia 15154-D and available locally in Gaffney by that summer.[79]

Back in South Carolina by week's end,[80] Parker and Woolbright returned to area appearances. On Friday, April 22, they were paid to entertain at Ross's "Old Time Fiddler's Convention" held at the county courthouse.[81]

On Saturday, July 16, Gossett Music announced that the first Parker and Woolbright record release was available for sale.[82] This further encouraged local interest in the duo, resulting in a spate of engagements. Mack was part of a musical group at a local home on August 4,[83] and Parker and Woolbright worked yet another Gaffney fiddlers' meet on October 28, this time under the auspices of S.S. Gaffney.[84] Mack and Charlie also appeared with Ross in early November, giving an "Entertainment" and "Fiddlers Convention" at Kings Creek on Saturday, November 5. A joint promotion by all three musicians, Parker and Woolbright promised to perform on guitar, mandolin, banjo and saw, "together with old-time and modern singing."[85]

Since their first record release was selling well, eventually moving almost 11,000 copies, a "hit" for those days, a second Columbia session was quickly arranged. The duo returned to Atlanta either on Wednesday, November 9, or Thursday, November 10, 1927. This time, all four recorded selections were issued. "The Man Who Wrote

What Earl Scruggs Heard

Home Sweet Home Never Was a Married Man," with the instrumental rendition of "Home Sweet Home" that inspired and informed Earl Scruggs, was issued in May of 1928 and paired on Columbia disc 15236-D with "Ticklish Reuben." Modern listeners can hear "The Man Who Wrote Home Sweet Home" on *The North Carolina Banjo Collection* (Rounder Records) and "Ticklish Reuben" on *Good for What Ails* (Old Hat Records). Originally titled "The Party That Wrote Home Sweet Home," Fleta Jan Brown's comedic composition about the trials and tribulations of married life was first published in 1908. Cal Stewart's turn-of-the-century recording of the novelty "laughing" song "Ticklish Reuben" launched the ditty into popular circulation and is possibly where the duo learned the piece. Their second 78 rpm disc wasn't issued until more than three years later in September of 1931 during the Depression. Columbia 15694-D included "The Old Arm Chair" backed with the narrative 19th-century ballad "Will the Weaver."[86] The nostalgic "heart-song" "Granny's Old Arm Chair" dates to the late 1870s, when both John Read and Frank S. Carr claimed the composition. The song seems to have achieved a modicum of popularity among country musicians indicated by the large number of groups that recorded the piece during the late 1920s and early 1930s.[87] Both Parker and Woolbright platters feature lead finger-picking banjo with guitar back-up accompanying two-part harmony singing rendered in a nasal folk style.

There's an unsolved mystery surrounding the second batch of recordings made by Charlie Parker and Mack Woolbright. Up until recently, it was always assumed that Mack played the majority of the banjo (if not all of it) on the second Columbia session. As opposed to the down-stroking banjo playing of the first Atlanta trip, which was assigned by Columbia to Parker, the second session exclusively featured heavily syncopated up-picked banjo. Those issued recordings fail to allocate the banjo playing to either Parker or Woolbright. Many years later, Tony Russell, the author of *Country Music Records: A Discography, 1921–1942*, the definitive published reference on these matters, assigned the banjo to Charlie Parker.[88]

Before Russell's book was issued, the only other publication describing these performances ascribed the banjo parts to Mack Woolbright. None other than banjo pioneer Earl Scruggs, who grew up just north of Gaffney in North Carolina, remembers hearing Mack play.

Writing in *Earl Scruggs and the 5-String Banjo*, Scruggs said the following:

Three: J. Ross, C. Parker and M. Woolbright Part One

> There were a few good three-finger banjo pickers I admired who lived near Flint Hill. Mack Woolbright, a blind banjo picker who recorded with Charlie Parker for Columbia Records in the late 1920s, stands out in my mind. I remember him from a visit he made to my Uncle Sidney Ruppe's home. Mack rocked in a rocking chair while picking "Home Sweet Home" in the key of C while in C tuning. The G7 chord he played in that tune sent chills down my spine. I was six years old then [circa 1930] and couldn't help but wonder how a blind person could pick a banjo so beautifully.[89]

These comments are reinforced by Earl's oldest brother Junie, who, many years later, told a local newspaper:

> There was a blind banjo picker named Mack Woolbright—he was born without any eyes.... I remember him playing at a show at the Flint Hill School the year Earl was born [1924]. Played "Home Sweet Home." When Earl plays "Home Sweet Home" it sounds exactly like him.[90]

Here's the problem with these stories. Both Mack Woolbright and Charlie Parker played multiple instruments, including the five-string banjo and the guitar. In period accounts from before his recording sessions for Columbia, Woolbright is credited with performing on "five different musical instruments,"[91] including the mandolin,[92] as well as being "in a class by himself as a guitarist."[93] Unfortunately, there aren't any newspaper articles predating his second Columbia session that specifically label Mack Woolbright as a banjoist.

On the other hand, Charlie Parker, before meeting Woolbright as well as during the early part of their collaboration, was consistently singled out for excelling on the banjo. From 1915 until the end of 1927, Parker won five first banjo prizes and two second places at area fiddlers' conventions. The *Gaffney Ledger* exclaimed, "There is no better banjoist to be found than Charley Parker."[94] Mack Woolbright's banjo playing is only explicitly cited after the second recording session by Parker and Woolbright.[95]

The other red flag involves the stand-out performance of Parker and Woolbright's second Atlanta trip. "The Man Who Wrote Home Sweet Home Never Was a Married Man" was a sort of theme song for Charlie Parker, and seemingly not associated at all with Mack Woolbright (Mack, the supposed harmony singer on their 78 rpm record, doesn't even appear to have fully learned the words). As early as 1916, Parker used the piece as his go-to selection for competitions.

Obviously, it is possible that Woolbright also played the song, either before or after Mack and Charlie rendered the composition for Columbia. Junie Scruggs dates hearing Woolbright play "Home Sweet

What Earl Scruggs Heard

Home" on the banjo to 1924, while Earl remembers his exposure first occurring around 1930. Regardless, we'll never know how accurate the Scruggs family memories were and if these recollections were strengthened with the ownership by Earl and his siblings of Parker and Woolbright's 78 rpm disc.

Which all adds up to this: I'm still not one hundred percent convinced of the banjoist's identity on the second and third Parker/Woolbright records.

Upon returning from their second recording session (which was to be their last), Woolbright and Parker competed at a fiddlers' convention held in benefit of the Cherokee Falls school. The Tuesday evening, November 15, competition drew forty contestants. That audience, five hundred strong, heard Woolbright take the banjo prize from eight other contestants, therefore winning $5.00. Charlie Parker beat six others to win the $5.00 guitar prize and the two won an additional $2.00 for "best duet."[96]

Charlie Parker and Mack Woolbright continued with their area appearances. They entertained February 10, 1928, at a private home[97]; promoted the Gaffney fiddlers' convention at the courthouse May 4[98]; played Charlie's family reunion outside of Statesville, North Carolina,

---

Musical Entertainment
Kings Creek School
Saturday, November 5th
7 O'CLOCK

Instruments: Guitar, Mandolin, Banjo and Saw. Old time and modern singing.

Ross, Parker and Woolbright in charge

ADMISSION 15c & 25c

Advertisement for "Musical Entertainment" with Ross, Parker and Woolbright, November 5, 1927. "Kings Creek Entertainment," (*Gaffney Ledger*, November 3, 1927).

Three: J. Ross, C. Parker and M. Woolbright Part One

Old Fiddlers' Convention

COURT HOUSE
FRIDAY NIGHT, MAY 4, 1928
8 O'CLOCK
GAFFNEY, S. C.

There will be a large number of Old Time Fiddlers, Banjo Pickers, Guitar Players as well as Fancy Dancers, including the Charleston and the Tangle Foot Orchestra.

CASH PRIZES

Cash Prizes will be awarded the winners in each contest.

This entertainment is being promoted by Charles Parker and Mack Woolbright, thus assuring you of plenty of fun and entertainment.

ADMISSION : 15c and 25c

Don't Forget the Date and Place

Advertisement for "Old Fiddlers' Convention," Friday, May 4, 1928, at the Gaffney courthouse, promoted by Parker and Woolbright (*Gaffney Ledger*, May 3, 1928).

What Earl Scruggs Heard

on August 3[99]; and performed at the Cherokee Falls High School auditorium on December 14.[100]

Without the promise of additional recording sessions, when the New Year's came, Parker and Woolbright went their separate ways. Charlie Parker performed solo at John Ross's convention in Blacksburg, South Carolina, on November 7, 1929,[101] and the pair co-managed the Gaffney contest on January 25, 1930.[102] Charlie lost his friend on March 28, when John W. Ross died after a short illness. Ross was seventy-seven years old and had lived as a bachelor for all his days.[103] Having enlivened the lives of countless area residents through his entertainments and fiddlers' gatherings, John Ross left behind a changing musical landscape. Home entertainments were being usurped by stage shows, with syncopated jazz rhythms hot-rodding local string band music.

After the death of John W. Ross, Charlie Parker continued to work in a local cotton mill[104] and promoted several fiddlers' conventions with Sam Gaffney.[105] Following a considerable period of declining health, Charlie Parker passed away June 8, 1931, and was buried in the Corinth Baptist Church Cemetery.[106] Parker, like his parents and siblings, died young, of heart disease at the age of forty-seven.[107]

Four

Mack Woolbright: Parts Two and Three

Parker and Woolbright's sessions for Columbia Records gave each musician a share of local celebrity. After his partnership with Charlie Parker ran its course, Mack's notoriety supplied him with a steady stream of area performances and opportunities. In 1929, for example, we know that Woolbright "entertained" March 12 at the home of Mr. and Mrs. Faye Pridmore.[1] However, for the next several years, the majority of Mack's playing was as the leader of what came to be known as Woolbright's Serenaders.

Woolbright's Serenaders

By August of 1929, Woolbright had enlisted three area musicians to back his banjo playing and singing. They included Richard Fox on violin, Erston (also called "Erskine" by the newspapers) Sprouse/mandolin and guitarist Ralph Patrick.

John Richard Fox was born April 28, 1903[2] in Hamblen County, east Tennessee, to farmer Louis (also spelled "Lewis") Maynard (October 8, 1880–November 28, 1950) and Nora Moyer Fox[3] (July 4, 1878–January 12, 1964).[4] Richard was the oldest of seven children, with the majority of his siblings arriving on a family sojourn to Missouri after his birth.[5] By the beginning of 1920, the Fox clan had relocated once again, this time to Spartanburg, South Carolina, where they resided in Cartwright Village. Louis worked as a carpenter, Richard as a weaver and his sister Bernice as a spinner in a local cotton mill.[6] By the time Richard joined the Serenaders, the Fox family had moved to the Hamrick Mill Village in Limestone.[7] John Richard Fox passed away in Gaffney October 5, 1971.[8]

Erston Young Sprouse and Ralph Patrick were next-door neighbors on Railroad Avenue in the Limestone section of Gaffney.[9] Erston, born

What Earl Scruggs Heard

in Spartanburg October 12, 1912,[10] came to Gaffney with his family in 1924. When he played with Woolbright, Sprouse was living with his parents Miller Young (February 2, 1880–February 22, 1959) and Nellie Lark Sprouse (June 5, 1883–October 16, 1965),[11] and working as a cotton mill hand.[12] Erston Sprouse died December 30, 1984, at the age of 72.[13]

Ralph Edward Patrick was from a cotton mill family as well. Ralph was born near Spartanburg in Glendale, South Carolina, October 10, 1910, to Alfonso Milton (January 11, 1876–April 2, 1960) and Isadora Stowe Patrick (October 5, 1878–December 17, 1951).[14] Like his friend Erston Sprouse, Ralph Patrick lived with his parents while playing with Mack Woolbright. Unlike the other band members, Patrick earned his living as a bookkeeper at Merchants and Planter National Bank.[15] Ralph Patrick passed away December 3, 1989.[16]

The Serenaders appear to have formed as the "house band" for the Palmetto Camp (i.e., chapter), one of the many South Carolina affiliates of the immensely popular Woodmen of the World. The Woodmen were a "mutual aid" organization, providing its members with affordable insurance coverage, as well as fellowship and entertainment. The camp was among at least three local W.O.W. clubs.

Mack Woolbright's connection to the Woodmen chapter, indeed, to the three younger musicians, may have come through fiddler Richard Fox. Fox had led the local camp's string band prior to Woolbright's participation.[17] While the previous members are unknown, it's not a stretch to believe that Richard had recruited Woolbright, Sprouse and Patrick for the W.O.W.

For the remainder of 1929, and into the following year, Woolbright's Serenaders would appear at Palmetto's weekly meeting on Thursday evenings, as well as for various outings sponsored by the organization.[18] Outside of their obligations to the Woodmen, Woolbright's Serenaders were kept busy with personal appearances.

On August 6, 1929, the quartet provided music for a meeting of the American Legion[19] and August 23, at E.R. Parker's restaurant.[20] September 3, they shared the stage with the Kennedy and Lovelace string bands at a street dance in Gaffney.[21] September 4, the Serenaders were responsible for the music at the Timber Ridge Community Club.[22] The following week, Woolbright's Serenaders entertained with "Mack's version of 'Turkey in the Straw' and his famous laughing song (possibly 'Ticklish Reuben')" at a chicken stew on the banks of the Broad River sponsored by the Palmetto Camp.[23]

In September of 1929, the band performed on the 13th at the closing of Holly Grove summer school[24] and for the Gaffney Lion's Club on the 23rd.[25] The Serenaders performed twice for Charlotte's Wayside Club, first traveling to the Queen City October 4[26] and then in the Gaffney high school auditorium on November 15.[27]

In 1930, Woolbright's Serenaders added Richard Fox's younger brother Roy on guitar. Daniel Leroy Fox was born on November 27, 1908, in Morristown, Tennessee. Roy moved with his family to South Carolina and, like his father and siblings, worked in textiles his whole life. Roy Fox died from acute pancreatitis October 15, 1945, at the age of thirty-six.[28]

The year of 1930 began with an engagement at the old Gaffney court house, where Mack reunited on January 25 with fiddlers' convention promoters Charlie Parker and John W. Ross.[29] In February, WSPA-Spartanburg, "The Voice of South Carolina," began regular broadcasts, and the Serenaders were summoned to the studios on top of the Montgomery building for the first of several appearances.[30] Woolbright's Serenaders repeated their performance on May 30 with a half-hour program at 10 p.m.[31] and again in January of the new year.[32]

For the rest of 1930, Woolbright's quartet played a mixture of schools and public concerts.[33] Mack and company also competed in area fiddle contests, winning the $10.00 (in gold) first prize at Gaffney's string band competition September 19,[34] as well as second place at the White Plains school contest on October 25.[35]

Once their tenure with the W.O.W. concluded, Mack Woolbright separated from his younger compatriots. Possibly his older style of music didn't mix well with the musical ambitions of the other Serenaders. With the addition of bassist Reese Hensley, Richard and Roy Fox became the Moonlight Dreamers and continued to regularly broadcast over WSPA.[36]

Martin Melody Boys

One band that appeared at the same venues and on the same programs as Mack Woolbright and company, as well as sharing his musicians, was Martin Melody Boys. The group predated Woolbright's Serenaders in their association with the W.O.W. and, with changing personnel, lasted into the 1940s. The Melody Boys are best known for their unique recording issued in 1929.

Even though the two bands drew from the same pool of pickers, the

What Earl Scruggs Heard

groups took a very different approach to the string band sound. While Woolbright's Serenaders looked back to the 19th century for its repertoire, the Melody Boys were firmly a 20th-century ensemble. As one can see from their repertoire that included the 1927 hit "My Blue Heaven" and "I'd Love to Live in Loveland (With a Girl Like You)," Martin Melody Boys leaned heavily on the popular songs and tunes of their day. It's obvious that A.D. Martin was trying for an audience outside of the one reserved for square dances and fiddlers' conventions.

The group formed at the end of 1928, when mandolinist Martin organized the first iteration of the Melody Boys.[37] Although his parents were from South Carolina, Alfred David Martin was born in Harris, Rutherford County, North Carolina, August 15, 1894. He was the next to youngest child of David Beauregard (December 6, 1861–January 3, 1896) and Martha Hester Quinn Martin (February 22, 1862–December 27, 1932).[38] Following David's passing, Martha moved her family back to South Carolina. By 1910, the Martin family were all living and working in the Limestone cotton mill village. The Martins had already begun making music at local homes, the group at that time including oldest brother Robert Pinkney (born June 20, 1882), Alfred and his sister Alice Eugenia (born October 16, 1890).[39]

Around 1913, A.D. Martin married Carrie Hyder Gowan (June 4, 1894–December 20, 1980).[40] During his thirty-five plus years of avocational music-making around Gaffney, A.D. Martin tried many professions. These included "laborer" for Shiplett Concrete,[41] running a confectionary and peanut butter manufactory[42] and working as a printer.[43]

Besides Martin leading on the banjo-mandolin, the original Melody Boys included Glenn Thompson on violin, Claude Thompson playing tenor banjo, as well as Joe Guthrie on the guitar.[44]

The brothers Thompson were the sons of Christenberry (circa 1875–August 1, 1962),[45] a farmer turned cotton mill weaver,[46] and Lavada Griffin Thompson (July 25, 1880–June 30, 1950).[47] Glenn Elbert Thompson (November 24, 1907–May 7, 1971)[48] and his older brother Claude (July 8, 1904–June 20, 1966)[49] grew up in Gowdeysville, moving with their parents by the late 1920s into the Limestone section of Gaffney. The boys worked at the local cotton mill by day and played music at private gatherings in the evenings. The Thompsons sometimes accompanied fiddler Richard Fox, who later played with Mack Woolbright, as well as Joe Guthrie on guitar.[50]

The family of Joseph Buren Guthrie (July 21, 1906–November 21, 1963),[51] like many musicians in this area, went from farming to jobs in area textile mills. The son of Wofford O. and Mamie Jennings Guthrie,[52] Joe married Helen Wheat around 1924 and had two children while playing music and working at a cotton mill in Limestone.[53]

Even though Glenn and Claude Thompson moved in 1931 to Anderson, South Carolina, for employment at Appleton (textile) Mills,[54] they continued their musical association with A.D. Martin. The Thompsons played with Martin through 1934, although Glenn took a break during 1932–1933 to perform with other musicians.[55] These included future Melody Boys Fletcher Blackwell/violin, Welford Gordon/mandolin and Ralph Patrick/guitar.[56] Glenn also used this hiatus to marry, taking Atrulia Brooks of Anderson as his bride on April 22, 1933.[57]

For much of their existence, Martin Melody Boys reserved Tuesday nights for the Cherry Camp of the Woodmen of the World meetings,[58] along with the occasional special W.O.W. event on Friday evenings.[59] The group was also "loaned out" to perform for the other local chapters of the Woodmen, as well as for additional community organizations.[60] During the band's initial years of 1929–1931, other times were filled with banquets, oyster stews, school concerts, restaurant appearances, church homecomings, religious revivals and birthday parties in a variety of settings.[61] Three especially important venues for Martin Melody Boys were radio, fiddlers' conventions and recording.

Alfred Martin, Glenn and Claude Thompson, and Joe Guthrie first broadcast over North Carolina's premier radio station WBT-Charlotte. On Thursday evening, January 3, 1929, the Melody Boys were scheduled to play live at 7:30 for one half hour. Instead, as reported in the *Gaffney Ledger*, listener requests by phone and telegram (numbering around seventy) required a full hour to fulfill. The Melody Boys played selections ranging from the planned "fight" song, "The Washington [and] Lee Swing"; "My Own Iona," the "Hawaiian" love song from 1916; "I'd Love to Live in Loveland [With a Girl Like You]"; "Down Yonder"; and "[My] Blue Heaven" (featured in the Ziegfeld Follies of 1927); to the requests "Red Wing"; "Golden Slippers"; and "The Sea [sic, C] March."[62]

The group was to broadcast three more times. On Wednesday, January 9, a repeat of enthusiastic listener response also expanded the Melody Boys airtime to an hour. It necessitated a return to the airwaves on Wednesday, January 31. For their third program that month, Martin Melody Boys treated the listeners to "Down Yonder," "Ain't She Sweet," "My Blue Heaven," the 1928 hit "That's My Weakness Now," "Washington and Lee Swing," "Over the Waves Waltz," as well as "Chinese Breakdown." Their fourth and final broadcast over WBT was on

Wednesday, February 20.[63] A year later, radio station WSPA-Spartanburg signed on the air and arranged for Martin Melody Boys to make several appearances.[64]

As is noted previously, fiddlers' conventions were major events for string musicians to share their music with other pickers as well as with local audiences. Martin Melody Boys either competed or were hired to perform (but not allowed to contest) at around a half dozen gatherings during the first three years of the group's existence. These included traveling to Harris, North Carolina June 15, 1929, to take on local favorites Snuffy Jenkins and his band in the local high school auditorium,[65] as well as a number of competitions held in Gaffney promoted by John W. Ross, Charlie Parker and Sam Gaffney.[66]

A high point for the quartet of Martin, Thompson and Guthrie was their recording session of April 16, 1929. The assumption is that the local Columbia Records dealer L.E. Weaver, as he had done for Charlie Parker and Mack Woolbright several years previously, arranged for Martin Melody Boys' Atlanta recordings. Four titles were rendered that day. The two issued on a 78 rpm disc were "An Old Sweetheart of Mine" and "The Donald Rag."

"Because You Were an Old Sweetheart of Mine," was written by

Advertisement for Martin Melody Boys' WBT broadcasts and Tolleson Music, local sellers of Gibson and Ludwig instruments. "Hit Made Over Radio By Gaffney Musicians," (*Gaffney Ledger*, January 5, 1929).

Four. Mack Woolbright: Parts Two and Three

> **"IT PAYS TO BUY THE BEST"**
>
> Says Mr. A. D. Martin, who, with his Melody Boys broadcasts from Station WBT. Mr. Martin uses a
>
> **GIBSON**
>
> MANDOLIN
>
> **J. R. TOLLESON & COMPANY**
>
> Gibson Agents for Cherokee County
>
> Opposite Peoples Drug Store

Advertisement, "Gaffney Musicians Score Second Hit Over Radio; Third Engagement Made," (*Gaffney Ledger*, January 12, 1929).

> **Martin's Melody Boys**
> At
> **Cherokee Falls School House**
> **"Something Different"**
> Friday Night, October 11th, 7:30 P. M.
>
> A large variety of songs from the oldest up to the very latest. "Martin's Melody Boys" have become famous throughout the U. S. A., for their sweet harmony and melody which has been broadcast over the Radio and recorded on Phonograph Records.
> This program will be worth your time for the "Melody Boys" always please their audiences everywhere. Admission 15c and 25c.

Advertisement for Martin Melody Boys' radio broadcasts and phonograph records (*Gaffney Ledger*), October 10, 1929.

Maurice L. Jacobs (words) and Harry I. Robinson (music) and published almost thirty years before. "The Donald Rag" seems to be derived in part from Percy Weinrich's "Persian Lamb Rag" of 1908. The two unissued pieces included "I'd Love to Live in Loveland (With a Girl Like You)," written by Will Rossiter and published in 1910, as well as the perennial fiddle favorite, "Twinkle, Little Star."

By July of 1929, Weaver was to advertise the record for sale in Gaffney.[67] The platter was an average seller for those issued on the cusp of the Great Depression, moving just shy of 3500 copies.[68]

In the wake of the local excitement caused by the Melody Boys recordings, several tours were organized by Alfred Martin. These included seven gigs at the end of September/beginning of October in Spartanburg County, South Carolina, as well as a run through nearby North Carolina at the end of 1929.[69]

Like many musical aggregations, A.D. Martin had a difficult time maintaining stable personnel. After their first year of existence, guitarist Joe Guthrie left the Melody Boys, to be replaced by O.B. Parker. Oris B. Parker (June 17, 1910–April 21, 1992) was the son of musician Charlie Parker and his first wife Jessie.[70] Before 1930, O.B. married Virginia Mozelle Davis (1913–May 23, 1988). A textile worker, Oris Parker and his family left the Gaffney area in the late 1930s for employment in North Carolina.[71]

A. D. MARTIN AND HIS MELODY BOYS

RECORDS

NOW ON SALE AT

Weaver's Music Store

N. Limestone St.   Gaffney, S. C.

Advertisement for Martin Melody Boys, "Record by Martin's Melody Boys Selling," (*Gaffney Ledger*), Thursday, July 11, 1929.

    Although Oris Parker brought duet singing to the Melody Boys, as he and Claude Thompson presented "Carolina Moon," a hit in 1928 for crooner Gene Austin,[72] and Jimmy Rodgers' ("the yodeling brakeman") "Soldier's Sweetheart,"[73] Parker's tenure in the band was short lived. Following the departure of O.B. Parker, guitarists included Herman Moore (1931–1932) as well as Ralph Patrick from Woolbright's Serenaders (1933–1935 and 1937). The two other members of Mack Woolbright's band also served stints with Martin's ensemble. Richard Fox fiddled in Glenn Thompson's stead for 1932 when the later took a hiatus. And mandolinist Erston Sprouse joined in 1933, staying with A.D. Martin for the next five years.

Patrick and banjoist Claude Thompson had both played with Fletcher Blackwell,⁷⁴ the Melody Boys' fiddler after Richard Fox. Coy Fletcher Blackwell (December 17, 1907–October 25, 1981)⁷⁵ was the son of fiddler N.J. Blackwell. Fletcher married Callie Hawkins (December 11, 1908–January 1, 1993) around 1929 and the couple lived in Limestone. During his association with Martin, Blackwell worked in a cotton seed oil mill.⁷⁶ Blackwell, Patrick and Claude Thompson additionally played with mandolinist Welford Gordon, who was a member of Martin Melody Boys from the fall of 1932 through 1934.⁷⁷

Other musicians that came and went from the Melody Boys in the 1930s included Alfred's oldest son Archie Durham Martin (October 21, 1915–October 25, 1992)⁷⁸ on tenor banjo (occasional member 1930–1931), C.S. Ballard/trombone (1931–1933) and Reese Hensley/string bass (1933–1937).⁷⁹

At the end of 1938, the Cherry Camp chapter of the Woodmen of the World ended their association with Martin Melody Boys.⁸⁰ Martin kept his hand in music, playing the occasional gig for the various fraternal organizations around Gaffney.⁸¹ Alfred David Martin died October 5, 1976.⁸²

Woolbright: Part Three

Once separated from the W.O.W. Serenaders, Mack Woolbright divided his time between the surviving relatives in his maternal line. His cousin, King David Garner (December 24, 1898–March 27, 1958),⁸³ worked in a Limestone cotton mill and gave Woolbright a home base for the 1930s.⁸⁴ David's mother, Emma Frances Gallman Garner (May 10, 1870–August 6, 1954),⁸⁵ was a sister of Mack's mother Louise.⁸⁶ Mack Woolbright often accompanied the Garner family for visits with Emma at her home in Star Farm, located close to where Woolbright was born.⁸⁷ It appears that one of the Garner daughters sometimes would back up Mack for his local appearances.⁸⁸

At other times, Mack Woolbright "visited" for extended periods of time at the Star Farm home of his uncle J.W. "Joe" Gallman.⁸⁹ The youngest of his mother's siblings, Joseph Wallace Gallman (October 29, 1878–April 28, 1937),⁹⁰ from all indications, was a musician, as were some of his offspring.⁹¹ Joe's son, Arthur Vanderbilt "Vannie" Gallman (March 18, 1899–February 6, 1977),⁹² seemed especially drawn to the music of his cousin Mack. For his annual appearance at the "closing" (commencement) of Star Farm School, Vannie Gallman would accompany

Four. Mack Woolbright: Parts Two and Three

Woolbright.[93] This would have led to, as an unknown writer in the *Gaffney Ledger* put it, "some grand music."[94]

While living in Limestone and visiting his Star Farm relations, Mack Woolbright continued with community performances. December 20, 1930, Woolbright was billed as "the banjo wizard" at the Christmas party for the American Legion of Pacolet Mills.[95] Mack played with an unknown band, "his S.C. Cavaliers," for a supper held on Monday, November 5, 1934, in the Palmetto hall of the Woodmen of the World. This group had purportedly been "broadcasting" over WBT-Charlotte and would "soon be on the air regularly over that station," although there isn't any evidence supporting those claims.[96] The group played the schoolhouse at Macedonia Friday, March 29, of the following year.[97]

For the 1935/1936 school term, Mack Woolbright explored another avenue for making a living from his talents. Woolbright decided to teach instrumental music to youngsters within the community.

There is evidence that Mack had mentored school age musicians as early as 1931.[98] This later stretch of teaching began in the summer of 1935. During that time, it was reported Woolbright was running a music class at Sarratt's by the end of July.[99] At the conclusion of the year, the *Gaffney Ledger* would report that "Mack Woolbright is now holding a school of instrumental music at night in the home of Mr. and Mrs. J.E. Humphries [in Macedonia]. A group of community young men ... are making up his school."[100] This ran over four weeknights; on weekends, Woolbright instructed in Thickety.[101] When Mack resumed after the holidays, "Four different instruments [were] being taught by Mr. Woolbright, violin, mandolin, guitar and banjo."[102]

Part of the instruction included public performances by his juvenile ensemble. On March 3, 1936, Mack and "his class of boys" provided the music for a "negro minstrel" at the Sarratt's schoolhouse. They also entertained "at the county home for the old people"[103] and provided music for the school "closing" (end of school) at Beaverdam.[104]

For the remainder of the 1930s into the early 1940s, area publications featured occasional notices of Mack Woolbright's entertainments. These included November 13, 1937, at Timber Ridge School[105]; February 11, 1940, for a birthday party in Pleasant Hill[106]; an August Reunion of the Whelchel family the same year[107]; August 7, 1943, bringing his mandolin to the Gaffney Church of God[108]; as well as providing a "one-man band" for the Cherry Camp of the W.O.W. on November 5.[109]

After 1943, notices of Mack Woolbright's musical engagements disappear from local papers. Around that time, Woolbright married for the

What Earl Scruggs Heard

Mack Woolbright and Ruby Pittman Woolbright, circa 1950s (courtesy George Hutchins / author's collection).

first and only time. His bride, the former Ruby Jeanette Pittman[110] (May 9, 1924[111]–January 10, 2004[112]), had contracted spinal meningitis as an infant, one of the results being the loss of her vision. Ruby's blindness, coupled with her family's itinerant lifestyle, resulted in Pittman's lack of formal education.[113] Mack and Ruby's only child, a daughter named Ruby Louise after her mother and grandmother, was born in 1946.[114]

From that point onward, the Woolbrights lived in various rented homes around Gaffney.[115] In September of 1956, their house was destroyed by fire.[116] Around the same time, Mack Woolbright's health began going downhill. That, combined with Mack's impoverished state, led to his death at the age of sixty-nine on June 2, 1960. Mack Woolbright was buried by the county in the Oakland cemetery, forgotten by the public that owned his records and the musicians he had influenced, without a stone to mark his grave because the family couldn't afford one.[117]

Thus passed one of the banjoists Earl Scruggs credits with influencing his playing. We'll next tell the story of two other area pickers that helped to shape the music of the young Scruggs.

Five

What Earl Scruggs Heard

When describing the music he heard in his youth, Earl Scruggs singles out banjoists Mack Woolbright, Rex Brooks, Smith Hammett and Fisher Hendley. These local musicians named by Scruggs as using three fingers to pick the banjo were not the only ones utilizing that method. In fact, this style, reminiscent of the "classic" city-bred players of the late 19th and early 20th centuries, was commonplace throughout the upland South. My research into the piedmont of North Carolina, previously published in *String Bands in the North Carolina Piedmont*, revealed that the generational changeover to Scruggs-style picking after World War II had its parallel in the shift from down to up-picking fifty years previously. Before Earl's birth, photographs of string bands show banjoists holding their right hand in an obvious up-picking rather than the downward stroking clawhammer position. For example, farmer Luther Gordon Haynes (September 29, 1891–November 18, 1980)[1] of the McKee band was obviously playing finger style when posing for a band photo made around 1920.

I've previously discussed Woolbright and his influence on Scruggs. We'll investigate Brooks and Hammett below and Hendley in the sections that follow this one.

Rex Brooks

DeWitt "Snuffy" Jenkins was born in Harris, North Carolina, on October 27, 1908. In 1927, [Jenkins] met two men who were playing in a three finger [*sic*] style. "One was Rex Brooks and one was Smith Hammett and they both lived in Cleveland County, North Carolina, right around where Earl Scruggs was born and raised. So I heard those fellas playing and that kind of stuck with me a little bit...." Rex Brooks was working at the local telephone company [*sic*], and played with his fingernails and a thumbpick. "It made a good clear sound, but it wasn't too loud, you know."[2]

Born on his family's farm August 23, 1899, Rex Brooks heard music from an early age. His father, Madison Monroe Brooks (May 19,

What Earl Scruggs Heard

Rex Brooks/fiddle and Verl Jenkins/harmonica (courtesy Judy Latham).

1873–June 29, 1958), operated a sawmill in the Corinth Community of Colfax Township in eastern Rutherford County. Matt was also a fiddler of some local renown. He had begun playing at the age of twelve or thirteen upon receiving a violin as a "premium" for selling Rosebud Salve (a not uncommon reward for these schemes). In addition to Rex, the elder

Five. What Earl Scruggs Heard

Brooks passed his love of music onto his numerous other children, most of whom took up a stringed instrument or two.³

When he came of age, Rex Brooks left the farmstead. First, he worked as a machinist in the cotton mill at High Shoals, where Brooks was listed as living in the 1920 Federal Census. That same year, Brooks married Verdia Hester Bridges, three years younger than himself. By 1921, the couple had moved back to the Brooks' family farm, where their first child was born.⁴

But farming didn't hold Rex's interest. By 1926, Rex Brooks had gone to work for the local electric utility and, therefore, moved closer to Mooresboro in western Cleveland County. Rex eventually rose to the position of manager for the Mooresboro unit of Duke Power.⁵ He and Smith Hammett became friends, with Brooks possibly drawn to the older man because of his knowledge of the three-finger technique. Brooks played the banjo, and, additionally, was adept on the guitar and the fiddle. It was the last instrument that Rex probably utilized for a string band featuring Hammett's banjo playing and a young Snuffy Jenkins on the guitar.⁶

Rex Brooks' life came to a sudden and sad end. On a rainy Sunday evening, October 20, 1935, the car Brooks was driving skidded on wet pavement, over-turning and crashing into a telephone pole at the Beaver Dam filling station. He was killed instantly.⁷

Smith Hammett

> As far as I'm concerned, Smith Hammett was the first man to come out with the three-finger style playing. I don't say he was the first, but I do say he was the first one that I heard do it. There's a lot of people give me credit, but that is not true. Smith Hammett and Rex Brooks were the first to my knowledge to play like that.
> —Letter, Dewitt "Snuffy" Jenkins to Paul Carpenter⁸

The next banjoist that Earl Scruggs and Snuffy Jenkins credit as an area pioneer in the three-finger style was Smith Hammett. Besides being a relative of Scruggs (Hammett's wife and Earl's mother were cousins⁹), Smith was somewhat of a musical father figure to Earl following the death of Earl Scruggs' father. Unfortunately for Earl, Smith Hammett, like his father and Rex Brooks, also died at an early age, depriving the young Scruggs of his further influence.

What Earl Scruggs Heard

Left to right: John W. Ross/fiddle, Smith Hammett/banjo and Brooker Self, circa 1920s (courtesy Larry Hammett).

Jessie Smith Hammett was born the fourth of six siblings, February 21, 1887, in Limestone Springs Township outside of Gaffney, Cherokee County, South Carolina.[10] Earl Scruggs writes that Smith's father John Martin "Mart" Hammett (April 15, 1851–April 17, 1927)[11] was a fiddler and obviously influenced his children in the playing of musical instruments. Earl also reports that, in addition to Smith, two of the Hammett brothers also played musical instruments. Scruggs' specific comment that Smith Hammett "could play almost any kind of instrument"[12] is borne out by other surviving recollections of Smith playing the fiddle, guitar, Hawaiian guitar, organ and buck dancing. Hammett's grandson Larry Hammett tells that the only time Smith lost a dance contest, it was to "a one-legged man." There are no surviving family stories of how Smith learned to play the banjo, although one tale tells of injuring his first finger, giving up clawhammer playing and causing the use of his second, third, and fourth finger for up-picking.[13]

Smith Hammett was married in 1907 to Essie Ola Harris, whose family helped found the Cherokee Church where they settled.[14] The couple eventually had nine children.[15]

One of Hammett's musical partners while residing in the Cherokee Church community was fiddler L.D. McCraw.[16] Lawson Davis McCraw was born in North Carolina April 29, 1869, to Chesley McCraw

Five. What Earl Scruggs Heard

(February 4, 1838–January 15, 1900) and Sarah Gaston (born circa 1832[17]). Chesley served as a "musician" during the Civil War, enlisting (and surviving) for the duration of the conflict.[18]

Around 1891, L.D. McCraw united with Rebecca Leanora "Nora" Jones[19] (October 2, 1875–May 29, 1949).[20] Their family eventually included nine children.[21] After renting farms on the Broad River in Cleveland County, North Carolina,[22] by the nineteen-teens, L.D. and Nora had moved their brood onto a homestead in Cherokee County, South Carolina.[23] For the remainder of his working life, McCraw would stay in South Carolina.[24]

The first documented public performance for the duo of McCraw and Hammett was at the school closing in Ashworth during March of 1910. Located northwest of Gaffney near the North Carolina border, the school was attended by members of both the McCraw and Hammett extended families.[25]

Once Smith Hammett moved to North Carolina, newspaper references for engagements with L.D. disappear. However, McCraw continued to make some limited local appearances without Hammett. L.D. and his daughter Euphra Frodie McCraw (née Goforth, June 20, 1898–August 24, 1987)[26] were advertised as contestants at John W. Ross's convention in Gaffney on March 1 of 1918.[27] However, it was McCraw's uncle, John C. McCraw (July 4, 1845–May 23, 1924) of Cliffside,[28] who accompanied L.D. For their part in the competition, the McCraws played "Julia Glover" and "Guard House."[29] John McCraw and his nephew had performed together as early as 1908, when the two musicians took first prize at the fiddlers' meet-up in Shelby.[30] The *Gaffney Ledger* notes L.D. McCraw's participation in two more local fiddlers' confabs, in 1920 and 1921,[31] lastly mentioning McCraw's appearance at S. Bridges' store in June of 1930.[32]

Interestingly, McCraw and Hammett seem to have, at least on one more occasion, made music together. Less than a month before his passing, Smith Hammett paid a visit to jam with Lawson McCraw.[33]

For the last five years of his life, L.D. McCraw lived in Forest City, North Carolina. On January 24, 1950, Lawson McCraw passed away at the age of eighty.[34]

By 1913, the Hammetts had migrated over the border to Caroleen in Rutherford County, where Smith worked for the local mill. Smith returned to farming by 1917,[35] although, like many farmers, he may have alternated toiling in the fields during good weather with employment by the mill in the winter. Hammett is also known to have been hired by the Seaboard Air Line railroad yard located in Bostic, North Carolina.[36]

What Earl Scruggs Heard

As share cropping cotton farmers (renting the land in exchange for a percentage of their yield), the Hammetts moved around the area a great deal. By 1920, the Smith Hammett family was residing on Webb Bridge and Bostic Roads in the Cool Spring Township of Rutherford County.[37] In 1922, they were living just over the county line in the Cleveland County township of Mooresboro, which the Hammetts left in June of 1929 for Gaffney, South Carolina.[38] By 1930, the Hammetts had also lived in the municipalities of West End and Limestone Mills.

Many area residents claimed to have played with Smith Hammett, or, like Earl Scruggs, to have learned some of their banjo style from him. Besides Earl and Snuffy Jenkins, they included Donnie Clifton Ruppe (November 17, 1907–August 9, 1983)[39] of Bostic and John Johnson (b.=1909) of Ellenboro, North Carolina.[40]

From a surviving photograph made around 1920, we know definitively some of Smith's other musical compatriots. They included a

Smith Hammett band. Standing, back row, left to right: Bernard "Big Mac" McDaniel, Dewey McDaniel, Rex Brooks and Smith Hammett. Front row, left to right: Will Grady, Jim Grady and Coley Fisher (courtesy Eula Bridges).

Five. *What Earl Scruggs Heard*

Dewey McDaniel band, circa 1930. Back row, left to right: Bernard "Big Mac" McDaniel/twelve-string guitar, Grady Wilkie/guitar, Solon Smart/banjo-guitar and Ode Jackson/twelve-string guitar. Front row, left to right: Paul Jackson/banjo-mandolin, Dewey McDaniel/fiddle and Coy Hammrick/banjo-mandolin (courtesy Larry Hammett).

number of musicians who worked at the Cliffside Cotton Mill at High Shoals: fiddler and mandolinist Dewey McDaniel (April 30, 1900–September 11, 1980[41]), a textile mill doffer[42] and piano tuner who once won a prize at the Hollis contest with a broken arm; twelve string guitarist and mill doffer Bernard Clement "Big Mac" McDaniel (March 6, 1901–September 11, 1955,[43] whose relationship to Dewey and H.B. is unknown); fiddler Rector Roland "Rex" McCraw (January 6, 1886–March 25, 1954), a speeder in the Cliffside mill[44]; and Coley Fisher on guitar. Smith may have known these men from his own time working in the Cliffside mill. Others in the Hammett band of unknown origins were Will Grady/fiddle and Jim Grady/guitar.[45]

Dewey McDaniel went on to lead his own band and compete against Smith Hammett at local fiddlers' conventions. "Big Mac" McDaniel joined Dewey's musical aggregation that also included Coy Hamrick/banjo-mandolin, Solon David Smart (October 15, 1908–March 10, 1999) of Cliffside/banjo-guitar,[46] Ode Jackson/twelve-string guitar, Paul

What Earl Scruggs Heard

Jackson/banjo-mandolin and McDaniel's nephew Grady (Lee) Wilkie[47] (February 16, 1912–April 2, 1991)/guitar. Wilkie, best friends with Coy Hamrick and the son of Dewey's sister Ollie, was taught to play by his uncle. A mill worker for all of his life, Grady was working as a doffer in the Cliffside cotton mill when he began playing with Dewey's band and later moved to Shelby to work for Lily Mills. Grady's daughter Pat remembers her father's story of helping a teen-aged Earl Scruggs get a wartime job at the Lily Mill in order to financially support his widowed mother.[48] Earl also lived with Grady and one cannot help but believe that the two played music together as well.[49]

During August of 1925, Okeh Records held sessions in Asheville, North Carolina, and it is possible that Hammett's band attempted to record at those sessions. According to family lore, the band's automobile broke down on the way to Asheville and the group never got the chance to make records, a great loss in documenting just how Smith's banjo style sounded.[50]

SPINNING, TWISTING, SPOOLING AND REELING DEPARTMENTS

FIRST ROW—Dave Revels and Fred Whitener.   SECOND ROW—Nina Beaver, Lona Sisk, Mae Patterson, Jewell Woods, Mamie Allen, Marjorie Humphries, Willie Mae Morehead, Lula Mae Pheagin, Bertha Canipe, Ethel Hardin, Blanche Poole, Elsie Jones, Ellie Parker, and Frankie Barrett. THIRD ROW—Pauline Poole, Corrie McSwain, Lula Mae Stidham, Lizzie Tritt, Ora Lou Poole, Grace Richards, Grace Price, Evelyn Cobb, Addie Morehead, Edith McMurray, Esther Adams, Gertie Byers, Pearl Lail, Ocie Sanders, Ocie Runyans, Grady Wilkie, and Ken Panther.   FOURTH ROW—Homer Jackson, Garnet Paxton, Kenneth Carter, Homer Pheagin, Earl Scruggs, Gidney Parker, Lloyd Self, North Warren, Junior Lail, Buren Humphries, Minnie Bivins, Carrie Bivins, Fred Bell, Lummie Canipe, George Melton, Carl McSwain, Glynn Panther, Alice Ellis, Alice Ward, and Lem Lail.   FIFTH ROW—Clevie Fortenberry, Charlie Bridges, Alvin Sisk, Lummie Philbeck, Smith Ledbetter, Marvin Lail, Hosea Bivins, Arthur Ledbetter, Monroe Smith, Clayton Poole, Woodrow Tesseneer, Arthur Poole, Charlie Jones, Osh Martin, Earl Price, H. K. Panther, and Gene Dover.

Workers at the Lily Mills include Earl Scruggs (third row, fifth from left) and Grady Wilkie (third row, second from right) (courtesy Tommy Forney).

Five. What Earl Scruggs Heard

Members of Smith's family inherited his musical talent. His children James Nathan (July 21, 1911–May 4, 1994),[51] Ruby (November 1914–March 9, 1993)[52] and Howard Luke (November 29, 1919–June 24, 1944)[53] all played the guitar; Tommy Thirston (May 7, 1913–January 1969) additionally mastered the fiddle and the banjo.[54] Smith's namesake grandson, Smith "Smitty" Irvin (1930–March 24, 2003), picked the banjo, first in a family band that included Roy Clark and later, with Bill Harrell and then, with Jimmy Dean.[55]

Around 1929, the young Earl Eugene Scruggs (born January 6, 1924[56]) came under the musical influence of Smith Hammett. Earl's father, bookkeeper and farmer George Elam Scruggs (b. January 10, 1876), had died the previous year, before his son could hear George's own clawhammer banjo playing and fiddling. Earl's oldest brother, Junius Emmett "Junie" Scruggs (September 9, 1911–December 15, 1995),[57] inspired by Smith, had already owned a banjo for several years (bought for $17.00 by mail order).

Earl attempted to play on both his father's open back and the instrument owned by Junie:

> When I was a little boy [wrote Earl] the only way I could pick Junie's banjo or the old banjo my father had played was to sit down with the body of the banjo resting to my right. I would slide it around quite a bit depending on which position on the neck I was trying to reach. That was pretty rough on a banjo if I happened to be sitting on the hardwood floor or outside on the porch or in the yard. Needless to say, Junie wasn't too pleased with me whenever he caught me playing his banjo.

The alternative for Earl was an instrument of reduced size owned by Smith Hammett. Earl recollects:

> Our families visited each other fairly often, and we always ended up playing some music before the visits were over. Smith's banjo picking inspired me, too, but what I remember most about him was a little banjo that he owned.
>
> The banjo head on Smith's little banjo was about nine inches in diameter, and the neck was quite a bit shorter than the length of a standard banjo neck. It always thrilled me to pick that little banjo because I could hold it in my lap and pick just like the grownups did with their regular-sized banjos. Anyway, he was going to give me that banjo, I thought he was, and then he got killed, and of course they never gave me the banjo.[58]

The instrument had, at one time, belonged to Rex Brooks, who ordered it through the store at Sunshine, North Carolina, just to the north of Bostic. Manufactured by the Henry C. Dobson Company of New York City, it is stamped with the patent date "11/08/1881." The instrument

What Earl Scruggs Heard

features a later metal "pie plate" resonator labeled "Bestone." Banjo collector and scholar James Bollman dates the Brooks/Hammett instrument to "the late 1880s–early 1890s."[59]

Phillip Shields, who played in a band with Thirston Hammett, tells a story about one aspect of Earl's musical schooling by Smith. The young Scruggs wouldn't know when to come in on a tune and so relied on Smith to step on his toe as a signal.[60]

After moving back to Gaffney, Smith Hammett had one more occasion to "pick" with L.D. McCraw. On Saturday, January 11, 1930, Smith and L.D. were joined in a music session by, among others, Snuffy Jenkins and his brothers. This gathering was repeated several months later.[61]

Unfortunately, circumstances intervened to keep Hammett from that second musical get-together. Like his friend Rex Brooks, Smith Hammett's time was cut short. Late in the evening of Saturday, February 1, 1930, an altercation took Smith's life.[62] The day of his funeral at Cherokee Church found the largest crowd ever assembled at that house of worship, proving the banjoist's local popularity. Earl's brother Junie was one of the pallbearers.[63]

Although Rex Brooks, Smith Hammett and other area banjoists failed to leave behind audio evidence of their banjo styles, Mack Woolbright, Charlie Parker and, later, Earl Scruggs give us valuable clues about how they sounded. Since Hammett spent his formative years in the same town as Woolbright and Parker, we can assume that each musician was aware of the other and that they either learned from similar sources and/or each other. Therefore, echoes of Smith Hammett are contained in the 78 rpm records of Parker and Woolbright, and both men helped to form the style that Scruggs came to use throughout his professional career.

There is one more banjoist that Earl Scruggs credits as an early musical influence. The remainder of this book is devoted to Fisher Hendley's story and his impact on area musicians.

Six

Crazy Crystals and Aristocratic Pigs
The Fisher Hendley Story

Earl: Take Two

Toward the end of the life of musician, songwriter (most notably, "Gentle on My Mind") and historian John Hartford (1937–2001), I spent an evening at the Hartford home. Besides John, two of his best friends, instrument dealer George Gruhn and banjo superstar Earl Scruggs, were in attendance. As we sat by the fire, exchanging small talk, Hartford, knowing that I was actively involved in country music research, asked what I was currently pursuing. When I replied, "Fisher Hendley," John, as he would have described it, "jerked his thumb" (pointed) at Earl, and retorted, "Here's someone who can tell you about Fisher Hendley."

After several uncomfortable moments with the three of us staring at Earl Scruggs and Earl staring back, he finally replied, "want to hear his lick?" I fetched one of Hartford's banjos and Scruggs proceeded to replicate Hendley's style. It turned out that, while growing up, Earl used to listen to Fisher Hendley's radio broadcasts out of Greenville, South Carolina (this would have probably been between the fall of 1935 and the spring of 1938 when Earl was in his early teens) to capture "his lick." During that time, Scruggs learned enough of the essentials behind Hendley's banjo method to remember them for the rest of his life. These included the use of "low bass" banjo tuning (gCGBD as opposed to the bluegrass tuning of gDGBD commonly used by Scruggs and his followers) as well as a syncopated style lacking Earl's continuous roll. Ironically, the Gibson instrument that later helped to define Scruggs' signature sound was played while Earl listened to him over the radio by its original owner, Fisher Hendley.[1]

What Earl Scruggs Heard

Fisher Hendley: Part One

When most of us think about old-time country music pioneers of the 1920s–1940s, we imagine overall-clad musicians fresh out of some mountain holler carrying a load of moonshine. The truth of the matter is much different from this fiction generated by the radio and record company publicists of the era.

Fisher Hendley's story helps illuminate something of the real history for early country music. Hendley was not from the mountains at all, but, rather, a sparsely populated farming area of the North Carolina Piedmont, a locale as rich in music as the better-known highland regions. Unlike the negative images of ignorant rural southerners, Fisher attended several institutes of higher learning, including the prestigious Trinity College in Durham. Hendley had extensive vocal training from traveling with choirs. Fisher's participation in dramatic presentations resulted in wearing, and insisting that his bands wear, full theater "pancake" make up and evening dress onstage.

Additionally, Fisher Hendley was a shrewd and successful promoter and businessman. He exhorted his children to "always buy the best" and kept his own council at the height of the depression by owning high-end musical tools, including those made by Gibson and a spectacular one-of-a-kind Epiphone Recording Deluxe "Dragon" banjo.

My initial interest in Fisher Hendley began through a fascination with "the Aristocratic Pigs," as one of his groups was labeled. As it turns out, the moniker was from a sponsor's contention that their pork products originated with high-class hogs and had nothing to do with Fisher or his musicians. I learned little more about Fisher Hendley and his group until the late 1990s, when I was assembling the two-CD set for Rounder Records, *The North Carolina Banjo Collection*. I included a cut of Fisher's banjo playing on this compilation, which triggered my research into his life for the album's booklet. A deeper investigation of Hendley's early years followed when, simultaneously, I was writing the book *String Bands in the North Carolina Piedmont* (McFarland, 2004) and researcher/musician Gail Gillespie uncovered some pictures of Fisher from his time at what is now Duke University. This period of inquiry ended with my inability to locate Fisher's family.

It was only after banjoist Jim Mills included Hendley in a *Bluegrass Unlimited* article that I discovered Fisher's daughter Hellen Hendley Permar was still living. Mills graciously supplied Mrs. Permar's contact information and she gave me access to two scrapbooks that provided

Six. Crazy Crystals and Aristocratic Pigs

a wealth of primary information, reopening my exploration into Fisher Hendley's interesting life.

Therefore, what follows is the fascinating chronicle of a musician's journey through early country music. Included in this tale are the story of the many players whose careers were aided by Fisher Hendley.

Ansonville, North Carolina

Walter Fisher Hendley, a native of Ansonville Township, Anson County, North Carolina, was born May 4, 1891, the sixth child of Charlotte Hellen Crump (born April 15, 1858, in Norwood, Stanly County) and the second born to Crump and farmer William Eugene Hendley (June 8, 1861–November 22, 1929). Hellen was the granddaughter of Dr. John S. Kendall, a famous Anson County physician, and daughter of Steven and Eliza Ann Kendall Crump. She had been previously married to Charles W. Hendley (March 19, 1857–March 1, 1886), whose familial relationship to her second husband is unknown.

Five children proceeded Fisher: the four produced by Hellen and Charles Hendley (Nona, in 1879; Bronnie, 1880; Raymond Theodore, 1883 and Amelia, 1884 or 1885) and one to William and Hellen (Wilma H., 1889). Fisher Hendley was followed by his youngest sister, Anna P., in 1895.

Fisher's daughter Hellen Permar related that her grandparents owned a spacious three-story home that sat under enormous trees on a hill overlooking the Rocky River. Hellen also remembered hearing tales that William Hendley was the "mathematician of the County." Relative Aileen Morris, during our phone conversation in July of 2005, recalled that William Hendley was a musician. His obituary called him "a great entertainer" who played a "big fiddle" (possibly a cello). A generation further back, William's father, James W. "Squire Jim" Hendley (November 1, 1828–December 5, 1898), who headed up a large family, worked as a blacksmith and served the community of Cedar Hill as postmaster. Squire Jim was reportedly a musician as well and said to be the source for the Hendley family's musical talent.[2]

Fisher Hendley's first banjo was similar to those played by many young aspiring musicians in his part of North Carolina. A promotional piece published almost forty years later gave the story:

> At the age of twelve [Fisher's] heart and soul was set on learning to play a five-string banjo. With no instrument on which to learn, he constantly asked

his father to buy him a banjo. His father thought best that he spend his time on his schoolbooks. So, one day Fisher went into the farm blacksmith shop, took a cheese box, and a stick of cord wood, and made for himself his first banjo, using a black cat's hide for the head, and sewing threads from his mother's machine drawer for strings.

Fisher recalled that this homemade instrument "whined" like a cat.

Rutherford College

In the fall of 1910, a nineteen-year-old Fisher Hendley left behind the family homestead for the halls of Rutherford College.[3] The Hendley clan was active in the Methodist faith, and Rutherford was allied with their brand of Protestantism.

The college preparatory school was located in the foothills of Burke County. A mile and a half from Connelly Springs, this stop on the Southern Railway was some one hundred twenty miles west of Hendley's Anson county home.

Rutherford College had its roots in the one-room Owl Hollow School founded in 1853 by Methodist minister the Rev. Laban Abernethy. The college specialized in providing an education for those students with limited financial resources.[4]

When Fisher Hendley first arrived at Rutherford in the winter of 1911, he found a beautiful, oak shaded campus of eight acres dominated by a large college building set upon a commanding hill. The structure contained spacious halls including four recitation rooms, two study rooms, a music room, a girls' hall, and, notably, a fine auditorium with the capacity for seating 600 people. Three acres of the grounds were dedicated to athletic fields, where the Rutherford baseball team played during both the fall and spring semesters.[5]

The teenaged Hendley had previously showed an aptitude for public speaking. This immediately propelled him into an involvement with one of the campus debate clubs, the Newtonian Literary Society, where Fisher Hendley served as secretary. Their contests were popular events at Rutherford College, and Fisher argued such topics as granting independence to the Philippines in front of large audiences.[6]

Fisher may well have had some informal musical training from his family, church, and community. We know that Hendley was already playing the banjo by the time he reached Rutherford and that the school offered a wide variety of musical and theatrical activities. Although not

Six. Crazy Crystals and Aristocratic Pigs

specifically mentioned by name, considering his aptitude with the banjo, Hendley, in all probability, participated in the 1911 and 1912 winter tours by the Rutherford College "Southern Minstrels." Sponsored by the Dramatic Club of the college, the Minstrels played surrounding towns such as Morganton and Hickory. These performances were given in financial support of the Rutherford athletic association.[7]

Minstrelsy was an immensely popular form of variety show entertainment that developed in America during the first quarter of the 19th century. Often featuring the banjo, the primarily white and male minstrel participants commonly wore black make-up on their faces and hands in an outward imitation of "Southern Negros." Although elements of this form persisted for over one hundred thirty years and was deemed "acceptable" by the morality of the day, the overt and covert racist content finally led to its death during the Civil Rights movement of the 1960s.

Fisher Hendley, school days (courtesy Hellen Hendley Permar).

The Southern Minstrels' March 1911 program in the Rutherford chapel

> was acknowledged by the largest audience present as the best entertainment of this kind given here for a long time. The program consisted of music by string band, negro songs, quartets, solos and colloquies by young men impersonating folks of the colored race.[8]

Another reason to suspect Hendley's involvement with the Rutherford Minstrels was Fisher's participation with one of the beneficiaries of the concerts, the college baseball squad.

Strangely, although family lore promotes his athletic abilities, Fisher Hendley is absent from baseball coverage until the end of his Rutherford College sojourn. Perhaps, as an underclassman, he was kept off the varsity squad by older, more experienced players?

What Earl Scruggs Heard

Finally, on Thursday, May 28, 1914, Fisher pitched under Coach Ledbetter. *The Charlotte Observer*'s sarcastic reporter, after commenting on the poor showing by the Rutherford nine during their season, criticized Hendley's performance thusly:

> [In] the game against the Asheville league ... he performed the remarkable feat of striking out nobody. And at no stage of the game was the ball any nearer the batters than when held in the pitcher's hands.

Trinity College

In the spring of 1914, Fisher Hendley graduated from Rutherford College and returned home to Anson County. Rutherford often served as a gateway to the Methodist-affiliated Trinity College. With Trinity's well-known baseball team and musical organizations, even at the age of twenty-three, it's no surprise that Fisher Hendley made the move to Durham after completing his three years at Rutherford.

Even though Hendley's performance on the Rutherford diamond appears to have gone badly, Fisher was still attractive to the Trinity nine. Claude Bascom "Crip" West, coaching his first year of College baseball, would have been disposed toward recruiting Hendley and procuring him a scholarship. An all-round athlete, C.B. West was born during 1888 in Anson County, only a few years before Fisher Hendley. West's father was a local Presbyterian minister, and Claude preceded Fisher at Rutherford College where, like Hendley, he participated in one of the debating societies.[9] Continuing on to Trinity, C.B. played shortstop for the baseball squad and was a member of the championship team during their 1908–09 season.[10] C.B. West continued with baseball while enrolled in the college's graduate program.[11] He also played professional ball during summer break, including a brief stint with the Baltimore Orioles and their farm system.[12] Since the fall term of 1911, West had taught at the Trinity Park School, the on-campus preparatory academy for the college, and managed both the basketball and baseball teams.

Fisher Hendley began at Trinity College during the 1914–15 school year and immediately acclimated himself to campus life. Fisher joined the Rutherford College Club lead by Professor West and reported on the group's activities for the college newspaper.[13] Hendley also signed up for the Glee Club and the Columbian Literary Society and he tried out for the baseball team.[14]

At first, it looked as if the freshman would have some success on the

Six. Crazy Crystals and Aristocratic Pigs

Rutherford College Club

OFFICERS

B. L. SMITH . . . . President
L. H. MCNEELY . . . . Vice-President
G. N. EARNHARDT . . . . Secretary-Treasurer
W. F. HENDLEY . . . . Press Reporter

MEMBERS

J. W. BENNETT
JOHN CLINE
D. E. EARNHARDT
G. N. EARNHARDT
L. FRAZIER
ROY W. GILES
J. W. HARBISON
W. F. HENDLEY
J. E. B. HOUSER
E. H. JORDAN
J. E. KANIPE
H. G. LOVE
L. H. MCNEELY
H. E. MYERS
M. A. OSBORNE
I. T. POOLE
B. L. SMITH
L. P. SMITH
W. C. STROUD
H. B. TEETER
PROF. W. W. PEELE
PROF. I. B. MCKAY
PROF. C. B. WEST

(165)

Rutherford College Club, Trinity College yearbook. Fisher Hendley is in the front row on the left (courtesy Duke University Alumni Archives).

What Earl Scruggs Heard

squad. Trinity was known to field tough teams and when Fisher tried out in September, Coach West told the college newspaper:

> There are also some good twirlers [period slang for pitcher] in the Freshman class. The Coach has not had an opportunity to work all the new twirlers out enough to know much about them, but says that ... Hendley [is] showing good form.[15]

Unfortunately, all references to Fisher Hendley's pitching end with this article. His daughter Hellen believes that, at some point, he switched to second base. Fisher is mentioned in the spring season coverage, although his playing position is not. In the two games covered by the *Trinity Chronicle* against arch Baptist rival Wake Forest, Fisher struck out twice, flew out twice, and got on base three times.[16] Fisher Hendley was not on the roster for a Virginia end-of-season road trip, nor pictured with the squad in the yearbook, and he was absent from any team lists printed in the college newspaper.

Fisher had more success with the Glee Club. He surely received vocal training as a club member and probably developed his somewhat formal tenor vocal style during this year. As shown in the Glee Club yearbook portrait, Hendley also got to employ his skills on the banjo and apply his experience with minstrel shows in Club performances. As "'Rag' Hendley and 'Diddie' Hall," he and another student utilized the blackface makeup and costume of early 20th-century minstrelsy as

A young Fisher Hendley holds his banjo in this photograph of the Trinity College Glee Club that appeared in the 1915 *Chanticleer* (yearbook). Although racist, the blackface makeup used by Fisher's guitar-playing partner was a part of minstrel shows and considered at that time to be acceptable (courtesy Duke University Alumni Archives).

a popular solo feature with the organization. Audiences for the Trinity Glee Club's annual ten-day fundraising tour of Piedmont towns such as Greensboro, High Point, Thomasville and Salisbury got to view the seventeen-member aggregation. After the Glee Club trip turned a profit, the Club assisted Fisher in procuring his first "real" banjo. Though he never graduated from Trinity, Fisher Hendley's achievements with the Glee Club would propel him toward a long and successful career in music.[17]

Asheville, North Carolina, and Hopewell, Virginia

By the conclusion of his freshman year, Fisher Hendley had reached his 24th birthday and the end of his college career. It's possible that Hendley's poor performance on the baseball squad resulted in a loss of scholarship funds, perpetrating his early exit from Trinity. One later promotional article mentions a season of professional baseball, the only time this possibility has arisen in my research.[18] At his age, Fisher may have just been ready to make his mark on the greater world. For the next ten years, Fisher Hendley tried out a number of professions before turning to music full-time.

Fisher's first stop was the city of Asheville in Western North Carolina. The mountain community was a hub for the Southern Railroad, whose promise of employment had drawn other members of the Hendley clan to the locale. Fisher's older half-brother Raymond had lived in Asheville since at least 1909, his first appearance in the City Directory. Besides Raymond, two Hendley sisters were also living in the metropolis when Fisher Hendley exited Trinity.

In the summer of 1915, Fisher moved into Raymond's West Asheville home. An engineer on the Southern, Ray Hendley may have paved the way for the employment of his younger brother as a newspaper salesman in the local railway depot.

It's unclear how long Fisher stayed in Asheville. However, by the time the United States entered World War I, Hendley was aiding the war effort by working at DuPont's facility in Hopewell, Virginia.

E.I. DuPont de Nemours Company, as it was officially known, had been at the site since 1912, when the firm purchased eight hundred acres near Hopewell Farm. Seeking to build a plant to manufacture dynamite, DuPont was attracted to the area by rail facilities as well as access to the deep-water port on the James River. By 1914, whether by coincidence or encouraged by the outbreak of World War I, the Company purchased sixteen hundred additional acres from the Eppes Estate. The resulting factory was, when built, the largest nitrocellulose (an explosive also known in the popular vernacular as guncotton) manufactory in the world. By the time Fisher moved to Asheville the following year, 40,000 workers were employed at what came to be known as City Point.[19]

In April of 1917, when the United States officially entered the World War, Fisher Hendley was working for DuPont.[20] While at E.I. DuPont, one newspaper article mentions acid burns that placed Fisher Hendley in the hospital.[21]

Joining Fisher in Virginia were his Anson County neighbors Earl and "Puett" Crump (of no close relation to Hendley's mother). Earl Fred, born a year after Fisher, lasted at DuPont until early 1918, when he entered the military. Puett was with Hendley at the end of World War I, when their jobs ended. Not surprisingly, Fisher had attended Rutherford College with a third Crump brother, Pet, who was another two years younger than Earl.[22]

The war didn't prevent Messieurs Hendley and Crump from engaging in a bit of high jinx. When home from Virginia visiting their families,

> Messrs. Fisher Hendley and Earl Crump two sporting dudes of this town drove a wild horse over the river one night last week to visit some of the fair damsles [sic] of Stanly [County], where they lingered till late hours. On their return they both were taken with a severe case of noctambulation and just as they started into the river the horse ran upon a high bank, turned the buggy over, threw them down the embankment, the horse ran into the river, demolished a new buggy which went down the stream and left them standing on the Stanly side wide awake. They arrived home about day with bruised and torn clothes and declared a thonjominaker had attacked them in the dark swamp on the river and badly bitten both of them. The whole male population of the town is looking for the critter, but nothing has been found but some empty [alcohol?] containers.[23]

Florida, Goldsboro, Carthage, Albemarle

At the end of World War I, DuPont closed City Point, and Fisher Hendley was again at loose ends.[24] After bouncing around for several years between Anson County; relatives in Miami, where he worked in a mill that manufactured staves for barrels[25]; and the like,[26] in April of 1921, Hendley took a job in Goldsboro. Two and half years later, Fisher was working in Carthage.[27] Eventually, Fisher Hendley settled in the

Six. Crazy Crystals and Aristocratic Pigs

town of Albemarle in Stanly County about twenty miles to the north of his birthplace.

By the fall of 1924, Fisher had taken a job with Mason and Melton's garage. Located just south of downtown Albemarle at "five points," Melton's was the local Studebaker dealer. In addition to automobile sales and general service for automobiles, the garage sold tires, batteries, and Gulf gasoline.

Hendley was nothing if not ambitious. After first working as Melton's bookkeeper, by the spring of 1925, Fisher was promoted to "business manager." In the summer of 1926, Hendley co-owned the concern, assuming full possession by 1928.

Fisher Hendley's success in business helped give him the financial stability to look for musical opportunities in the surrounding area. Toward this end, Hendley renewed his rounds of community events that were the traditional outlets for his style of string band music. Foremost among those were fiddlers' conventions, which were used as community fundraisers. Fisher had competed at these conventions for all of his adult life, where the winning of prizes might bring the attentions of those needing to hire entertainment. Fiddlers' conventions also were gathering places for area musicians, and it was here that Fisher began to meet the fiddlers, banjo players, guitar pickers, and other string instrumentalists that he would eventually come to rely on for events of his own making.

Audience members describe Fisher Hendley's early act as extremely entertaining. Dr. William H. Boyce, a retired vascular surgeon born in 1918, grew up about three miles from the Hendley family's home in Anson County and remembers Fisher Hendley coming to the school auditorium in Wadesboro (circa 1924–1930). Boyce recalls that Fisher would "throw the banjo in the air as the music went on, catch it and it was still right in tune."

The earliest documented prizes by Fisher Hendley occurred April 24, 1923, when he took first place at a gathering held at the Ansonville School,[28] and May 21, in Albemarle at the courthouse.[29]

Fisher's first big win came in 1924 at the self-proclaimed "North Carolina State Fiddlers' Convention." Promoted by J.C. Sell, publisher of the *Cooleemee Journal*, the convention was held each September in the Davie County mill town of Cooleemee.

On Saturday, September 20, 1924, Fisher mounted the stage of the new school building and, using a borrowed banjo, played "Let Your Shack Burn Down," a piece that he would later wax at his first recording session. The song drew from several different sources, including "Hesitation Blues," a composition associated with W.C. Handy. When Fisher was awarded the first banjo prize, Hendley was roundly praised by one of the judges as being the best picker he had ever heard. For nine years, Fisher was to take first place at this contest and to capture many other prizes well into the 1930s. These wins provided Fisher Hendley the momentum toward the expansion of his musical career.

Seven

WBT-Charlotte

"Watch Buick Travel"

His first musical successes led to Fisher Hendley's being summoned by Charlotte broadcaster WBT for an appearance over their airwaves. North Carolina's premier station had squealed to life during April of 1922. Amateur radio buff Fred Laxton carried the seeds for the original 100-watter from his home to the Independence Building on the downtown square of the Queen City. When C.C. Coddington, the local dealer of Buick automobiles, purchased Laxton's property in 1925, he claimed its call letters, WBT, stood for "Watch Buick Travel." WBT was still a small, local concern when Fisher first performed from "the Interstate Radio Studio" at 7 West Fourth Street at 9:00 in the evening of April 15, 1925.

Newspaper reports of Fisher Hendley's presentation intimate that Victor Records was using Fisher's appearance on WBT as an audition. However, no Victor recording session was immediately forthcoming.

Fortunately, one of Victor's rivals, the Okeh Company, was interested in Hendley. When that concern brought portable recording equipment to the mountain town of Asheville, North Carolina, Fisher Hendley was invited to make a "test" or audition recording that Okeh could use to gauge his sales potential. At the end of the last week in August of 1925, Fisher traveled to Asheville to record. His two selections were a medley of the aforementioned "Let Your Shack Burn Down" and "All Night Long," along with a version of Shepherd N. Edmonds 1901 composition "I'm Going to Live Anyhow 'Til I Die."

Fisher's two sides, featuring his formal singing backed by finger-picked banjo, were released on a 78 rpm record by October of 1925. Albemarle residents could sample the disc at the jewelry store of W.J. Rowland.[1] Alas, it made little impression in the marketplace and Okeh never recalled him into its studios.

What Earl Scruggs Heard

Fisher Hendley proudly holds his "first good banjo," purchased with the help of the Trinity College Glee Club. This photograph was probably made around 1925 on the occasion of his first radio broadcasts over WBT-Charlotte, North Carolina (courtesy Hellen Hendley Permar).

Seven. WBT-Charlotte

The Albemarle Novelty Amusement Company

Hendley returned home on August 30 to his service station, continuing with solo engagements and those with the group he had assembled following his first big contest victory. This loose association of musicians was titled the Albemarle Novelty Amusement Company. It was among Fisher's earliest attempts, if not his earliest, at putting together a program of entertainers that he would lead as manager, promoter, performer and master of ceremonies.

Initially, Fisher recruited three players—Preston Mayberry, Worth Allen and Gowan Cole—to fulfill local obligations.[2] All came from families that held working-class cotton mill occupations. For these men, music was never their main pursuit, but, provided a leisure-time activity and a bit of additional funds. As Guy Swaringen wrote in the *Charlotte Observer*, their "advocation outdistanced their vocation."[3]

Guitarist Preston Lee "Press" Mayberry (January 3, 1893–June 1, 1978) had been born in Wilkes County.[4] Mayberry followed his family to Jerusalem Township, outside Coolemee in Davie County, where Preston worked as a weaver in the local cotton mill.[5] By 1917, Mayberry had moved to Salisbury's Kesler Mill.[6] The following year, Press Mayberry changed occupations, taking advantage of Salisbury's proximity to the Southern Railroad to gain employment.[7] Married in the spring of 1918,[8] by year's end, Preston's wife had succumbed to the "Spanish" influenza.[9] Press Mayberry's relocation to Albemarle, where he was engaged as a stonecutter, was predicated on his remarriage, in 1922, to local resident Terry Morris.[10]

Worth T. Allen (October 28, 1904–June 5, 1953)[11] came from Albemarle and was a cotton mill worker all of his life.[12]

Four string banjo and mandolin picker Gowan Wesley Cole (April 12, 1891–August 26, 1970)[13] started out his life in Albemarle. After a period working in the local cotton mill,[14] Cole was drafted in June of 1917. He spent the next three years in the United States Army, including service in Europe.[15] Before Gowan left for France, he made music daily, writing to his mother, "I took my mandolin out one night and played and since then some one [sic] is after me every time I go out to come and play at their house."[16]

Returning to Albemarle in September of 1920,[17] Gowen Cole first went to work for D.W. Snider, whose sewing and talking machine repair business was based within the Cole home.[18] By the time Gowan joined the Amusement Company, he was employed locally by his father at the Southern Power Company.[19]

What Earl Scruggs Heard

If newspaper coverage is to be believed, Fisher Hendley and an expanded eleven-member troupe played a total of thirty local engagements in the spring of 1925, including those at the Albemarle Graded School Auditorium and the Opera House in Badin. After emphasizing that the group was made up of talented locals, the *Albemarle Press* described their presentation as "[the] Latest Popular Music by a Novelty Orchestra." There were Hawaiian selections by Gowan Cole (on "jazz" banjo), trombonist Worth Allen and steel guitarist Hugh Barrier. Barrier also performed on tenor banjo and saxophone, danced and participated in minstrel skits. Press Mayberry brought along his guitar.

Besides these players, the full orchestra included Richard Clyde Simpson on saxophone, clarinetist George Russell, Hoyle Lowder/piano, and Grover Thompson (known as "Doodly Squat") on drums. Hendley and Grover Thompson also performed in blackface.[20] While trying to make his living from music, Thompson was working for Hendley at Mason and Melton's.[21] Clyde Simpson (April 22, 1890–January 26, 1946) was the only musical professional of the bunch.[22]

Additionally, Prince Furr and his family band made an appearance, as did the Frisky Four Quartette, composed of cotton mill worker[23] Ray Ezra Ballard (May 21, 1903–May 24, 1973),[24] Fisher Hendley, Frank Smith and Frank Mabry, who worked as a bookkeeper at the aluminum plant in Badin. The Quartette often won prizes by singing "The Farmer Song," in which Hendley crowed like a rooster.

The Albemarle Novelty Company was obviously not a country string band, but a variety show ensemble catering to popular tastes. The above descriptions go a long way toward disavowing another stereotypical image, of country folk sitting around singing British ballads and playing Irish and Scottish fiddle tunes!

Fisher Hendley brought his Novelty Company for a return visit to the Cooleemee fiddlers' convention. Resolving to defend his banjo prize, Fisher also hoped to bring home the silver loving cup awarded to the county with the most prize winners. When the September 1925 contest ended, Hendley and his musicians had captured all but one first place, forcing the surrender of the trophy by Rowan County, the 1924 champion. Fisher Hendley had again emerged with the first prize in the banjo contest, P.L. Mayberry captured the guitar honor, Hugh Barrier received first for "buck and wing" dancing, and 11-year-old Belvin Furr, whose family had taken the 1924 prizes for juvenile players, once more won for violin. Earl Hatley, a member of Fisher's later string band, garnered the second fiddle prize. Other contestants from Stanly County included

Seven. WBT-Charlotte

fiddlers DeWitt Hudson and T.F. Crowell, guitarist John Crowell and mandolinist Tom G. Whitley, all from the New London area.

Prince Furr Family

Multi-instrumentalist Prince Alexander Furr was born January 25, 1888, on a farm in Almond Township, Stanly County. The oldest child of Marshall F. and Laura Jane Morton Furr,[25] family lore has Prince traveling as a teenager with a carnival band. It was Prince's second marriage, in 1912,[26] to Carrie Ila Byrd (July 4, 1894–June 5, 1971),[27] that yielded the musical progeny who were to join him in a family ensemble. Carrie and Prince had probably met at the cotton/hosiery mill where they were both laboring. Prince was to work as a machinist in area mills for much of his adult life and his offspring followed Furr into similar employment. Furr's

Prince Furr and His Musical Sons at the start of their career, circa 1925. Left to right: Belvin/fiddle, Marvin/fiddle, Prince/guitar, Thad/banjo and Rayvon Furr/ukulele (courtesy Bill Furr and *Stanly News and Press*, November 23, 1984).

What Earl Scruggs Heard

musical sons eventually included William Belvin "Pee Wee" (born July 18, 1913),[28] Marvin Deamus (born November 22, 1915[29]), Thaddeus Alexander (born January 19, 1917[30]) and Rayvon Elbert (born October 8, 1918).[31]

In 1921, Furr began teaching his eldest to play the fiddle. The following year, Belvin and Prince performed as a duo at a fiddlers' convention in the Albemarle courthouse, bagging the $5.00 first prize. Belvin, backed by his father on mandolin, captured an award in 1923 by fiddling "Katie Kline."[32]

These victories started the Furr family on a circuit of local fiddlers' conventions, political rallies, birthday parties, and dances. As each son came of age, he in turn joined the group. In 1922, Marvin started on the mandolin, later switching to the fiddle. The following year, Thad began playing the tenor banjo, and then, another year later, Rayvon took up the ukulele and the mandolin.[33] In the course of their studies, all the boys learned to read music.

In 1925, Prince Furr and His Musical Sons, as the band was locally known, began their association with Nehi beverages. Nehi had

The Furr family as the Nehi Orchestra at a trade show, circa 1925–1929. On the left side of the photograph are Thad/banjo (partially outside the frame), Marvin/fiddle, Belvin/fiddle and Prince/guitar (courtesy Bill Furr).

introduced a line of fruit-flavored sodas in 1924, and Prince represented the local manufacturer. A visit by the district manager prompted a trip by the ensemble to a national convention of soft drink manufacturers. There, the group performed in the Nehi booth twice a day. Furr and Sons changed its name to the Nehi Orchestra and traded their stage outfits of white sailor suits for military band–style uniforms. In 1925, the Furrs were sent by Nehi to Kansas City; in 1926, to Buffalo; and, in 1927, to the Columbus, Georgia, home of the Nehi Company. However, with the arrival of the 1929 Depression, soft drink sales also crashed, ending the Furr's association with Nehi.

Thereafter, the family began the changeover to a more modern horn- and reed-led dance band. The Furrs took up other instruments— Prince the bass fiddle, Marvin the sax and Rayvon the drums—and the group became known as Prince Furr and His Orchestra. In 1933, the family band ended its run. Three of the brothers, led by Belvin, formed their own big band, dubbed the Tar Heel Club Orchestra, one of many ensembles sharing that name.[34] By 1937, Thad Furr was gigging on his own, including weekends at the Ocean Plaza Hotel in Myrtle Beach,[35]

Prince Furr died on September 15, 1968, at the age of 80.[36] Marvin passed away September 24, 1984,[37] Belvin February 1, 2004,[38] Rayvon followed on May 4, 2007,[39] and Thad succumbed March 25, 2012.[40]

Following the Cooleemee convention, Fisher Hendley was elected to the post of secretary/treasurer for the fiddlers' contest. In 1927, Hendley ascended to its chairmanship and brought the event to Albemarle. It was with this association that Fisher first proved his skill as an event organizer, which was to serve him well once he moved into music on a full-time basis.

Before Hendley could take further advantage of his successes with the Albemarle Novelty Amusement Company, Fisher again struck out on his own. Following several solo appearances for civic clubs in Charlotte,[41] Hendley performed during the first week of 1926 at the local Keith's Vaudeville theater.[42] This trial proved successful, and Fisher joined S.T. Abbott and Company's vaudeville troupe in Chicago.[43] While in the windy city, Fisher Hendley also broadcast over radio station WGN.

Wedding Bells

By summer's end, Hendley was back in Albemarle running Hendley's Auto Service. He also got married. Fisher Hendley's bride was the

What Earl Scruggs Heard

Hendley's Auto Service, Albemarle, North Carolina, 1927. Mr. and Mrs. Fisher Hendley stand in the foreground with baby Graham Hendley (courtesy Hellen Hendley Permar).

V.C. Edminister on fiddle, Hayes Williams/guitar, mandolinist Conrad and J.C. Howell on banjo, circa 1935 (courtesy Marcus Howell).

former Margaret Estelle Carroll, born June 18, 1899, in Duplin County. Maggie, as Mrs. Hendley was known, was the daughter of Kenansville tobacco farmer John Carroll, who also ran a country store. Fisher had met Maggie ten years previously through her brother-in-law Thurman Wells, with whom Hendley had worked at DuPont. Maggie Carroll had a modicum of education and business experience, which would later come in handy when the Hendley's entered music on a full-time basis. She had followed an older sister into the teaching profession and then a brother into an office job at the Atlantic Coastline Railway headquarters in Wilmington, North Carolina.

Fisher and Maggie tied the knot on August 21, 1926. The ceremony took place at the home of Maggie's sister Sally in Winter Park outside of Wilmington. The Hendleys then took up residence near the service station in Albemarle. A year later, the couple's first child, Graham Fisher Hendley, was born June 19, 1927. A daughter, Margaret Hellen, followed on November 12, 1928.

Even as he ran the Mason and Melton garage, Hendley continued in his pursuit of a musical career. At some point, Fisher decided to ally himself with a local country string band. This ensemble included fiddler V.C. Edminister, cotton mill worker J.C. Howell on banjo, Howell's son Conrad on mandolin, Hayes Williams/guitar, comedian Rolly Forte, and comedian and dancer Happy Harris. Fisher probably took this band along for his continuing broadcasts over WBT, even if the radio audience couldn't see Harris's dancing or Hendley's banjo stunts. And it didn't hurt that Hendley's Auto Service was sponsoring the band's programs.

Fisher Hendley initially called this group the Badinean Minstrel Troupe, possibly because the other musicians lived in the town of Badin, and/or because the group mixed string selections with those from blackface minstrelsy familiar to Fisher Hendley.

James (Mc)Coy Howell was born April 25, 1889, in Gold Hill, a Rowan County community located half-way between Badin and Salisbury.[44] In 1908, Howell married Ida Cristie Crowell (1890–1965)[45]; their son Conrad Therian arrived the following year.[46] Originally, James worked in one of the local mines. However, by the time America entered World War I, J.C. was employed by the American Aluminum Company in Badin, moving his family there by the beginning of 1920.[47] Conrad Howell left home to marry in 1928. He held a variety of jobs throughout the 1930s,[48] ending up by 1940 managing the Roxy, a local movie house.[49]

This group's association with Fisher was probably short-lived. However, according to family lore, the two Howells, along with Edminister and Williams, continued throughout the 1930s to play as an ensemble. Conrad told his offspring that the band had performed every Sunday morning on a broadcaster in Charlotte, which I assume was WBT (although I haven't found evidence to back that claim). He also asserted that the group was good enough to consistently win prizes at fiddlers' conventions throughout the region and that those winnings helped to get them through the Depression.[50]

James Howell died in Badin on August 30, 1955.[51] Conrad passed away April 25, 1989.[52]

James Coy Howell with Gibson Mastertone-model banjo, circa 1930 (courtesy Marcus Howell).

Carolina Tar Heels

By the end of 1928, with a shuffle of personnel, Fisher's group became known as the Carolina Tar Heels (not to be confused with the more famous band of the same name nor the sports teams at the University of North Carolina). Hayes Williams, joined by Dan J. Harris on fiddle and Badin resident Marshall Small, second banjo, was the only surviving member from the old ensemble.

Daniel Jefferson Harris (November 15, 1856–March 9, 1940)[53] and his wife Julia Ann Hatley owned a large farm near Oakboro in Stanly County. The couple produced twelve children, several of whom played banjo, fiddle, guitar and Hawaiian guitar and competed at local fiddlers' conventions. A schoolteacher[54] of varied musical interests, Harris had also organized and led Stanly County's first brass band in the 1890s and early 1900s.[55]

Seven. WBT-Charlotte

Marshall Small, strangely enough, was related by both marriage AND blood to banjoist James C. Howell, whom he succeeded in Hendley's band.[56] Like Howell, Marshall Albert Small (August 27, 1887–February 27, 1947)[57] was born in the Gold Hill community.[58] And, like James Howell, Marshall started out as a mine worker.[59] By 1918, Small had married Howell's sister Ethel Mae, worked as "constable" for Gold Hill[60] and served in the military during the end of World War I.[61] Soon after his release from the service, Marshall and Ethel left Gold Hill, first moving south of Albemarle to Norwood and then to Badin. In both locations, Small ran his own auto repair shop.[62]

Dan Harris with fiddle, 1929 (courtesy Katharine Berger).

The Tar Heels eventually grew to include seven members and at one time comprised Spencer B. Hatley on guitar, Earl Hatley on fiddle, James Russell/guitar, Claude Eudy/mandolin, Hawaiian guitarist Fred Russell and Sam Poplin on fiddle.

Earl Alonzo Hatley (May 25, 1893–August 5, 1975)[63] held many jobs: farmer, cotton mill carpenter,[64] mechanic, stone cutter in a monument yard,[65] tombstone delivery man for Palmer Stone Works in Albemarle, road worker, bakery driver and home builder.[66] His son, Spencer Bruin Hatley (December 19, 1913–September 2, 1997[67]), a teenager when first appearing with Hendley,[68] left mill work behind[69] to study music.[70] After World War II, Spencer directed the Albemarle High School Band[71] and went on to run music stores in Salisbury and Statesville.[72] The brothers Russell, Fred Tyler (July 20, 1891–May 7, 1978)[73] and James (born January 1888), grew up on a farm in the Stanly County town of Tyson.[74] Fred followed his father into farming,[75] marrying twice: first at the age of twenty and, after his wife died six years later,[76] at the end of 1924 to Pallie Lillie Furr Kimrey, sister to Marshall Furr mentioned previously.[77] Sam Wesley Poplin (April 9, 1915–January 24, 2000) was from Norwood in Stanly County.[78]

What Earl Scruggs Heard

The Carolina Tarheels, March 1929. Back row, left to right: Spencer Hatley, Dan Harris, Earl Hatley and James Russell. Front row, left to right: Fisher Hendley, Fred Russell and Claude Eudy. This photograph appeared in the *WBT Radio Log*, "WBT Offers Splendidly Arranged Radio Log," *Charlotte Observer*, April 21, 1929 (author's collection).

The Carolina Tar Heels documented their existence by donning evening dress and visiting Leonard Alexander Hitchcock's local photographic emporium to have their picture made. Hendley had held onto the style of costume used in performances by the Trinity Glee Club, which always appeared in publicity photographs clothed in formal attire. Fisher passed this belief in formality onto to his bands, which mostly bucked the country music tradition of "dressing hillbilly," therefore differentiating themselves from scores of other entertainers. One of the uses for these photographs were to advertise broadcasts by the Carolina Tar Heels over WBT.

By 1929, WBT-Charlotte had a 50,000-watt signal that covered two-thirds of North Carolina, where one out of every seven families owned a radio.[79] Before that time, published radio listings are either vague or non-existent. Therefore, it is hard to track the exact amount of country music broadcast over WBT. However, it's for certain that, judging from the programming publicized between 1929 and 1933, from the 1920s to the advent of the Crazy Water Barn Dance in the spring of 1934,

Seven. WBT-Charlotte

the station never prominently featured fiddlers, banjoists and rural singers. Instead, a variety of music and talk programming graced the Charlotte airwaves, with an emphasis on the high-class and the popular.

Someone at WBT must have decided that there was an audience for string bands, for several, including Hendley's Carolina Tar Heels, began broadcasting at the start of 1929. In order to reach rural and working-class folks, these programs were scheduled in the mid- to late hours of the evening. However, if the radio listings are to be taken literally, there was no consistency to when these groups would appear or something different would be scheduled in their place. The bands that broadcast during 1929 were initially allowed an hour of airtime, which quickly diminished to half-an-hour per appearance. It is unknown whether the WBT string band schedule was limited by excessive demands on the radio waves or by the parameters of the musician's schedules. After all, most of these players worked primarily outside of music, and, before sponsored programs, radio appearances were unpaid. Therefore, a busy aggregation such as Hendley's wouldn't want to miss the opportunity for the remuneration from live performances or the cash prizes at fiddlers' conventions.

The bands that appeared alongside the Tar Heels were Martin Melody Boys of Gaffney, South Carolina; the W.O.W. String Band and the Woodlawn String Band. In January and February of 1929, A.D. Martin and His Melody Boys made four appearances on WBT,[80] and the W.O.W. String Band (it's unclear which one, for a number of W.O.W. chapters sponsored groups) was a late Saturday-night favorite from April to June.[81] The most consistent group for 1929 was the Woodlawn String Band. Besides appearing photographically in the Spring *WBT Radio Log*, nothing else about this group is known except that, because Woodlawn is a neighborhood of Charlotte, that the members lived in the metropolitan area. The band disappears from the published listings by the end of the year.[82]

As for Fisher Hendley's Carolina Tarheels, after a handful of broadcasts in January, February and March, as well as appearing in the April *Radio Log*, they vanish from the newspaper schedules for WBT and don't return for the rest of 1929.[83] In fact, spot checking the *Charlotte Observer* and *News*, with the exception of the Wayside Program, no rural string musicians consistently appear through 1930.

Despite his earlier lack of success with the Okeh recording outfit, Fisher continued to work all the angles in procuring a record contract for the Tar Heels. In this regard, at the beginning of 1930, Hendley wrote

What Earl Scruggs Heard

KALAMAZOO, MICHIGAN
January 28, 1930

Carolina Tar Heels
Box 565
Albemarle, N. C.

Attention: Fisher Hendley

Dear Friend:

We surely were tickled to receive your good letter of January the 22nd and many congratulations on the Shriners Convention job.

I am going to tell all the folks around the Gibson factory what time you go on the air so that they can tune in and of course, we will make note of this in the MASTERTONE Magazine.

We certainly would like to have a cut of which you sent us an illustration as we could make good use of it in the MASTERTONE Magazine and I know you would find the publicity very valuable.

We have been hearing a lot about the Carolina Tar Heels these days and I hope that you are successful in lining with some good record company. I will notify Mr. Peacock to give you a lift if he possibly can.

You certainly have an organization to be proud of, Mr. Hendley, and believe me, Gibson, Incorporated is mighty proud too of the fact that you are 100% Gibson.

Keep up the good work and send us this cut as soon as possible.

Best wishes.

Sincerely yours,

GIBSON, INC.

George H. Post
BL

Letter from Gibson, Inc., to Fisher Hendley, January 28, 1930 (courtesy Hellen Hendley Permar).

Seven. WBT-Charlotte

to the Gibson Company. He and his band mates were exclusive users of Gibson musical instruments, and Fisher Hendley hoped that the company would help with the record business.

Here's the answer from Gibson:

Gibson Inc.
Mastertone Fretted Instruments
Kalamazoo, Michigan.

January 28, 1930

[to] Carolina Tar Heels
Box 565
Albemarle, N. C.
Attention: Fisher Hendley.

Dear Friend:

We surely were tickled to receive your good letter of January the 22nd and many congratulations on the Shriners Convention job.

I am going to tell all the folks around the Gibson factory what time you go on the air so that they can tune in and of course, we will make note of this in the *Mastertone Magazine*.

We certainly would like to have a cut of which you sent us an illustration as we could make good use of it in the *Mastertone Magazine* and I know you would find the publicity very valuable.

We have been hearing a lot about the Carolina Tar Heels these days and I hope that you are successful in lining with some good record company. I will notify Mr. Peacock to give you a lift if he possibly can.

You certainly have an organization to be proud of, Mr. Hendley, and believe me, Gibson, Incorporated is mighty proud too of the fact that you are 100% Gibson. Keep up the good work and send us this cut as soon as possible. Best wishes.

Sincerely yours,

George H. Post
[Salesman for Gibson]
Gibson, Inc.

Fisher hadn't realized what a serious effect the Depression was having on all businesses, including the recording companies. It took an arrangement with Henry Whitter, a guitarist with a measure of prior successes, to gain a new contract, this time with Victor Records.

Whitter had formerly made discs with fiddler G.B. Grayson for A&R (Artist and Repertoire) pioneer Ralph Peer. With Grayson's untimely death, Henry wrote Peer in August announcing his new partnership with Hendley and asking for a session. Approval was forthcoming, although it is unknown if Ralph Peer remembered Fisher from Hendley's prior Asheville recordings when Peer was employed by Okeh.[84]

Henry Whitter arrived in Albemarle in October of 1930 for rehearsals and local performances with Hendley and Marshall Small in preparation for their recording session. Whether the musicians had prior commitments, or Whitter didn't see the need for the other members of the Carolina Tar Heels, is impossible to say. Limiting the ensemble to a trio had some sonic benefits. It does allow us to hear just how good Small was on the banjo. Although grateful for these four sides, I wish they had cut more so we could further enjoy Marshall Small's playing.

After appearing at local high schools in nearby Montgomery County, the trio, announced in local newspapers as recording in Atlanta,[85] left for Memphis, Tennessee, the real site for their session. On November 28 and 29, 1930, Whitter, Hendley and Small waxed six tunes for Victor in their temporary studios. One coupling was released the following spring: the instrumentals "Shuffle, Feet, Shuffle," (a medley of "Will the Roses Bloom in Heaven" composed by Charles K. Harris, author of "After the Ball"; and the 1870 song "Little Old Log Cabin in the Lane" from Will S. Hays) and "Tar and Feathers" (based on the 1894 pop tune "Sweet Bunch of Daisies"). Whether the record's appeal or the effects of the Depression determined its success, Victor waited another five and a half years to issue "Another Man's Wife" (aka "Girl with the Waterfall" played as a medley with the 19th-century pop tune "The Merriest Girl That's Out"), backed with "A Pretty Gal's Love," on its budget Bluebird label. All the released recordings feature the up-picking finger style banjo duets of Hendley and Small. The Trio plugged their first Victor 78 rpm record with March appearances on WBT.[86]

These recordings did not have much effect on Fisher's musical aspirations. He continued to promote fiddlers' conventions, appear for civic organizations and to sporadically broadcast over WBT-Charlotte, WWNC-Asheville and WSOC-Gastonia.[87]

One notable event of this time period was held in Statesville. The local newspaper offered this report:

> Fiddler's [sic] Contest. P.O.S of A. Will Stage Musical Treat Here Saturday Night. The Patriotic Orders [sic] Sons of America, which has staged splendid fiddlers conventions here in the past, are bringing a special contest here Saturday night at 7:30 o'clock, at the Court House, which will afford another opportunity to hear old-time music. Mack Crow's band and Fisher Hendley's Tar Heel Serenaders will engaged [sic] in a musical contest here, and the

Seven. WBT-Charlotte

FISHER HENDLEY

General Manager, North Carolina String Musicians' Association, and Champion Banjo Player of the State, will be there and have charge of the program. This will be a County Championship Convention. Every musician in New Hanover County is urged to be there and take a part in this contest. Championship awards will be given for best string band of four or more musicians; best vocal quartet, male, ladies' or mixed; best duet of any two instruments; best violin; five-string banjo; best tenor banjo; best standard guitar; best Hawaiian guitar; best mandolin; best clog and buck dancer. The winners selected at this time will represent New Hanover County in the State Championship contest to be held in Charlotte, N. C.

Advertisement for Fisher Hendley as "General Manager, North Carolina String Musicians Association," circa December 1932 (courtesy Hellen Hendley Permar).

local order's proceeds will be used in charity work. The contest is stated to be for the State championship.

The two bands are well known here. Mack Crow, known as "The Banjo King" was manager and master of ceremonies at a fiddlers convention early in September, sponsored by the P.O.S. of A. and Fisher Hendley's band was one of the outstanding aggregations in the convention. That occasion filled the court house to capacity and the program was termed one of the best ever held here.[88]

One of the Tar Heels few engagements where they yielded to the country bumpkin stereotype was in New York City. Summers were a slow time in the pre-air-conditioned South. The schools and halls that served as venues for itinerant country musicians were closed. Therefore, radio performers would go on hiatus. So Fisher began the practice of bringing his band to New York City during the summer and early fall for performances both live and on the radio. If they were lucky, recording sessions were also arranged.

Fisher Hendley's Carolina Tar Heels made at least two trips to New York, in 1933 and 1935. There, they worked at the Brown Derby, the Washington Heights Club and the Paradise Restaurant. At the Village Barn Theatre, the Tar Heels, opening for Paul Whitman's band, wore "hillbilly" garb for the engagement. To publicize their appearances, Hendley and company broadcast over a series of radio stations, including WMCA, WOR and finally, WEAF.[89]

Although being in a large city like New York must have seemed glamorous, the Tar Heels certainly didn't get rich from their engagements. Members of Earl Hatley's family remember that the family struggled with their breadwinner gone, especially as Earl wasn't sending much money home.

The Tar Heels did manage to land a session for ARC's Vocalion label, but mostly waxed a series of fairly standard fiddle tunes. Fisher did get to show off his vocalizing on "Answer to the Big Rock Candy Mountain," a reply to the 1906 song, as well as "Work in 1930." These recordings hit the market fairly quickly, at the end of 1933 and into the first part of 1934.

Unfortunately, as their Vocalion discs were released, the Carolina Tarheels disbanded. By this time, other musical opportunities had come to Fisher Hendley. It was time for Hendley to sell his business and leave Albemarle behind. Fisher Hendley and his young family was headed for Charlotte, for a job with Crazy Water Crystals and WBT.

Eight

Crazy Water and Crazy Bands

Country Music has had a long association with patent medicine companies. In the late 19th and early 20th centuries, "doctors" in traveling "medicine" shows included crowd-pulling musical performers in their pitches. This developed into the radio sponsorships of the 1920s–1940s by the myriad of tonics and miracle cures gracing drugstore shelves. One such concoction, Crazy Water Crystals, was a popular "natural" laxative salt distilled from water originating (the company claimed) in Mineral Wells, Texas.

Crazy Water's relationship with string band music in the Carolinas began with James Wesley Fincher's move to Charlotte, North Carolina, in August of 1933. As president of the local Crystals office, Fincher arranged to underwrite broadcasts on WBT's 50,000-watt signal. The original Crazy Water program was carried over the airwaves on Tuesday and Thursday just after noon and Monday, Wednesday and Friday at 8:15 a.m.[1] The first mention of this schedule appeared in local Crazy Water ads on Thursday, August 17, 1933. By the fall, Fincher had also added to their sponsorship popular dance band appearances over WPTF-Raleigh and WWNC-Asheville.[2]

In March of 1934, at the same time J.W. Fincher was aggressively expanding his dealer network,[3] Fincher added a country "barn dance" program a la WSM-Nashville's Grand Ole Opry variety show to the Crazy Water radio schedule. Initially broadcast from the studios of WBT, the Crazy Barn Dance aired each Saturday night between 8:30 and 9:30.

By May, in order to accommodate exploding audiences, the Crazy Water Barn Dance had moved into an auditorium owned by the *Charlotte Observer* newspaper. The original one-hour presentation was expanded into a two-and-a-half-hour extravaganza from 9:30 until midnight.[4] The Barn Dance eventually morphed into a traveling show. For

What Earl Scruggs Heard

Eight. Crazy Water and Crazy Bands

the better part of a year, the Crazy Barn Dance toured North Carolina, adding talent contests to their program. A live audience paid to witness performances by a dozen amateur bands eager for the opportunity to broadcast their music over the Charlotte powerhouse.[5] Only a portion of the live show was carried by WBT on Saturday evenings at various times until the show's demise. Ultimately, many of the Crazy Water broadcasters, including WPTF, WWNC, as well as WHAS-Louisville, Kentucky, carried their own, localized version of the Saturday night Barn Dance program.[6]

The success for all of their transmissions resulted in Crazy Water's expansion of their sponsored programming to WSOC-Gastonia and

Opposite: Cast of the Crazy Barn Dance, WBT. Front row, left to right: (standing) Master of Ceremonies Fisher Hendley/banjo, (sitting) Dick Hartman (Tennessee Ramblers)/guitar, "Pappy" (Kenneth Wolfe, Tennessee Ramblers)/fiddle, Excell Stallings/comic singer, J.W. Fincher/president and general manager, H.T. Fincher/assistant manager, "Harry" (Blair, Tennessee Ramblers)/guitar, "Curley" (Cecil Campbell, Tennessee Ramblers)/plectrum banjo, Claire Shadwell/announcer. Second row: Ray Broome (Broome Brothers)/fiddle, Leroy Broome (Broome Brothers)/guitar, Robert Broome (Broome Brothers)/mandolin, Arthur Goodman (Shell Allen's Kannapolis W.O.W. String Band)/guitar, Harue Suther (Shell Allen's Kannapolis W.O.W. String Band)/banjo-mandolin, Shell Allen (Shell Allen's Kannapolis W.O.W. String Band)/fiddle, Carl Dayvault (Shell Allen's Kannapolis W.O.W. String Band)/guitar, Raymond Thornburg (Shell Allen's Kannapolis W.O.W. String Band)/string bass, Zeke Robinson/fiddle, Everett Tabor/mandolin, F.H. Camp, Lawrence Mills/banjo, Henry Tabor/string bass. Third row: Homer Broome (Broome Brothers)/mandolin, Henry Broome (Broome Brothers), Joe Broome (Broome Brothers)/guitar, Hebert Lipe/mandolin, Sam Poplin/fiddle (Fred Russell's Hillbillies), Earl Hatley (Fred Russell's Hillbillies)/fiddle, Fred Russell (Fred Russell's Hillbillies)/mandolin, Hawley Perry/banjo, Dewitt "Snuffy" Jenkins (Jenkins String Band)/banjo, Tom Kimrey/string bass. Fourth row: Pete Scarboro, Howard Leigh/guitar, Cordell Smith (Moonlight Serenaders)/guitar, James Russell (Fred Russell's Hillbillies)/guitar. Fifth Row: J.E. Mainer (Crazy Mountaineers)/fiddle, Lester Leigh/guitar, Dorsey Dixon (Dixon Brothers)/guitar, Howard Dixon (Dixon Brothers)/Hawaiian guitar, Howard Cole (Jenkins String Band)/guitar, Dennis E. Jenkins (Jenkins String Band)/guitar. Back row: Wade Mainer (Crazy Mountaineers)/banjo, Roy Smith (Moonlight Serenaders)/mandolin, Mrs. Roy Smith (Moonlight Serenaders)/guitar, Floyd Bailey/banjo, Wade Cranford, Mrs. Maud Byars/ukulele, Miss Mary Byars/Hawaiian guitar, Mack Byars/guitar, Verl Jenkins (Jenkins String Band)/fiddle. First published *Charlotte Observer*, May 20, 1934 (courtesy Rachel Wiles).

What Earl Scruggs Heard

WBIG-Greensboro, as well as other stations in North and South Carolina and Georgia. Ultimately, Crazy Water and WBT had an immensely effective (albeit short) partnership, lasting into 1935, when a downturn in sales ended the Crazy Water collaboration.[7]

With the addition of the Barn Dance, Crazy Water needed a manager/agent/talent scout to wrangle performers and fill slots on Saturday nights. Fisher Hendley took on that role in the spring of 1934, bouncing between Crazy Water broadcasters WWNC-Asheville,[8] where he still had siblings residing, and WBT-Charlotte, which became the new home for the Hendley family.

Fisher's job with Crazy Water finally enabled him to enter the music business full-time. On May 10, 1934, Fisher, along with his wife Maggie and children Graham and Hellen, left their garage in Albemarle and Stanly County behind for life in the big city of Charlotte.

Fisher Hendley was uniquely positioned to take advantage of the advertising muscle that the Crazy Water company brought to the station. Fisher's work for Crazy Water capitalized on all his talents. He was a masterful master of ceremonies, a colorful entertainer, and an excellent organizer of live events. His experience

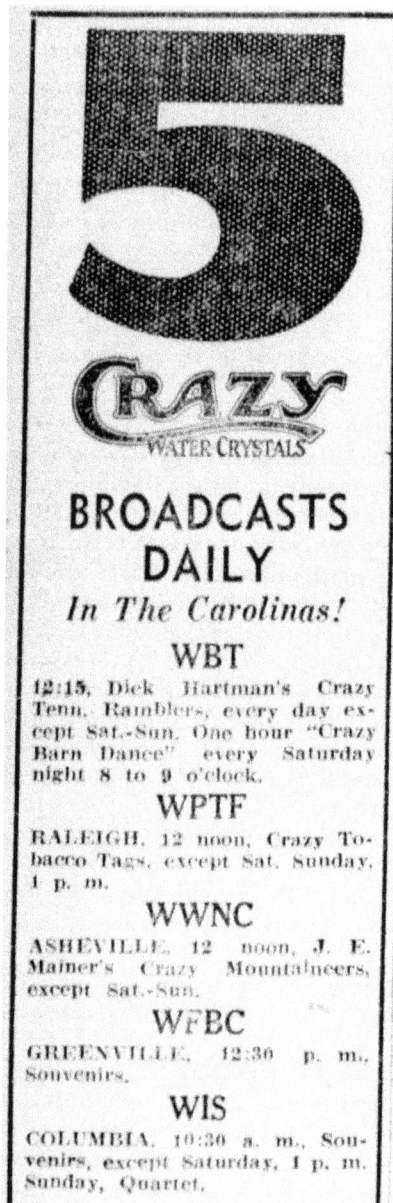

Advertisement for Crazy Water broadcasts (*Charlotte Observer*, October 7, 1934).

Eight. Crazy Water and Crazy Bands

promoting fiddlers' conventions stood him in good stead as a talent scout, and he brought a number of bands into the Crazy Water fold.

The Crazy Water Cast: Tennessee Ramblers

One group already working for Crazy Water was the Tennessee Ramblers. Of all the bands the company brought to the airwaves, it was the only aggregation exclusively earning a living from personal appearances generated by a daily spot on WBT. Led by Dick Hartman, the ensemble, which played both Western swing and old-time string music, had already worked for Crazy Water in Pittsburgh, Pennsylvania, and Rochester, New York, before relocating to Charlotte.[9]

The Ramblers personnel that came to WBT included guitarist Dick Hartman (June 12, 1898–April 15, 1962), born in Burlington, West Virginia[10]; William John "Horse Thief Harry" Blair, born in New Martinsville, West Virginia, August 26, 1912[11]; and fiddler Kenneth "Pappy" Wolfe. The only North Carolina native in the Ramblers was tenor banjoist Cecil Robert "Curley" Campbell. Born March 22, 1911, in the Stokes County community of Danbury,[12] at the age of fourteen or fifteen years old, Campbell had taught himself to play the guitar minding the family's tobacco curing barn.[13] Cecil's first occasional radio job was over WSJS–Winston-Salem. Cecil Campbell worked on his father's farm until at least 1930, when the family was living in the Forsyth County town of Belews Creek.[14] In 1932, while visiting his brother in Pittsburgh, Cecil met Dick Hartman,[15] then broadcasting over KDKA,[16] and was asked to join Hartman's group.[17]

The Tennessee Ramblers were appearing for Crazy Water in Rochester, New York, over the airwaves of WHEC, when the call came for the move to Charlotte. The Ramblers first surfaced in WBT's radio listings at the beginning of 1934, hitting the airwaves during the last week of January. WBT chose to introduce the group to the public with a live event held in the Charlotte Armory on Saturday, January 27. The following Monday, the Crazy Tennesseans began their broadcasts, commanding a daily spot in the radio schedule.[18]

Of course, broadcasting was just a gateway for musicians to paid public performing (it is unclear if the Ramblers were salaried by Crazy Water or just given free airtime through a sponsorship arrangement). After a sporadic spring,[19] Hartman and the Ramblers had secured a scattering of area bookings publicized in the local newspapers through the

The Tennessee Ramblers in Rochester, New York, broadcasting over WHEC for Crazy Water Crystals, September 1933. Back row, left to right: Kenneth "Pappy" Wolfe/fiddle, Harry Blair/guitar and Cecil "Curley" Campbell/guitar. Front row, left to right: unknown and Dick Hartman/banjo (courtesy http://mcnygenealogy.com/pics/picture.php?/4267/categories).

Eight. Crazy Water and Crazy Bands

The Tennessee Ramblers at WBT-Charlotte, North Carolina. Back row, left to right: Harry Blair/guitar, Cecil "Curley" Campbell/banjo and Fred "Happy" Morris/guitar. Front row, left to right: Dick Hartman/tenor guitar and Kenneth "Pappy" Wolfe/fiddle (author's collection).

end of the year.[20] Other opportunities came along as well. At the beginning of 1935, the band traveled to New York City for a mammoth recording session with the Bluebird record label.[21] They were augmented by the newest Rambler, Jack Gillette.

"Montana" Jack Gillette hailed (strangely enough, considering his stage sobriquet) from Providence, Rhode Island. Born around 1908, he began performing in vaudeville, traveling with a group called the Rodeo Boys. Jack played the violin and many musical novelties, such as the saw, balloon, bass drum, bicycle pump, hot trumpet and even an instrument he created himself, a "slip horn" which Montana called the "poobaphone." Gillette had originated the instrument in 1928 when a member of Louis Prima's band.[22]

Bluebird, a subsidiary of RCA-Victor, brought the Tennessee Ramblers to Atlanta (with additional band member Fred "Happy" Morris) in August for further transcription work.[23]

Under Fisher's leadership, the following bands were added to the Crazy Water fold and featured within the pages of their promotional publications. Some were previously known to Hendley, others he found after being hired by the Barn Dance, and some, in all probability, independently made their way to WBT.

The Broome Brothers

The Broome Brothers (and father) were a string band bridging the gap between amateur community and professional stage performances. While broadcasting over WBT, the older Broomes maintained other professions. After the Crazy Barn Dance folded, the younger brothers established careers as polished entertainers.

The family patriarch, Joseph Henry Broome (March 28, 1878–February 3, 1963[24]), worked as a blacksmith in the Wingate Village section of Monroe, north of Charlotte.[25] Henry married Mary Jane Stegall (March 12, 1884–August 9, 1966) on September 2, 1900.[26] Their large family included five musical sons. Mandolinist Joseph Homer (October 28, 1909–August 24, 1977) worked at the Louise Cotton Mill[27] and guitarist Robert Henry (May 13, 1915–March 25, 1976) built roads for the WPA.[28] The youngest brother, Joe Neal (May 20, 1923–November 30, 1993),[29] was originally a mandolinist; Marshall Ray (June 11, 1917–November 7, 1993) played the fiddle[30] and Leroy "Lee Roy" Broome (December 9, 1919–March 31, 2003)[31] the guitar.

Eight. Crazy Water and Crazy Bands

After leaving WBT, the first professional engagement for Leroy and Ray that I've discovered was in the fall of 1940. Both brothers found employment with the O.L./H.N. Sykes traveling show. Operating out of Garfield, Georgia, that October, Sykes was based in Sussex, Virginia.[32]

At some point between the fall of 1940 and July of 1941, after their stint with the Sykes show had concluded, at least Lee Roy Broome had joined the Lazy K Ranch Boys, with other evidence pointing to the eventual addition of his brother Ray.[33] There were many groups that utilized the Lazy K name. Newspaper listings either omit the names of band members or use their rather widespread, generic stage names such as "Scotty," "Elmer," and "Curley." So it's a bit difficult to precisely track engagements for any specific group of musicians. Additionally, at least two of the Broome's served in the military during World War II, therefore, interrupting stateside performing.

The version of the Ranch Boys that included the Broome Brothers

The Lazy K Ranch Boys featuring the Broome Brothers. I believe the Brothers are standing in the back row, left and right (*Daily Times*, April 16, 1942).

What Earl Scruggs Heard

was initially led by Blackie Skiles. Skiles was based throughout 1940 in Richmond, Virginia, making the transition from radio station WRNL to WRVA at year's end.[34] Skiles' Ranch Boys performed in an area stretching from Newport News to the east, to Danville to the southwest and Mt. Solon to the northwest.[35] Among the highlights of their stay in the Virginia state capitol was sharing the stage with Sunshine Sue and the Tobacco Tags for the Dixie Jamboree.[36]

By April of 1942, the Lazy K Ranch Boys had shifted their base of operations to Salisbury, Maryland, working indoor and outdoor movie theaters between there and Frederick.[37] In July, Lee Roy Broome left for the military[38] and, as is appropriate for a Western band, the trail then goes cold until after World War II.

Meanwhile, Broome brother Joe Neal appeared separately from Lee Roy and Ray. In June of 1942, he worked at the Steel Pier's Dude Ranch, a Western-themed nightclub located in Atlantic City, New Jersey.[39] Joe Neal Broome then entered the service for the remainder of the war.

At the conclusion of World War II, the Broome Brothers reassembled in Los Angeles as a trio a la the Sons of the Pioneers. Luckily, their music fit right in with the California country and western music scene of the post-war period.

During their West Coast sojourn, the three Brothers maintained an active schedule of "personals" and appearances in B movies. Their films included 1949's *Square Dance Jubilee* with a musical cast including the Spade Cooley Band, Herman the Hermit, Claude Casey and Cowboy Copas; *Kentucky Jubilee* (1951) with Claude Casey and Fred Kirby of WBT; and 1952's *Buffalo Bill in Tomahawk Territory*,

Marshall Ray Broome, circa 1950s (author's collection).

starring Clayton Moore, aka television's The Lone Ranger.[40] Several of the films are available on YouTube[41] and feature the Broome's performances. These songs include "Moon Over Texas" and "The Old Panhandle Trail" in three-part harmonies, the trick-fiddling of "Pop Goes the Weasel," as well as the theme-song for "Square Dance Jubilee." The last was a co-write between Ray Broome and June Carr.

The Broomes recorded for Crystal Records under their own name in 1948 ("Someday You'll Pay" b/w "Holiday for Guitar") and also backed the singer Carolina Cotton for the label ("You've Got Me Wrapped Around Your Finger").[42] In 1950, they made a second Crystal paring ("So Why Should I Be Blue?" b/w "Gabriel's Valley").[43] Their final single ("The Old Trail" b/w "The Mandolin Waltz") was cut in 1953 for Flair, an imprint owned by the Bihari Brothers, who also controlled Modern, both early pioneering Rhythm and Blues labels.[44]

By the 1960s, as their schedule slowed, it appears that the Broome brothers went on to other pursuits. Ray Broome taught art classes,[45] and Joe sold Oldsmobile automobiles.[46]

Shell Allen's Kannapolis W.O.W. String Band

In an area rich with textile mills, one would expect that at least some of the local amateur musicians employed by the Crazy Water Barn Dance would also be cotton mill workers. One such musician was Shell Allen. Fiddler Shelley Kaylor Allen (May 14, 1897–November 10, 1976) was either born in his father's hometown of Birmingham, Alabama,[47] or his family's later address in the China Grove community south of Salisbury, North Carolina.[48] His father, Jerry Martin Allen, was, unusually for the time, not a mill worker but a professional photographer.[49]

By the beginning of 1918, Shell had followed his two older brothers into textile work. He found a job with the powerhouse Cannon Mills that, for all intents and purposes, ran the surrounding town of Kannapolis.[50] Shell Allen would spend the rest of his professional life employed by Cannon.

From August 26, 1918, to early March of 1919, Allen served in the United States military.[51] In the October following his service, Shell Allen married Nellie McClamrock.[52] The couple eventually had three sons.[53]

Shell had begun playing the fiddle by his teenage years, appearing at area home entertainments backed by guitarist Dolph Dayvault.[54] Adolphus Wilson Dayvault (December 9, 1893–June 28, 1976) was the

What Earl Scruggs Heard

youngest of eleven children from the union of Paul Monroe Dayvault (1848–1911) and Hettie Margaret Walter Alexander (1858–1930).[55] Born on a Rowan County farm,[56] Dolph married Ruth Esther Cashion (1894–1971) in 1913. The couple ultimately produced three offspring.[57]

By mid-1917, Dayvault was farming for his stepfather Charles Wesley Alexander.[58] Eventually, the lure of the mills became too great, and, after a spell fixing textile machinery in China Grove, Dolph ended up, along with his wife Ruth, following Shell Allen to Kannapolis and employment at Cannon Mills.[59]

By 1916, Dolph Dayvault was playing for local gatherings, sometimes with Shell Allen, and, at other times, in the company of carpenter and farmer John Franklin Hileman (March 16, 1885–July 7, 1955),[60] Wade Hampton Krimminger (October 15, 1885–March 21, 1961)[61] and a Mr. Christy, probably an in-law of Krimminger's.[62]

Shell Allen's String Band won the so-called State Fiddlers' Convention run by Fisher Hendley, held in Albemarle during the fall of 1927. This is possibly how they came to Hendley's attention and were later employed by Crazy Water Crystals.

By the spring of 1929, Shell Allen and Dolph Dayvault had become associated with the Kannapolis chapter of the Woodmen of the World (W.O.W.). Founded in 1890, this fraternal order and mutual benefit society was prevalent throughout North and South Carolina. Surprisingly, many of the local chapters sponsored string bands and the Kannapolis branch was no exception. In fact, at least two Woodmen ensembles competed for airtime on the Crazy Water Barn Dance and over WBT.

The earliest mention of the Kannapolis chapter's band, albeit without the names of specific musicians, occurred in August of 1912. At that time, the W.O.W. subsidized both a string band AND a cornet band.[63] By 1929, the Kannapolis W.O.W. String Band, partially underwritten by the Clint Coal Company of Spartanburg, South Carolina, was broadcasting Saturday evenings over WBT.[64]

Over the life of Shell Allen's Kannapolis W.O.W. String Band, as they were locally known, the group went from the original trio up to a septet. One of the earliest additions, on guitar, was, not surprisingly, Dolph's nephew Carl Dayvault.

Carl Henderson Dayvault (June 10, 1903–November 9, 1981)[65] experienced personal tragedy at a young age. His mother perished from heart disease when Carl was four and a half months old,[66] resulting in his father leaving the child with his grandparents, Paul and Hettie Dayvault, to raise.[67] Eight years later, Paul Dayvault died. A year later, Carl's

Eight. Crazy Water and Crazy Bands

Shell K. Allen's Kannapolis W.O.W. String Band as they appeared in the mid–1930s. Back row, left to right: Harue Suther/banjo-mandolin and Shell Allen/fiddle. Front row, left to right: Arthur "Kid" Goodman/resophonic guitar and Carl Dayvault/guitar (courtesy Rachel Wiles).

What Earl Scruggs Heard

grandmother married Charles W. Alexander, who also passed away, in 1919.[68] Even in the days before antibiotics, that's a lot of losses for one child to experience.

Carl married in 1926, and, like his uncle Dolph, became a cotton mill mechanic.[69] Dayvault also imitated his uncle by learning the guitar and joining Allen's string band.

At various times, Shell Allen's band also included cellist and Cannon employee Raymond L. Thornburg,[70] Arthur Goodman on guitar and banjo-mandolinist Harue Franklin Suther. Suther (November 10, 1908–July 11, 1989),[71] the youngest child of Charles Griffin Suther (December 24, 1861–April 7, 1945) and Sarah Elizabeth "Bettie" Pence (June 17, 1866–July 20, 1950),[72] was part of a family of textile mill laborers that, as did

Allen's W.O.W. String Band, circa 1934, with the addition of Raymond Thornburg on cello, in the WBT-Charlotte radio studio. The announcer is labeled as being "Fritz" Hurst, although he strongly resembles Charlie Crutchfield. Left to right: Carl Dayvault/guitar, Raymond Thornburg/cello, "Haywood" [sic] Suther/banjo-mandolin, Shell Allen/fiddle, Carl "Dolph" Dayvault/guitar and "Fritz" Hurst/announcer (courtesy Rachel Wiles).

Eight. Crazy Water and Crazy Bands

Shell Allen's band, at the W.O.W. clubhouse in Kannapolis, February 4, 1932, expanded to a septet. Left to right: Carl Dayvault/guitar, Shell Allen/ fiddle, Harue Suther/banjo-mandolin, Raymond Thornburg/string bass, unknown/banjo-mandolin, unknown/fiddle, Dolph Dayvault/guitar (courtesy Rachel Wiles).

many workers, moved from mill to mill seeking better wages and working conditions. After Harue's birth in the Iredell County town of Mooresville,[73] Charles Suther moved his family just south of Bessemer City to Crowders Mountain, then to Cooks Cross Roads outside of Kannapolis.

Charles Suther serviced mill machinery, like the Dayvaults with whom Harue performed in the Kannapolis W.O.W. ensemble. The Suthers and Dayvaults became acquainted either at Cannon Mills or through the local W.O.W. chapter, of which Harue was a member.[74]

Dewitt Wheless

The other Woodman of the World-sponsored string band appearing on the Crazy Barn Dance was led by banjoist Dewitt Wheless.

What Earl Scruggs Heard

Dewitt Talmadge Wheless (born October 2, 1889) was the eleventh of thirteen offspring from the union of Emma Tyson and Arthur Benjamin Wheless.[75] Arthur (February 23, 1832–January 1, 1906[76]) was born in Franklin County, North Carolina, moving southwest to Anson County to farm with his brother John Washington sometime before the Civil War.

In 1862, the brothers enlisted in the Anson Regulators, which fought on the Confederate side during the conflict. Arthur's musical talents were soon recognized, and he was transferred by April of 1864 to the company band and promoted to full musician by the end of that year. Although we do not know when and where Arthur Wheless learned music, nor what instrument he played with the army band, it appears that both he and his brother John were fiddling before the Civil War.

By the time the war was over, Wheless had returned to Anson County, married, and resumed playing for community functions. With his group, which included the brothers Adolphus A. "Dolph" and John Birdson Waddill (or Waddell) on guitars, Arthur Wheless played for dances in Ansonville and at the local female college. The sons of a Wadesboro tavern-keeper, the Waddills had also served during the war.

Growing up around a musical father, it is no surprise that Dewitt took up the banjo; his first was made, like Fisher Hendley's, from a cheese box. He also sang and played a bit of piano, guitar, mandolin, and fiddle. "It came natural to him," recalled Wheless's daughter Mildred.[77] After serving in World War I,[78] Dewitt married schoolteacher Osie Belle Lee of Norwood in 1921.[79] The Wheless family grew cotton, eventually switching to dairy farming in the 1950s. Dewitt also carried the mail before marrying[80] and worked for the railroad, running watering stations at Brown Creek and Wadesboro for steam locomotives until around 1937. Additionally, Wheless was a silent partner in his brother Jim's grocery store located in Ansonville.

Weekends were reserved for music, with Dewitt Wheless providing musical accompaniment for community functions. However, none paid very well, remembered later Wheless group member Jack Harrington.[81]

Possibly through his friendship with Fisher Hendley, Wheless's band, first sponsored by the local Woodmen of the World chapter and later called "Skillet Lickers" (not the group from Georgia that recorded for Columbia and RCA), journeyed out to WBT in Charlotte and WPTF-Raleigh to broadcast for Crazy Water Crystals. This musical ensemble, beside Dewitt Wheless on banjo, included Blake Hildreth and Lee Morris on guitars, Milton T. White/mandolin and fiddler David Lear.

Eight. Crazy Water and Crazy Bands

The Wheless band as pictured in the Crazy Water book from 1934. Back row, left to right: Blake Hildreth/guitar, Dewitt Wheless/banjo, Milton T. White/mandolin. Front row, left to right: Lee Morris/guitar and David Lear/fiddle (courtesy Wheless family).

What Earl Scruggs Heard

Guitarist Blake Eason Hildreth (August 22, 1913–August 11, 1986)[82] was the son of William Harrison (October 29, 1860–February 12, 1939) and his second wife, Mary Jane Caudle Hildreth (March 20, 1875–December 31, 1955).[83] Blake Hildreth spent his life farming.[84] Blake's older brother, guitarist Joseph Leroy (February 4, 1903–September 13, 1988), drove a delivery truck out of Wadesboro for Carolina Ice and Fuel.[85] Younger brother James Dunlap (November 15, 1917–November 21, 2005)[86] served in World War II.[87] Like Blake, James, who started on mandolin and later learnt to fiddle, spent his life farming.[88] Milton Thompson White (born November 13, 1911)[89] was raised on an Anson County farm and had settled in South Carolina by 1940. Before joining the military during World War II, Milton White worked for United Candy of Charlotte.[90]

For their programs over WPTF, James Hildreth replaced Milton White and Jack Harrington came in to fiddle. Edwin Jackson Harrington (April 20, 1914–March 6, 2007)[91] first heard a violin played around 1920 by his maternal grandmother Jenny McCaskill of Wadesboro, North Carolina. Jack's eighth grade teacher also played the violin, and he took four lessons from her, learning how to read music in the process. However, Harrington acquired most square dance tunes by ear, finding

Family group with Jack Harrington's grandmother Jenny McCaskill at the center with fiddle (courtesy Jack Harrington).

Eight. Crazy Water and Crazy Bands

inspiration in recordings by the likes of Clayton McMichen and Riley Puckett (including their disc of "Alabama Gals"/"Fire on the Mountain"). When his father Stonewall Jackson Harrington died in 1940, Jack took up his profession of running a crane at Bonsal Gravel.[92]

Jack Harrington met Dewitt Wheless around 1936 through the Hildreth brothers. The two men hit it off, and, as well as acquainting Wheless and Harrington, Joe Hildreth introduced Jack to his two younger brothers. Harrington would often visit the Hildreth family in Ansonville, and so it was natural that all would eventually become members of Dewitt Wheless's string band.

Jack Harrington with fiddle, in front of his old home place outside Lilesville, North Carolina, circa 1940 (courtesy Jack Harrington).

Every Saturday, the Wheless band would drive to Raleigh and play on the radio for the Crazy Barn Dance over WPTF. There was a studio audience at the show, and a number of groups, including J.E. Mainer and Wade and Zeke, played three or four tunes each. "That was a big thrill to even play at that time, radio was [so] new," remembers Jack Harrington.

World War II effectively ended the local weekend square dances where the Wheless band provided the musical accompaniment. However, during the 1950s, Dewitt responded to family need to call his group back together. One series of dances, held in 1953 in an empty storefront in Polkton, benefited his daughter's high school senior class trip. The last organized events where Dewitt Wheless performed were in 1956 and '57: benefit square dances to support a local semi-pro baseball team, of which his son Buck was a member. The dances were held outside of Ansonville at the National Youth Administration Camp, which is no longer standing.[93]

Dewitt Wheless died February 16, 1961, from cancer.[94]

Zeke Robinson/Uncle Joe Robinson/Wayside

There isn't much information that has emerged about Zeke Robinson. He appears, possibly holding a fiddle, in the Crazy Barn Dance cast photograph. The one newspaper reference that I could find describes him as the manager of the Grove String Band from Gastonia performing over radio station WSOC.[95] WSOC appears to have begun broadcasting around the beginning of 1931.[96]

The event Robinson was publicizing, featuring Zeke and the Grove band, was sponsored by the Wayside organization of Charlotte. Wayside was a local supporter of radio programming and public concerts.[97] According to *North Carolina: A Guide to the Old North State*, Wayside raised money to care for "shut-ins." Its headquarters was at the Wayside Cottage in Charlotte.

The March 25, 1932, program with the Grove String Band also included Uncle Joe Robinson, a banjoist that played an active role in Wayside's variety entertainments.[98] From 1931 through at least 1940, Uncle Joe is featured in Wayside's frequent newspaper columns, on their WBT broadcasts,[99] as well as at area appearances from Rowland to Taylorsville to Gaffney and back home in Charlotte.[100] Robinson was also a regular on the local fiddlers' convention circuit,[101] where he often performed as a "one man band," "playing a mouth harp, piano and banjo all at the same time."[102]

Eight. Crazy Water and Crazy Bands

J.E. and Wade Mainer's Mountaineers

> **SEE AND HEAR THE**
> **Crazy Water Crystals Mountaineers**
> BROADCAST THEIR REGULAR RADIO PROGRAM
> **Saturday Night, Sept. 14th**
> DIRECT FROM THE STAGE OF THE
> LUMBERTON HIGH SCHOOL AUDITORIUM
> AFTER THE SHOW ANY TIME COME HERE FOR
> **Crazy Water Crystals**
> TWO SIZES 60c AND $1.00
> **LUMBERTON DRUG CO.**

Advertisement for "Crazy Water Crystals Mountaineers," broadcasting live, Saturday, September 14, 1935, from the Lumberton (North Carolina) High School Auditorium (*Robesonian*, September 12, 1935).

Fisher Hendley's biggest discovery for Crazy Water were the Mainer brothers. Wade Eckhart Mainer was born April 21, 1907, near Weaverville, just north of Asheville in the North Carolina mountains.[103] After following his older brother J.E. (Joseph Emmett, July 20, 1898–June 12, 1971[104]) to Concord in the mid–1920s, Wade joined him working in a cotton mill and making music. By the early 1930s, the Mainers became popular at local parties and fiddlers' conventions, with J.E. on the fiddle, Wade on banjo and guitarists such as B.A. Blackwelder.[105]

Initially broadcasting over WSOC-Gastonia,[106] the Mainers caught the attention of Hendley and Crazy Water Crystals in 1934. Originally named J.E. Mainer and His Carolina Mountaineers, after adding "Daddy" John Love and Claude Edward "Zeke" Morris (May 9, 1916–August 5, 1999), J.W. Fincher dubbed them the Crazy Mountaineers. Starting in September of 1934, in addition to their appearances on the

What Earl Scruggs Heard

COMPLIMENTS OF "THE CRAZY COMPANY"
Broadcasting Daily 12:00 Noon over WWNC
(Except Saturday and Sunday)
Also

| WWNC Asheville | CRAZY BARN DANCE
WBT—Charlotte
Every Saturday Night | WWNC Asheville |

For

THE  CO.

CHARLOTTE, N. C.
See Your Local "CRAZY" Dealer

Eight. Crazy Water and Crazy Bands

Barn Dance, Crazy Water sponsored the band's noon broadcasts over WWNC-Asheville.[107]

In 1935, Mainer's Crazy Mountaineers moved their radio program back to Charlotte and WBT. Their fifteen-minute daily broadcast over WBT occurred at 12:15 p.m.[108]

Other Performers

At various times and locales, the Crazy Barn Dance also included harmonica specialist M.P. Medford of Asheville,[109] the Tobacco Tags (George Wade, Luther Baucom, and Reid Summey) of Gastonia, Rockingham's Dixon Brothers duo, the Jenkins String Band of Harris (banjoist Dewitt "Snuffy" Jenkins, October 27, 1908–April 30, 1990; fiddler Verl Jenkins; Dennis Jenkins/guitar and Howard Cole/guitar), fiddler Homer Lee "Pappy" Sherrill (March 23, 1915–November 30, 2001) and the East Hickory String Band aka Crazy Hickory Nuts,[110] Salisbury's Hilo Hawaiians, Leroy Smith's Moonlight Serenaders of Mt. Gilead High School,[111] the Rambling Trio from Granite Falls, Fred Russell's Hillbillies featuring ex–Tar Heels Fred and James Russell along with Sam Poplin and J.A. Farrington's Carolina Melody Boys of Davidson.[112]

The Beginning of the End for Crazy Water

By the closing days of 1934, things began to unravel for Fincher and Crazy Water Crystals. The company's rapid expansion in the Carolinas had flooded the marketplace with merchandise, necessitating several price reductions for the Crystals products.[113] Not surprisingly, in Charlotte, a southern city that mostly distanced itself from the stereotypical "hillbilly" label, Crazy Water's broadcasts had generated some criticism. A letter to the *Charlotte Observer* wished the Barn Dance and other programs sponsored by Fincher would be terminated:

> I think something should be done about that Crazy Water Crystals program and other so-called hill-billy programs which disgrace the air so many times

Opposite: **J.E. Mainer's Crazy Mountaineers. Back row, left to right: Fisher Hendley/announcer, Wade Mainer/banjo and J.E. Mainer/fiddle. Front row, left to right: John Love/guitar and Zeke Morris/guitar. The Gibson-brand banjo held by Fisher supposedly became the signature instrument for Earl Scruggs (author's collection).**

a day! Hill-billy songs make me positively ill, and I wish all those lukewarm, washed out, dragged in the mud hill-billies would go back to the mountains (or wherever they came from) and do their squawking somewhere besides on the radio.[114]

Crazy Water also ran into problems with local governments and labor unions. On August 20, 1935, Rowan County's Department of Health cited J.W. Fincher and the Barn Dance for violating laws designed to control the spread of polio.[115] And, at the end of August, the North Carolina Federation of Labor proposed boycotting Crazy Water events if their labor practices didn't improve.[116]

As Crazy Water began its slow decline in the Carolinas, Fisher Hendley's relationship with Crazy Water Crystals soured. In the fall of 1935, Hendley relocated to Greenville, South Carolina, where he gained a new sponsor for his radio program.

Fisher Hendley managed his exit just before Crazy Water's implosion could have ruined his musical career. Several months later, Fisher sued James Fincher and Crazy Water, alleging he was owed almost $11,000.00 in back pay for his talent scouting and hosting work on the Crazy Barn Dance.[117]

Along with other subsidized programming, the Crazy Water Barn Dance broadcasts for WBT concluded around the end of 1935.[118] Fincher continued to sponsor airtime over WSOC, but those too disappear from the newspaper listings by early May of 1937.[119]

Nine

Aristocratically Yours, Fisher Hendley

WFBC

In the fall of 1935, Fisher Hendley moved his base of operations to WFBC-Greenville, South Carolina. Fisher's new radio home, owned by the local newspaper, was just an infant, having signed on the air two years previously.[1] The station had recently moved to 1330 on the dial and upped its power from 250 to 1000 watts, which might have encouraged Fisher's relocation.[2] Hendley possibly learned about WFBC through its former program director, Charlie Crutchfield, now making his mark at WBT. Another connection between the two stations was the underwriting by Crazy Water of programming in Greenville, most notably for the brother duo of Bill and Charlie Monroe.[3]

Besides a new station, Fisher Hendley had a different sponsor as well: the Balentine Packing Company. Presided over by W. Louis Balentine, the concern was founded in 1888 as a meat market run by Louis's father, William Hampton Balentine. In 1917, William Balentine opened a meat processing operation to supply army bases in South Carolina. Balentine Packing had been a WFBC sponsor since the beginning of the station's existence.[4] Considering Balentine based their pre-existing advertising campaign around a mascot in evening dress complete with a top hat and monocle, Fisher's formally outfitted ensemble fit right in with the company's branding. Upon returning from summer engagements in New York City, on Wednesday, October 9, 1935, Hendley's band made their first 1:15 to 1:30 p.m. broadcast as the "Aristocratic Pigs."[5]

Rather than recruiting from area talent, Fisher Hendley's first hires were seasoned radio and stage professionals. These included the Dutch-born duo of "Zeb" Janssen and "Zeke" Shippers, comedian Joseph "Elmer" Lenzer (whose big piece of stage business was playing "Home

What Earl Scruggs Heard

on the Range" with escaping air from a balloon),[6] alongside North Carolinians Eddie Smith (from Shelby) of Otto Gray's Oklahoma Cowboys and Boyden Carpenter, "The Hillbilly Kid."[7]

Janssen, Shippers and Lenzer had been performing as members of the Village Barn Hill Billies in New York City, which is probably where Hendley had first seen them. Zeb, Zeke and Elmer also appeared with Lita Grey Chaplin and a very young Sammy Davis, Jr.,[8] in *Seasoned Greetings*, a 1933 Warner Bros. Vitaphone short.[9] Hildreth Boyden Carpenter (February 26, 1909–May 25, 1995)[10] was raised in Cherry Lane, North Carolina. By 1930, he was making his living from music,[11] and recording for Gennett Records. Carpenter only stayed with Hendley through the fall,[12] and, by January's end, Boyden had joined Mainer's Crazy Mountaineers for their broadcasts over WPTF-Raleigh.[13]

For 1936, in order to accommodate the demands of a growing live audience for their country music broadcasts, WFBC moved Saturday's programs by the Monroe Brothers and the Aristocratic Pigs from their radio studios to the Butler Guards armory on Laurens Street.[14] Additionally, the Pigs' broadcasts first went to six afternoons a week and then to twice an afternoon.[15] Paid public appearances were on the uptick as

By January 26, 1936, the Pigs had shifted personnel slightly. The band was photographed at the station's new radio tower. Back row, left to right: Eddie (Smith) and "Zeb" (Janssen). Front row, left to right: "Lonesome Luke" (Joseph "Elmer" Lenzer), Fisher Hendley and "Zeke" (Shippers) (*Greenville News*, January 26, 1936).

Nine. *Aristocratically Yours, Fisher Hendley*

BALENTINE'S "ARISTOCRATIC PIGS"

EXTEND THEIR BEST WISHES TO

WFBC

and

THE GREENVILLE NEWS-PIEDMONT

Since the very beginning of WFBC—back when 100 watts looked mighty big to us, we have been more or less a consistent advertiser . . . we have seen improvements made—every one of them toward a big and better WFBC and today we heartily join hands with every true and loyal Carolinian and congratulate The Greenville News and Piedmont upon the magnificent station they have given to us in a little less than three years.

Every day we present our program to WFBC's listeners. The popularity of our "Aristocratic Pigs" is born out in the tremendous amount of mail they receive weekly and the request for personal appearances in churches and schools throughout the Piedmont section. If you are not a listener to this popular program, we invite you to join our thousands of friends who enjoy it every day.

BALENTINE PACKING CO.

Advertisement for the Aristocratic Pigs, Balentine Packing and WFBC. *Greenville News*, March 1, 1936 (courtesy Hellen Hendley Permar).

What Earl Scruggs Heard

well. And WFBC had once again increased their power (this time to 5000 watts) and reach, as well as adding an affiliation with the NBC Network.[16]

This possibility of permanency motivated Fisher to advertise for an apartment. Hendley may have also planned to move his family to Greenville, who appear to have, for the moment, stayed behind in Charlotte.[17]

On September 19, 1936, following their summer break, Fisher Hendley returned to the airways with a completely new group of Aristocratic Pigs. Hendley had been advertising for musicians, especially a "bass fiddler that sings, plays other instruments [and] Guitar player that sings, plays other instruments."[18] Fisher convinced Sam Poplin, from his home area in North Carolina and the only holdover from Hendley's earlier groups, to lead the ensemble with his fiddle. The other musicians were, as described by the *Greenville News*, "new faces" in town. After holding auditions, Fisher Hendley chose "Handsome" Bill Bennett from Rock Hill, South Carolina, on violin, mandolin and guitar; as well as Emerson "Black

Just add a bit of photographic trickery and, "voila," the accordionist and the names on the pig cutouts magically change. Shown here is a different/fourth version of the "new" Pigs line up. Left to right: "Cousin" Ezra Roper/accordion, Hampton "Little Boy Blue" Bradley/vocalist, Fisher Hendley/banjo, Sam Poplin/fiddle and Dixon "Baby Ray" Stewart/bass (*Greenville News*, April 25, 1937).

Nine. Aristocratically Yours, Fisher Hendley

Sheep" Rednour and Hampton "Little Boy Blue" Bradley from Gastonia.[19]

Guitarist Emerson Orley Rednour (January 22, 1904–January 23, 1975)[20] came from a cotton mill family and Orley followed them as a teenager into a local mill.[21] Rednour's short time with Hendley's Pigs was but a brief respite from mill work, although, later in life, Orley was known as a music teacher and performer.[22] Guitarist Hampton Lorance Bradley[23] (October 8, 1910–January 1, 1996),[24] like Rednour, came out of a family of cotton mill workers and from a textile mill job to the Aristocratic Pigs.[25] Hendley's offer of employment provided many musicians an escape from the cotton mills to a life in radio and of live performing.

The personnel of the Aristocratic Pigs had not yet stabilized and December 1936 brought new band members and instrumentation.[26] Bennett and Rednour were out, replaced by George Dixon "Baby Ray" Stewart (March 16, 1916[27]–December 2, 1971[28]) of Saluda County[29] on bass and Harold Compton/accordion.[30]

After the new year, bookings continued to flood in. The *Greenville News* reported, with two radio broadcasts a day,[31] a full February and March of personal appearances. Typical invites for concerts came from schools and churches looking to raise funds for various projects.[32] By that time, Bill Bennett had left the Pigs, reducing the band to a quartet.[33] Harold Compton also only lasted two to four months. By the end of April, "Cousin" Ezra Roper had replaced him on accordion.[34]

Ezra Leroy Roper (September 29, 1914[35]–June 25, 1980[36]) was born on a farm in Anderson County, South Carolina.[37] By 1920, Roper's father

Photograph of Fisher Hendley in evening dress with his Gibson-brand banjo (*Greenville News*, June 20, 1937).

What Earl Scruggs Heard

R.Q. Glass (left), sales manager for Balentine, and Fisher Hendley, in Glass's office, with weekly mail numbering 5000 pieces per week. Published in *Greenville News*, June 30, 1937 (courtesy Hellen Hendley Permar).

"Aristocratic Pigs leaving Columbia for a show date in Conway, South Carolina. The State Capitol Building forms the backdrop." Trailer holds sound system, instruments and stage costumes. Along with the automobile, the trailer was utilized for transport to and from personal appearances. Notice the band in the vehicle and the logos painted on the trailer's sides (courtesy Hellen Hendley Permar).

Nine. Aristocratically Yours, Fisher Hendley

and three oldest siblings were all working in a cotton mill to support the family,[38] Ezra's mother having died several years previously.[39] By the time of the 1930 Federal Census, Ezra and his father had moved with his widowed oldest sister and her children into the Monaghan Mill Village in Greenville to work at that facility.

Hand colored photograph of Hellen and Graham Hendley wearing their stage costumes, circa 1938 (courtesy Hellen Hendley Permar).

What Earl Scruggs Heard

Top left: **Sam Poplin, dressed in hillbilly "character" for a stage skit (*Greenville News*, April 17, 1938).** *Top right:* **Dixon "Baby Ray" Stewart, in evening dress, with WFBC microphone (*Greenville News*, April 24, 1938).**

Five years later saw a change in Roper's fortunes. Throughout 1935 into the spring of 1936, Ezra Roper led His Serenaders at scattered dances in the Greenville area.[40] Then came his big break and full-time employment when the call came to join the Aristocratic Pigs. Ezra Roper stayed with Fisher Hendley until he entered the military at the conclusion of 1942.[41]

At the end of May 1937, Fisher Hendley closed out the season with a prestigious appearance at the "Big State Fiddler's Contest," where the Aristocratic Pigs shared the stage with performers from Atlanta radio station WSB.[42] For their efforts, Hendley and company took the "grand prize."[43] After their last broadcast on June 30, 1937, it was then time for a two-month summer vacation.[44]

When Balentine renewed their sponsorship of the Aristocratic Pigs for another season,[45] Fisher Hendley felt confident enough to advertise for a house in order to permanently move his family to Greenville.[46] Monday, September 6, 1937, at noon marked the return of regular

Nine. Aristocratically Yours, Fisher Hendley

programs by Hendley and Pigs Roper, Bradley, Poplin and Stewart to the airwaves of WFBC.[47] Additionally, Fisher had booked a full fall schedule of public appearances.[48] The membership for the Aristocratic Pigs had finally stabilized and this configuration would last for two seasons until the spring of 1939.

In December of 1937, Fisher Hendley's Aristocratic Pigs played two Christmas-themed events, one to benefit the Salvation Army and the other an annual Kiwanis-sponsored party for underprivileged children. Both were arranged by WFBC, with the Kiwanis concert broadcast during the Pigs normal afternoon time slot.[49] The Aristocratic Pigs received their own Christmas present in the form of, as reported in the *Greenville News*, "a modern, streamlined trailer [that] carries the $2,000.00 worth of instruments, costumes and make-up that go along on each show date."[50]

"Baby Ray," dressed in "character" for a stage skit (*Greenville News*, May 29, 1938).

By the start of 1938, both Hendley children had joined the act, albeit for weekend appearances. From an early age, they had been groomed as performers, awakened backstage in order to take their turn on the boards dressed in the costumes their mother had sewn. Ezra Roper of the Pigs taught Hellen to play the mandolin, and between Graham and his sister, the duo handled tap dancing, tenor saxophone, clarinet, mandolin and guitar.[51]

Along with a public address system, new stage outfits joined the contents of the Pigs' trailer[52] for personal appearances. "Balentine's standard colors are represented in the new costumes," bragged an article published in the local newspaper. "The shirts with blouse sleeves are a balanced blend of orange and royal blue. The trousers are red without any other color.... A sash of two-tone color completes the ensemble.... They have a costume for each individual act. A show, in its entirety, contains several different acts."[53]

Mr. and Mrs. Fisher Hendley with Pig cutouts, Fisher with his Gibson banjo (courtesy Hellen Hendley Permar).

Fisher Hendley and the Aristocratic Pigs were booked solid throughout the Carolinas and Georgia.[54] They had reached the height of their success. On July 2, 1938, Hendley's band made its last broadcast and appearance before taking its yearly two-month summer break.[55] The future for the upcoming season looked rosy. It seemed that permanent musical success had finally graced Fisher Hendley's family.

WIS: Singing, Playing, Dancing, Yodeling, "Red Hot" Fiddling and High-Class Comedy

In September of 1938, Hendley's Pigs added three other stations to their broadcasting network. These included WIS-Columbia, WOLS-Florence and WCRS-Greenwood. Additionally, the band moved their base of operations to Columbia, South Carolina, continuing their daily broadcasts at 12:15 p.m. from the studios of WIS.[56]

Fisher also led what was to be his last string of commercial recordings. When Vocalion came to town at the end of October, the younger

Nine. Aristocratically Yours, Fisher Hendley

"FIVE ARISTOCRATIC PIGS" Compliments BALENTINE PACKING CO., Greenville, S. C. Broadcasting Daily (Except Sunday) Over WIS, Columbia, S. C,—12:15 P. M.

The Aristocratic Pigs appear in their finest bib and tucker in this 1938 promotional shot, taken during their third year of broadcasting. In white tie, left to right: "Cousin Ezra," "Little Boy Blue," Fisher Hendley, Sam Poplin and "Baby Ray" (author's collection).

members of the Aristocratic Pigs starred on most of the selections. Showcasing the more modern side of the band, Sam Poplin and Hampton Bradley "covered" Wade Mainer's and Zeke Morris's recording of "Brown Eyes." But Hendley got his own features, lending his finger-picked banjo to the religious "Walking in the Shoes of John," "I'll Meet My Precious Mother" and the much recorded "Blind Child's Prayer." Vocalion also had Fisher cut one of his solo numbers, "Weave Room Blues," which he had picked up from Dorsey Dixon, a former member of his WBT cast. Fisher Hendley fronted the Pigs on two songs with their roots in minstrelsy, "Push Them Clouds Away," a Percy Gaunt composition from 1892 that was recorded by Harry C. Browne for Columbia Records in 1917, and "Hop Along Peter."[57] It was then back to a regular daily schedule of radio programs, driving, performances, driving, sleeping, and more of the same.[58]

What Earl Scruggs Heard

Graham and Hellen Hendley, the children of Fisher and Margaret Hendley, pose with their porcine friends and the WIS microphone, circa fall 1938 (courtesy Hellen Hendley Permar).

Since the spring of 1937, the Pigs line-up had included Sam Poplin/fiddle, Ezra Roper/accordion, Hampton Bradley/guitar and Dixon Stewart/string bass. Stewart married in November of 1939, taking for his bride Sybil Imogene "Sue" Moore (September 9, 1919[59]–September 23, 2000), an aspiring musician from near Greenville, South Carolina.[60]

Nine. Aristocratically Yours, Fisher Hendley

Top left: Fisher Hendley with WIS-Columbia, South Carolina microphone, in black tie, circa 1939 (courtesy Southern Folklife Collection, UNC–Chapel Hill). *Top right:* Ezra Roper in evening dress, with WIS-Columbia, South Carolina, microphone, circa 1939 (courtesy Ancestry Family Tree).

A scant three months later, Dixon Stewart exited the Aristocratic Pigs.[61] Dixon had gained an affiliation with Vim Herb, one of the many challengers for Crazy Water Crystals' market share. Hampton and Sue moved to Spartanburg, hired some local musicians and began broadcasting on either WSPA-Spartanburg or WFBC-Greenville. The Stewarts and their band mates all bedded down within the same dwelling. Dixon Stewart's affiliates included Colin Ivydale, Buddy Chapman and a nineteen year old who later became famous as Arthur "Guitar Boogie" Smith.[62] Stewart called this band "His Country Cousins."

By the fall of 1940, Dixon and Sybil's base of operations had shifted to nearby Greenville,[63] and, again, to WBT-Charlotte in February of 1943.[64] His music making was cut short by War World II. Dixon Stewart entered the army at the beginning of October 1943 for the duration of the conflict.[65]

After the war, Stewart returned to Greenville. For at least a part of the 1950s, Dixon worked as an announcer for his former employer, radio station WFBC.[66] Eventually settling in Taylors outside Greenville proper, Dixon Stewart was active in community life, helping to organize the local

What Earl Scruggs Heard

The Rockin' Chair Rythm Blues
A Fast Stepping Swing Tune
BY EZRA L. ROPER

PUBLISHED BY HENDLEY MUSIC CO.
RADIO STATION W IS
COLUMBIA, SOUTH CAROLINA

Sheet music cover for "The Rockin' Chair Rythm [*sic*] Blues," with Ezra Roper dressed as above, circa 1939 (courtesy Ancestry Family Tree).

fire department and water district.[67] Stewart continued his music making at the Rhythm Ranch, a barn he built to host country music jam sessions and dancing, until his premature death at the age of fifty-five.[68]

Upon the departure of Dixon Stewart, Fisher Hendley hired two new musicians. Along with Poplin on fiddle, Bradley on guitar and

Nine. Aristocratically Yours, Fisher Hendley

Roper/accordion, Hendley added another accordionist, Henry Gaston, and James J. "Jimmie" Colvard (born circa 1921) from Abbeville on bass to replace the exiting Stewart.[69]

Henry Lewis Gaston (December 27, 1916[70]–March 3, 2010) grew up the youngest of nine children on a farm outside of Belmont, North Carolina.[71] From an early age, Gaston sang to make his chores go faster. In high school, Henry joined the glee club and performed at the weddings of family, friends and classmates.[72] Graduating from public school in the mid–1930s, Henry Gaston attended Berea College in Kentucky, choosing the institution because students were allowed to trade their labors for tuition. While at Berea, he took formal voice lessons and learned folk songs like "Barbra Allen," which

Dixon Stewart with what looks to be a Martin-brand guitar, sponsored by Vim Herb (*Greenville SC News*, February 14, 1943).

Gaston claims he performed at the 1937 National Folk Festival in Chicago. His vocal coach at Berea, Gladys Jamison, sent Henry to Frantz J.E. Proschowski, a famous instructor based in New York City. Gaston spent summer vacations during his college years studying voice with the eminent "professor." It was then on to membership in the Aristocratic Pigs.[73]

By the spring of 1940, Sam Poplin had also quit the Pigs. Like Dixon Stewart, Poplin was offered his own radio sponsorship by Adluh Flour of the Allen Brothers Milling Company. Adluh (pronounced "Add-loo"), was named for the daughter of the mill's original owner ("Hulda" spelled backwards is "Adluh").[74] Sam Poplin's group, the Musical Millers, began broadcasting on WIS six mornings a week and booking area appearances.[75] The Adluh Millers lasted at least until the beginning of 1942.[76] Eventually, Sam Poplin joined up with the WBT Briarhoppers, continuing to make his living from music.[77]

Sam Poplin's replacement on fiddle was Robert Lee "Bob" Smith

What Earl Scruggs Heard

The Aristocratic Pigs, circa 1940. Left to right: Henry Gaston/accordion, Graham Hendley/guitar, "Jimmie" Colvard/string bass, Fisher Hendley/Epiphone "Dragon" banjo, Hampton "Little Boy Blue" Bradley/guitar, Maggie Hendley/rolling pin, "Bob" Smith/fiddle, Hellen Hendley/mandolin and "Cousin" Ezra Roper/accordion (courtesy Southern Folklife Collection, UNC–Chapel Hill).

(January 15, 1918[78]–December 21, 2012[79]). Smith was born on a farm in Campobello, South Carolina, outside of Spartanburg.[80] Bob had received violin instruction in school and featured classical compositions in his performances.[81] After the end of his career in music, Bob Smith went to work for the local Sears store in Columbia.[82]

Fisher Hendley, with Bradley, Gaston, Colvard, Roper and Smith as Aristocratic Pigs, finished out the season of broadcasts and performance. After a summer break in July and August, the newly configured band would once again resume this cycle in the fall.[83]

The year of 1940 marked the sixth year for Hendley's Balentine sponsorship as the Pigs returned to the airwaves of WIS and WFBC.[84] Colvard was gone from the band by the time fall came along. He was replaced on string bass, guitar and comedy by "Hillbilly John" Ingold.

Nine. Aristocratically Yours, Fisher Hendley

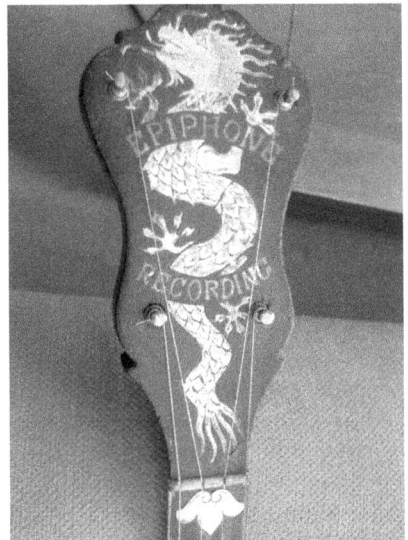
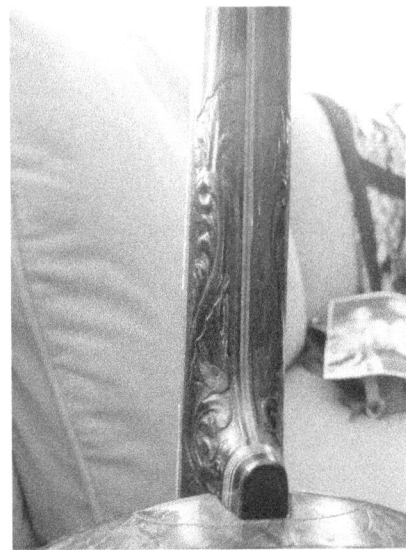

Top left: Circa 1940, Fisher Hendley traded in his Gibson Mastertone for a used top-of-the-line instrument from Gibson's competitor Epiphone. This Deluxe Art Model was more commonly known, because of its headstock inlay, as the "Dragon" banjo. Made between 1925 and 1927, the Dragon was a part of Epiphone's Recording line and produced in extremely small quantities, especially in this five-string configuration. This is the headstock of Dragon banjo as it appeared several years ago (photograph by/courtesy Gail Gillespie). *Top right:* Neck carving on the Dragon banjo (photograph by/courtesy Gail Gillespie).

John Martin Ingold (November 14, 1919[85]–June 18, 1987[86]) grew up on a farm in Fisher Hendley's hometown of Ansonville, North Carolina.[87] Ingold left a job in one of the local cotton mills to join Hendley's group. During his first season with the Aristocratic Pigs, Ingold married his hometown sweetheart, musician Helen "Miss Honey" Burgess (May 27, 1925–December 16, 2014),[88] who promptly joined Hillbilly John in the act.[89] The couple stayed with Hendley through World War II, although it appears that John sometimes had to take outside work in textiles or photography to supplement his income from music.[90]

Another musician that worked in the spring of 1941 with Hendley's Pigs, possibly on a fill-in basis, was James Eidson.[91] James William Eidson (February 27, 1922[92]–June 29, 1995[93]) grew up in a cotton mill family in Greenwood, South Carolina.[94] Eidson lost his father at age eleven.[95] By 1940, James Eidson was playing music on the radio,

What Earl Scruggs Heard

Dragon banjo held by descendant of later owner China Poplin (photograph by/courtesy Gail Gillespie).

probably over WFBC-Greenville,[96] and, therefore, came in contact with musicians such as Dixon Stewart, who had worked for Hendley. After his brief tenure with the Aristocratic Pigs, Eidson performed for Vim Herb maker Herb Products in South Carolina and, by the end of 1942, over WJHP-Jacksonville, Florida.[97]

Fisher Hendley capped the 1940–1941 broadcast season by returning to his roots and promoting a fiddlers' convention at Textile Hall in Greenville. On May 31, the Pigs were joined by a number of performers who journeyed from WBT-Charlotte for the show.[98] Hendley held a repeat performance of the spring 1941 fiddlers' event in April of 1942, at that time bringing "Judge" George Hay over from the Grand Ole Opry to be the master of ceremonies.[99]

War Years

World War II made it difficult to keep a band together, as young musicians kept getting drafted or joined up to fight in the military. The war also brought rationing and shortages that limited travel for both

Nine. Aristocratically Yours, Fisher Hendley

Pictured above are Fisher Hendley and his "Aristocratic Pigs," popular radio entertainers who return to the airwaves tomorrow, Monday, at 12:15 p. m. over WFBC. The group has been off the air for most of the summer, enjoying a well-earned vacation. Sponsored by the Balentine Packing company of Greenville, their radio programs will again originate in the studios of WIS, Columbia, and will be carried by special wire facilities to Greenville for broadcast over WFBC. Hendley and his troupe have been broadcasting for the past five years under the sponsorship of the Balentine Packing company.

The circa 1941 Aristocratic Pigs. Back row, left to right: Hampton Bradley/guitar, Henry Gaston/string bass, "Hill-Billy" John Ingold/guitar, Bob Smith/fiddle and Ezra Roper/accordion. Front row, left to right: Graham Hendley/guitar, Fisher Hendley, Maggie Hendley and Hellen Hendley/guitar (courtesy Southern Folklife Collection, UNC–Chapel Hill).

musicians and their audiences. By the time Balentine discontinued their sponsorship mid-way through World War II, a number of additional musicians had worked with Hendley.

The first to go in the army was fiddler Bob Smith, who left in October of 1941.[100] Smith was replaced by "Curley" Patterson.[101] Next to be claimed by Uncle Sam was Ezra Roper and his accordion. Roper entered the military on Thanksgiving of 1942.[102]

It's unclear how long Henry Gaston's tenure lasted with the Aristocratic Pigs. Although Gaston stayed in Spartanburg at least through 1945, the last apparent references to Gaston appearing with the band date to the end of 1940.[103] All newspaper listings show Henry Gaston limiting his performing to singing at weddings[104] and in church choirs.[105] By mid–1947, Gaston had returned to Belmont, North Carolina, the area of his upbringing, where Henry continued to perform songs from

What Earl Scruggs Heard

TOMMY NOLAN
PRESENTS
FISHER HENDLEY
ON THE HILL BILLY JAMBOREE
THE CROSS ROADS STORE
TEXTILE HALL Friday Night March 24

FISHER HENDLEY Champion banjo picker of the South will appear in person together with Hillbilly JOHN, at the CROSS ROADS STORE ... Hillbilly Jamboree, Friday. March 24th. 8:00 P. M., TEXTILE HALL, GREENVILLE. Fisher Hendley is well known in these parts for his playing, singing and as master of ceremonies. He promises to bring you the "Weave Room Blues." Mr. Hendley will be supported by a large number of famous radio Hillbillies on this ALL TIME ... ALL STAR ... FUN FEST. DON'T MISS IT!

FISHER HENDLEY
TICKETS
On Sale at Bruce & Doster Drug Store.
(Save 1-3) **50ᶜ**

Advertisement from March 24, 1944, for a performance at the Cross Roads Store Textile Hall, featuring Fisher Hendley and Hillbilly John (*Greenville News*, March 22, 1944).

a light classical repertoire such as "Because" and "I Love Thee."[106] Henry and his wife became public school teachers,[107] and also acted and sang in the summer outdoor drama *Horn in the West*.[108] After he retired from instructing, Henry Gaston became somewhat of a regional celebrity through his prizes from the National Hollerin' Contest,[109] as well as his weekly homespun columns for the *Charlotte Observer*, which ran from 1989 to 2002.[110]

By the fall of 1942, Balentine Packing had severed their relationship with Fisher Hendley. Wanting to associate with all the previous goodwill generated by the Aristocratic Pigs name, Fisher had to come up with a new moniker that evoked their old title. Thenceforth, the Aristocratic Pigs became the Rhythm Aristocrats.[111]

At the end of the 1942–1943 season, the Hendley children left the act. They both entered–the University of South Carolina, Hellen to study music and Graham, medicine. Although Fisher's offspring

Nine. Aristocratically Yours, Fisher Hendley

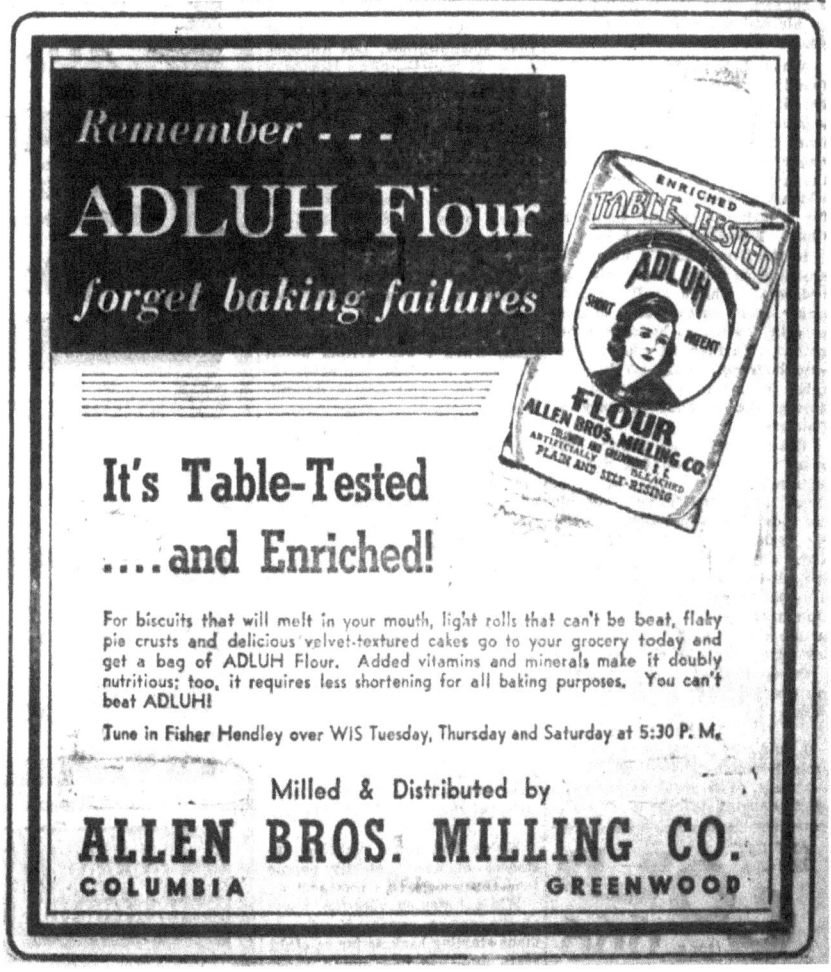

This advertisement for Adluh Flower mentions Fisher Hendley (*Index-Journal*, November 25, 1943).

would make the occasional appearance with their father, from this point onward, Graham and Hellen Hendley would pursue careers apart from their parents.

The loss of Balentine as a sponsor temporarily had a negative effect on Fisher Hendley's broadcasts and performances. After several months attempting to make new arrangements, in June of 1943, Hendley procured stopgap underwriting from Vick Chemical, as well as Lydia E. Pinkham's compound, a patent medicine originating in the 19th century

What Earl Scruggs Heard

A World War II–era promotional shot for the Rhythm Aristocrats. Left to right: "Clinton"/fiddle, Hosea (Chandler)/mandolin, Miss Ollie (Helen Ingold)/guitar, announcer Peterson (Curley Patterson), S.W. (Swamp Water) John/fiddle, Fisher Hendley and H(ill) B(illy) John Ingold/guitar, at the WIS microphone (courtesy Southern Folklife Collection, UNC–Chapel Hill).

that promoted women's reproductive health.[112] Both would sponsor some of the Rhythm Aristocrats broadcasts into early 1944.[113] However, Hendley's main sponsor for the rest of his radio career became Adluh Flour. The Aristocrats joined the Adluh gang at the end of November 1943.[114]

Post-War Years

Hendley persevered on, emerging from World War II with "His Rhythm Aristocrats," and the sponsorship of Allen Brothers Milling. Listeners to WIS heard the Aristocrats six days a week at 12:45 p.m. Fisher Hendley filled his bands with whatever musicians were available. The Rhythm Aristocrats featured at one time or another: Hosea

Nine. Aristocratically Yours, Fisher Hendley

Advertisement for appearance by Fisher Hendley's Rhythm Aristocrats at Mellichamp High School (*Orangeburg Times and Democrat*, November 28, 1945).

Chandler on mandolin and guitar; "Hill-Billy" John Ingold/guitar; Arthur "Sandy" Watts on guitar or bass; "Greasy" Medlin/bass, guitar and black face entertainment; Bob Smith on fiddle or string bass; Cecil Bowers on fiddle; Tommy Faile/guitar; George Berry/guitar and mandolin; Dewey Price; "Red" Bennett playing violin, mandolin and guitar; and Al Wall/bass.[115]

Hosea Clarence Chandler (December 3, 1918–April 5, 2005) was born in Williamston, South Carolina.[116] Hosea was the middle child in a large family of cotton mill workers.[117] After playing with Hendley, Chandler moved to Georgia, where he worked on aircraft for the military and

What Earl Scruggs Heard

finally, at DuPont's nuclear reactor in Savannah.[118] The Arthur Watts who played with Fisher Hendley may have served in the army during World War II, where he spent a year and a half in a Nazi prison camp.[119] Watts later repaired pianos.[120] Julian Leonard "Greasy" Medlin (September 18, 1910–July 5, 1982[121]), from Dentsville, Richland County, South Carolina, began learning music on guitar at age of eight, playing for local dances until he was thirteen years of age.[122] By the spring of 1930, Medlin had joined his brother working in the Winnsboro cotton mill, where, when not pursuing a career in music, Julian labored for the next ten years.[123] In April of 1931, Greasy left home to join Dr. H.E. Foxworth's Medicine Show. Ten years later, as a member of Byron Parker's WIS Hillbillies, Medlin met Snuffy Jenkins. Greasy Medlin then went from the Hillbillies to Hendley's Aristocrats in 1944, exiting Fisher's group by the end of 1945.[124] Thomas Edward Faile (September 15, 1928–August 2, 1998)[125] was born in Lancaster, South Carolina, another child in a family of mill workers.[126] It appears Tommy's first professional work in music was with Fisher Hendley immediately following World War II. Of course, he then went on to a distinguished career with Snuffy Jenkins,

Fisher Hendley with his Bacon banjo is front and center with the Rhythm Aristocrats, circa 1946. Left to right: George Berry/guitar, Gene Goodwin/steel guitar, Cecil Bowers/fiddle, Hendley/announcer, Tommy Faile/guitar, and Alvin Wall/bass (courtesy Hellen Hendley Permar).

Nine. Aristocratically Yours, Fisher Hendley

Pappy Sherrill and the Hired Hands, as well as Arthur "Guitar Boogie" Smith. Beginning in 1951, Faile became a fixture in Smith's Crackerjacks, as well as on his own programs over WBT-Charlotte, achieving enduring local fame.[127] Dewey Price worked with Hendley in the fall of 1945 before joining the Tennessee Ramblers.[128] By the summer of 1946, Price was a Briarhopper and stayed with WBT radio into 1950.[129]

In the fall of 1946, if you went to see Fisher Hendley at your local high school in upstate South Carolina, you would hear the version of the Rhythm Aristocrats including "Orangeburg's Own" Gene Goodwin on steel guitar, guitarist Tommy Faile, Cecil Bowers providing the fiddling, George Berry playing guitar and mandolin, Al Wall on the string bass, as well as (occasionally) the two Hendley siblings Graham and Hellen.[130]

Gene Randolph Goodwin (March 20, 1928–July 22, 2011) grew up in Orangeburg.[131] While still in high school, Goodwin began leading a band, "his Carolina Serenaders featuring Cliff Parker and his electric guitar," in local dance halls and theaters.[132]

The ninth of eleven children born to William Harvey Wall, Alvin Jerome "Slim" Wall (March 19, 1926–August 31, 2012) was born in Marion, North Carolina. Al was influenced by his father's and eldest brother's song leading in church, learning to play on a neighbor's guitar because he couldn't afford one of his own. Many well-known musicians who helped define early bluegrass music were from or based around Marion when Al was growing up. These included Luke Balcom of the Tobacco Tags, fiddler Art Wooten and guitarist/singer Clyde Moody, who were both members of Bill Monroe's early Bluegrass Boys, along with Jay Hugh Hall, J.E. and Wade Mainer, and the Morris Brothers.

Al graduated from high school in the spring of 1943 and immediately went to seek out Fisher Hendley, to whom Wall had been listening over WIS. Over that weekend, Fisher gave the young aspiring musician advice about running a band, had him appear with Hendley's group on their Monday radio program and promised to hire Al Wall after his military service. When Wall made it home from visiting Fisher, he took the $50.00 graduation present he had received from one of his brothers and bought a string bass. The aggregation of local players Wall then assembled had known each other throughout Al's high school years. Ken Sowers, on electric guitar, had dropped out of school in order to support his family. Mandolinist Charles Lindsey was initially too old for the draft, but when his number came up, was replaced by guitarist Rast Harvey, who was around ten years older than Wall. Faye Mainer, a niece of J.E. and Wade, came in on piano, with her brother B.J.

Advertisement for Gene Goodwin's band broadcasting over WRNO (*Times and Democrat*, March 21, 1947).

Nine. Aristocratically Yours, Fisher Hendley

The Blue Ridge Hillbillies, 1946. Back row, left to right: Carl Sauceman/guitar, Willie Carver/steel guitar and Al Wall/string bass. Front row, left to right: Benny Sims/fiddle and J.P. Sauceman/mandolin (courtesy Alvin Wall).

occasionally sitting in on clarinet. The final member was Clifford Johnson, a young multiple-instrumentalist from Old Fort who had faced Wall's band in local talent contests.

In order to support his family and his music making, Al Wall took a job with Drexel Furniture. Drexel gave him most of his weekends off for radio appearances and live performances. The band alternated Saturday evenings at the WHKY barn dance in Hickory as a hillbilly band called the Carolina Cut-Ups and as a swing group titled Sugar Hill at the local country club, but it was a tough time to run a band, as rationed gasoline severely limited travel.

By early 1944, Al's time had to come to enter the service. He joined the navy and his band broke up. While in the military, Wall kept busy on board the USS *Achernar* playing with a make-shift band.

When Al Wall was discharged in the summer of 1946, he joined the Blue Ridge Hillbillies, then performing over WWNC in Asheville, North Carolina. Led by the Sauceman brothers Carl/guitar and J.P./mandolin, in addition to Wall on string bass, the Hillbillies also included Benny Sims on fiddle (later with Flatt and Scruggs) and Willie Carver/steel guitar. Al played their *Midday Farm Hour* show five days a week to a live audience. He also appeared on average about four nights a week with the Saucemans for show dates.

By the fall of 1946, Wall had left the Saucemans to fulfill his promise made during the war to Fisher Hendley. Fisher, suffering from recurring back problems, often missed the live shows. Therefore, fiddler Cecil Bowers would MC and Al would handle the business of collecting admission fees.[133]

Goodbye, Aristocrats; Hello, Radio Pals

By 1947, the Rhythm Aristocrats had moved over to WRNO-Orangeburg, South Carolina. Hendley's current band included Gene Goodwin, Al Wall and Tommy Faile, along with Johnnie Bishop, "Featured Comedian 'King of the Ivories' Singer and Dancer"; Larry Ruff, "Red Hot Guitar Popular Singer and Comedian"; as well as fiddler Cecil Bowers.[134] Cecil Augustine Bowers was born September 1, 1926[135] on a farm in Dekalb, Kershaw County, South Carolina.[136] Before working for Hendley, Bowers fought with the Marines from July 6, 1944, to June 21, 1946.[137]

Unfortunately, Hendley either couldn't or wouldn't maintain a band, and, in January of 1947, the Aristocrats were disbanded.

Nine. Aristocratically Yours, Fisher Hendley

Fisher Hendley's band in the radio studio, circa 1946. Left to right: Cecil Bowers/fiddle, Tommy Faile/guitar, Hendley/announcer, George Berry/mandolin and Alvin Wall/string bass. They are wearing their stage clothes because, after the radio program, the group were headed to a photography studio for publicity photographs (courtesy Alvin Wall).

Without the Rhythm Aristocrats, a group of his former band members formed their own ensemble. Called the Radio Pals, it included returning military veterans Ezra Roper and Bob Smith, along with Hampton "Little Boy Blue" Bradley and "Hillbilly" John Ingold. Technically, under government regulations, musicians hired to replace those serving during World War II would have to yield those positions to the returning vets that once held them. Therefore, Roper and Smith may have assumed that they were owed their jobs by Fisher Hendley. However, with the breakup of the Aristocrats, those spots disappeared.

The earliest articles mentioning the Radio Pals date to March of 1947.[138] The band seems to have continued through 1949, with some vestiges of the ensemble working under John Ingold into at least 1950.[139]

After the Pals disbanded, Ezra Roper briefly was engaged as an

What Earl Scruggs Heard

Circa 1947–1950 photograph of the Radio Pals in the broadcast studio. Left to right: Bob Smith, Ezra Roper, Helen Ingold, Hampton Bradley and John Ingold (*Orangeburg* [South Carolina] *Times and Democrat*, December 13, 1987).

announcer on WIS, worked as a printer, and retired to Florida.[140] John Ingold became a radio engineer.[141]

Gene Goodwin continued his local performances. Goodwin's ensemble, first titled after his high school group, the Carolina Serenaders, quickly was renamed the Dixie Hillbillys.[142] Broadcasting over WRNO, with a mid-day slot on Saturdays, Gene Goodwin's original band included Floyd McDaniel singing lead and playing guitar, Franklin LaFrance/guitar and tenor vocals, along with MC and "Old Time" fiddler Elmer Martin.[143] By the beginning of 1948, Gene Goodwin had enough of performing and advertised "Hillbilly equipment" trailer, bass, guitars and "musical supplies" for sale.[144] Goodwin still played the occasional gig,[145] but, seems, by all reports, to have exited the music business.[146]

After his stint in the Marines, Cecil Bowers continued playing local gigs. In May of 1948, Bowers fiddled with Slim Mims and the Dream Ranch Boys, which included Julian "Greasy" Medlin,[147] a group that was still performing several years later.[148] Cecil Bowers became an owner of radio stations in Camden and Bishopville, South Carolina. Bowers served three terms (from 1975 to 1982) as Kershaw County coroner before his appointment to the state public service commission.[149]

Nine. Aristocratically Yours, Fisher Hendley

Advertisement for an appearance by Slim Mims with fiddler Cecil Bowers, May 11, 1948, at the Carolina Theater (*Florence Morning News*, May 9, 1948).

Radio with Madame

As Fisher Hendley approached the age of 60, the prospect of traveling to performances became less and less appealing. Country music was also changing, leaving behind the music of Fisher's youth for

What Earl Scruggs Heard

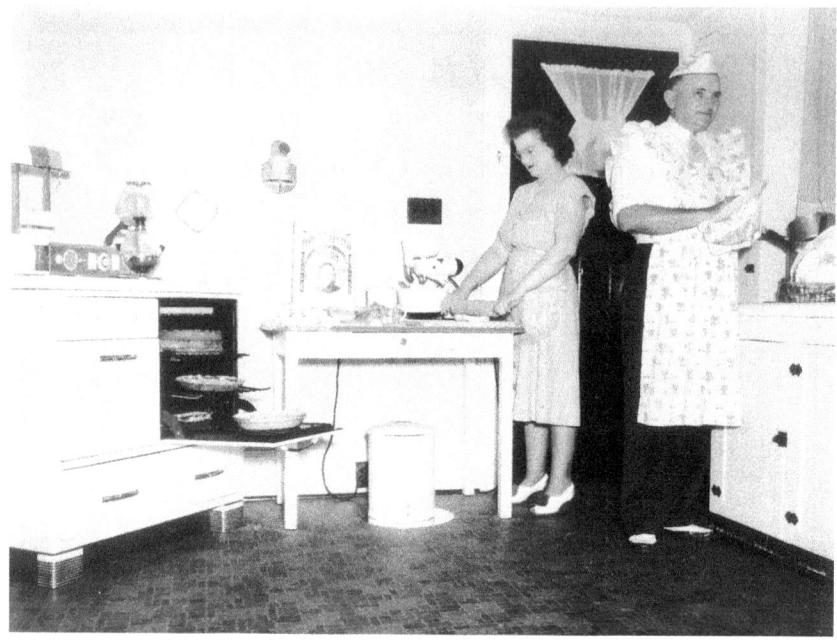

Publicity shot for "Fisher Hendley and The Madam" radio program, circa 1948. Kitchen scene includes the sponsor's Adluh Flour bag on table, and Fisher in an apron (courtesy Hellen Hendley Permar).

either the more up-tempo sound of bluegrass or slick, modern crooning country music. Luckily, the opportunity emerged for the raconteur to stay home and host an early morning talk show with Mrs. Hendley. They kept their sponsorship from Allen Brothers Adluh Flour and over WKIX-Columbia, "Fisher Hendley and the Madam," as the show was titled, filled fifteen minutes, six days a week, with chat and humor. The Hendleys were syndicated to WTND-Orangeburg, WLBG-Laurens and WCRS-Greenwood.[150] The program ran from September 1948 until the end of January 1949.[151] By that time, Graham Hendley, having just finished his undergraduate degree in the spring, was living with his parents while performing with the Woody Woodword Orchestra.[152]

Florida

Finally, Fisher Hendley was ready for a rest. In the spring of 1949, he sold his spacious West Columbia home and retired to Florida. Hendley

Nine. Aristocratically Yours, Fisher Hendley

built a motel, the Gulf Palms, in Venice[153] and then moved to Apopka in 1954[154] to live closer to his daughter and grandchildren. Fisher Hendley lived another ten years, passing away on February 27, 1963,[155] while his wife Maggie died April 15, 1977.[156]

Graham Hendley attended medical school at Virginia Commonwealth University, graduating with a pharmaceutical degree in 1954.[157] He spent the three years following his graduation in the army medical corps.[158] Graham Fisher Hendley died July 5, 1995.[159]

After graduating in 1950 from the University of South Carolina, Hellen Hendley moved to Apopka, Florida, just north of Orlando, to teach high school chorus.[160] Margaret Hellen Hendley Rogers Permar passed away August 12, 2017, in Apopka.[161]

Conclusion
Post-History "A.E." (After Earl)

At the end of World War II, Earl Scruggs was ready to try his hand at earning a living from music. During September of 1945, Scruggs left his job at Lily Mills in Shelby, North Carolina, to join the band of Lost John Miller. He stayed with Miller's Allied Kentuckians in Knoxville, Tennessee, until Miller disbanded the group after thanksgiving.

At the beginning of November 1945, while Earl Scruggs was still a member of Lost John's ensemble, Bill Monroe found himself without a banjoist. When Bill queried his fiddler Jim Shumate for replacements, Shumate recommended Earl. Jim then attempted to recruit Earl Scruggs for Monroe's Bluegrass Boys. However, Scruggs was not yet ready to leave Lost John.

However, once his gig with Miller ended, Earl was on his way to Nashville, where he was quickly asked to join up with Monroe's ensemble.[1] Fortunately for Earl Scruggs (and, consequently, for Bill Monroe and every banjo player since that time), his updating of the pre-war up-picking technique fit into and helped to define the new string band music being created by Monroe and his group.

The country version of classic banjo heard by Earl Scruggs in the 1920s and 1930s was highly syncopated. It utilized a different rhythm and flow then the three-finger style eventually developed by Scruggs. Earl fit the banjo into the modernized tempos and arrangements being developed by professional string bands, ultimately, by smoothing out and standardizing the "picking" hand. He limited and regularized the right-hand patterns to a basic roll, incorporating the melody into that roll rather than allowing his left hand to dictate the movement of his right. During his time with the Bluegrass Boys, Earl further refined and honed this technique.

Earl Scruggs' two-year tenure with Bill Monroe lasted until early in 1948, when Earl returned home to North Carolina. However, his

Conclusion

retirement from music was brief, as another former Bluegrass Boy, Lester Flatt, contacted Scruggs with the goal of co-leading their own band. Flatt & Scruggs begun working together in early March. Their twenty-year partnership furthered the spread of Scruggs-style banjo playing.[2]

First with Monroe and later with Flatt, Earl Scruggs captured lightning in a banjo. His broadcasts and recordings galvanized musicians. Scruggs' roll was a method whose basics could be replicated and repeated. Even though, in the rush to learn Earl's style of playing, very few musicians played with Earl Scruggs' subtleties, enough identifiable "Scruggisms" were retained to make their picking discernable as originating with Earl. String band music was replaced by bluegrass, with "Scruggs Picking" at its center. Even though Bill Monroe led the band that defined this new musical genre, Earl's banjo playing was the one feature that easily distinguished bluegrass from what had come before it. Consequently, there's country string music before Earl and then there's completely different country string music after Earl.

The rise of Earl Scruggs and what was to become known as bluegrass signaled the eventual marginalization for the older forms of southern string band music. Bluegrass with Scruggs Picking banjo replaced country string music in the public's consciousness. Nobody thought anymore about Smith Hammett, Charlie Parker, Mack Woolbright, Rex Brooks or Fisher Hendley. Scruggs crowded them all out of the picture. The "Scruggs Style" was to revolutionize the southern string band and, from that point onward, change country music forever.

Discography

All discographic information based on Russell, Tony. *Country Music Records: A Discography, 1921–1942.* New York: Oxford University Press, 2004; Meade, Guthrie T., Jr., et al. *Country Music Sources.* Chapel Hill: University of North Carolina Press, 2002; *Gaffney Ledger*; *Charlotte Observer*; and www.45worlds.com.

All reissues are compact discs.

Broome Brothers

Crystal Records, Los Angeles, CA, Ray: fiddle, Lee Roy: guitar and Joe Broome: string bass/mandolin
"Someday You'll Pay (Lee Broome)," Crystal 158, 1948
"Holiday for Guitar" (Schelb/Bryant), with Buddy Bryant/guitar, Crystal 158, 1948
"You've Got Me Wrapped Around Your Finger" (Cooley/Porter), backing Carolina Cotton, Crystal 157, 1948
Crystal Records, Los Angeles, CA, Ray: fiddle, Lee Roy: guitar and Joe Broome: string bass/mandolin. With Johnny Howard.
"So Why Should I Be Blue?" Crystal 273, 1950
"Gabriel's Valley," Crystal 273, 1950
Flair Records, Los Angeles, CA, Ray: fiddle, Lee Roy: guitar and Joe Broome: string bass/mandolin
"The Old Trail (Koury/Spencer)," Flair 1002, 1953
"The Mandolin Waltz (Deb Dyer)," Flair 1002, 1953

Hendley, Fisher

Okeh Records, Asheville, NC, August 27 or 28, 1925, Hendley: vocal/banjo
"Let Your Shack Burn Down," Okeh 45012, October 1925. Reissued, *Fisher Hendley* (BACM Records, 202)
"Ni**er, Will You Work?" Okeh 45012, October 1925
Victor Records, Memphis, TN, November 28–29, 1930, Hendley: vocal/banjo; Marshall Small: banjo; Henry Whitter: guitar
"Shuffle, Feet, Shuffle," Victor 23528, spring 1931. Reissued, *The North Carolina Banjo Collection* (Rounder Records 0439/0440; 1998).
"Tar and Feathers," Victor 23528, spring 1931. Reissued, *Fisher Hendley* (BACM Records, 202)

Discography

"Another Man's Wife," Bluebird B-6555, November 1936. Reissued, *Fisher Hendley* (BACM Records, 202)
"A Pretty Gal's Love," Bluebird B-6555, November 1936. Reissued, *Fisher Hendley* (BACM Records, 202)
"My Yellow Gal," unissued
"The Possum Hunt," unissued
"Pretty Little Girl," unissued
"Whitter's Rabbit Hunt," unissued
ARC/Vocalion Records, New York, NY, August 11, 1933, Carolina Tar Heels: Hendley: vocal/banjo; possibly Earl Hatley, Sam Poplin: fiddles; Claude Eudy: mandolin; Spencer Hatley or James Russell: guitar
"Answer to the Big Rock Candy Mountain," Vocalion 02543, October 1934. Reissued, *Fisher Hendley* (BACM Records, 202)
"Work in 1930," Vocalion 02543, October 1934. Reissued, *Fisher Hendley* (BACM Records, 202)
"Cindy/Soldier's Joy/Mississippi Sawyer," Vocalion 02612, April 1934
"Going Downtown," Vocalion 02612, April 1934
"Greasy Possum," Vocalion 02530, December 1933
"Peek-A-Boo," Vocalion 02530, December 1933. Reissued, *Fisher Hendley* (BACM Records, 202)
"Under the Double Eagle," Vocalion 02679, July 1934. Reissued, *Fisher Hendley* (BACM Records, 202)
"Hook and Line," Vocalion 02679, July 1934. Reissued, *The Vocalion Label* (BACM Records, 140)
"Rooster's Comb," unissued
"Katie Cline," unissued
ARC/Vocalion Records, Columbia, SC, Oct. 31–Nov. 2 and Nov. 11–12, 1938, Aristocratic Pigs: Hendley: vocal/banjo; Sam Poplin: vocal/fiddle; Ezra Roper: accordion; Hampton Bradley: vocal/guitar and Dixon Stewart: vocal/string bass. Possibly Hellen Hendley: mandolin; Graham Hendley: guitar
"Walking in the Shoes of John," Vocalion 05216, January 1940
"I'll Meet My Precious Mother," Vocalion 05095, October 1939
"Blind Child's Prayer," Vocalion 04658, April 1939. Reissued, *Fisher Hendley* (BACM Records, 202)
"Brown Eyes," Vocalion 04556, February 1939. Reissued, *Fisher Hendley* (BACM Records, 202)
"Weave Room Blues," Vocalion 04780, June 1939. Reissued, *Hard Times in the Country* (County Records, CO 3527-CD)
"Push Them Clouds Away (Percy Gaunt)," Vocalion 05216, January 1940
"Hop Along Peter," Vocalion 04780, June 1939. Reissued, *Fisher Hendley* (BACM Records, 202)
"Raindrop Waltz," Vocalion 04937, August 1939. Reissued, *Fisher Hendley* (BACM Records, 202)
"It Makes No Difference Now," Vocalion 04516, February 1939 (https://www.youtube.com/watch?v=JLaQHb3YWMw)

Discography

"If It Wasn't for Mother and Dad," Vocalion 04881, July 1939. Reissued, *Fisher Hendley* (BACM Records, 202)
"Come Back to the Hills," Vocalion 04718, May 1939. Reissued, *Fisher Hendley* (BACM Records, 202)
"Blue Eyes," Vocalion 04718, May 1939. Reissued, *Fisher Hendley* (BACM Records, 202)
"She'll Be There," Vocalion 04658, April 1939. Reissued, *Fisher Hendley* (BACM Records, 202)
"To Leave You Would Break My Heart," Vocalion 04556, February 1939. Reissued, *Fisher Hendley* (BACM Records, 202)
"I'm Going Back to the Mountains," Vocalion 05095, October 1939
"You Make My Heart Go Boom," Vocalion 05016. Reissued, *Fisher Hendley* (BACM Records, 202)
"My Angel Sweetheart," Vocalion 05016. Reissued, *Fisher Hendley* (BACM Records, 202)
"Won't Somebody Tell My Darling," Vocalion 04937, August 1939. Reissued, *Fisher Hendley* (BACM Records, 202)
"Darling, Do You Know Who Loves You?" Vocalion 04516, February 1939. (https://www.youtube.com/watch?v=UYWUjufpXRw)
"My Family Circle," Vocalion 04881, July 1939. Reissued, *Fisher Hendley* (BACM Records, 202)
"Memories in the Moonlight," unissued
"I'm Thinking Tonight of You Dear," unissued
"Down by the Moss Covered Spring," unissued
"When I Was Born," unissued

Martin Melody Boys

Columbia Records, Atlanta, GA, April 16, 1929, A.D. Martin: banjo-mandolin; Glenn Thompson: violin; Claude Thompson: tenor banjo; Joe Guthrie: guitar
"An Old Sweetheart of Mine (Maurice L. Jacobs [words], Harry I. Robinson [music])," Columbia 15413-D, July 1929 (https://www.youtube.com/watch?v=Z3wTrFjMd8A)
"The Donald Rag," Columbia 15413-D, July 1929 (https://www.youtube.com/watch?v=DOM0YZLxRLY)
"I'd Love to Live in Loveland [With a Girl Like You; Will Rossiter]," unissued
"Twinkle, Little Star," unissued

Parker, Charlie, and Woolbright, Mack

Columbia Records, Atlanta, GA, April 6, 1927, Parker: lead vocals/banjo; Woolbright: harmony vocal/guitar.
"Where Shall I Be," unissued

Discography

"While Eternal Ages Roll," unissued
"Give That Ni**er Ham," Columbia 15154-D, July 1927 (https://www.youtube.com/watch?v=HwpNGopN1lE)
"Rabbit Chase," Columbia 15154-D, July 1927 (https://www.youtube.com/watch?v=3DaVGNMQJgk)
Columbia Records, Atlanta, GA, November 9 or 10, 1927, Parker: lead vocals/banjo?; Woolbright: harmony vocal/guitar?
"The Man Who Wrote Home Sweet Home Never Was a Married Man (Fleta Jan Brown)," Columbia 15236-D, May 1928. Reissued, *The North Carolina Banjo Collection* (Rounder Records, 0439/0440; 1998)
"Ticklish Reuban," Columbia 15236-D, May 1928. Reissued, *Good for What Ails* (Old Hat Records 1005)
"The Old Arm Chair," Columbia 15694-D, September 1931 (https://www.youtube.com/watch?v=-fRAgIVSHWc)
"Will the Weaver," Columbia 15694-D, September 1931. Reissued, *In the Pines* (Old Hat Records 1006)

Tennessee Ramblers

Bluebird Records, New York, NY, January 3, 1935, Kenneth Wolfe: fiddle; Jack Gillette: vocal/fiddle; Dick Hartman: vocal/tenor guitar; Cecil Campbell: vocal/steel guitar/banjo/guitar; Harry Blair: vocal/guitar
"When I Take My Vacation in Heaven," Bluebird B-5796, March 1935
"Silver Threads," Bluebird B-5796, March 1935
"Wolfe's Trail," Bluebird B-5797
"From the Palms of Hawaii," Bluebird B-5962, August 1935
"March of the Roses," Bluebird B-5962, August 1935 (https://www.youtube.com/watch?v=wYV1-QjRayc)
"Still Talkin'," Bluebird B-5992, September 1935
"Long, Long Ago," Bluebird B-5992, September 1935. Reissued, *Dick Hartmann's Washboard Wonders* (BACM 259)
"I Got the Carolina Blues," Bluebird B-5909. Reissued, *Dick Hartmann's Washboard Wonders* (BACM 259)
"Take This Message to Mother," Bluebird B-5891, June 1935
"My Little Hut in Carolina," Bluebird B-6003, September 1935
"Pappy's Breakdown," Bluebird B-5797
"She's Long She's Tall," Bluebird B-5909. Reissued, *Dick Hartmann's Washboard Wonders* (BACM 259)
"Beautiful Heaven Must Be," Bluebird B-6003, September 1935
"She's My Curly Headed Baby," Bluebird B-5891, June 1935. Reissued, *Dick Hartmann's Washboard Wonders* (BACM 259)
"Loveless Love," Bluebird B-5876, March 1935
"When It's Harvest Time in Peaceful Valley," Bluebird B-5837, April 1935
"Dad's Favorite Waltz," Bluebird B-5876, March 1935
"South Bound Train," Bluebird B-5837, April 1935

Discography

"Hot Time," Bluebird B-5875, April 1935
"Don't Go 'Way, Doggone Ya," Bluebird B-5875, April 1935
Bluebird Records, Atlanta, GA, August 4–5, 1935, Kenneth Wolfe: vocal/fiddle; Dick Hartman: vocal/tenor guitar; Cecil Campbell: vocal/steel guitar/banjo/guitar; Harry Blair: vocal/guitar; Fred Morris: vocal/guitar/string bass
"Mountain Dew Blues," Bluebird B-6105, December 1935 (https://www.youtube.com/watch?v=kNqMD5zbyf8)
"Back to Old Smoky Mountain," Bluebird B-6105, December 1935
"New Red River Valley," Bluebird B-6162, January 1936 (https://www.youtube.com/watch?v=hApVqiPrCg8)
"Beautiful Texas," Bluebird B-6226
"New How-Do-You-Do," Bluebird B-6089
"Little Green Valley," Bluebird B-6180
"This Train," Bluebird B-6135, January 1936
"Little Sweetheart of the Mountain," Bluebird B-6180
"New River Train," Bluebird B-6162, January 1936 (https://www.youtube.com/watch?v=QZEsk36IOUs)
"These Bones Gonna Rise Again," Bluebird B-6089
"Birmingham Jail," Bluebird B-6207, February 1936
"Pennsylvania Hop," Bluebird B-6122, December 1935. Reissued, *Dick Hartmann's Washboard Wonders* (BACM 259)
"Kentucky Jig," Bluebird B-6122, December 1935
"Who Broke the Lock," Bluebird B-6207, January/February 1936 (https://www.youtube.com/watch?v=Xsje93Ry778)
"Ramblers' Rag," Bluebird B-6274, April 1936
"Leechburg Polka," Bluebird B-6274, April 1936. Reissued, *Dick Hartmann's Washboard Wonders* (BACM 259)
"Goin' Down the Road," Bluebird B-6135, January 1936
"Memories of Old," Bluebird B-6227
"Dick's Hoedown," Bluebird B-6227
"Step Light Ladies," unissued
"Melody of Hawaii," unissued
"Give Me Back My Texas Home," unissued

Chapter Notes

Preface

1. John Hartford, "The Boys From North Carolina," 1992, John Hartford Music, BMI, track 8 on *Goin' Back to Dixie*, Small Dog A-Barkin,' compact disc. Used by permission.
2. Wikipedia.
3. *Red River Blues* (Urbana: University of Illinois Press, 1986); *Crying for the Carolinas* (London: Studio Vista, 1971).
4. John Thomas Fowler, *Trotting Sally* (Spartanburg, SC: Kennedy Free Press, 2014).

Chapter One

1. Joe L. Hughes II, "Crowds will convene this weekend," *Gaffney Ledger*, November 4, 2011; Wikipedia.
2. ttp://www1.cpdl.org/wiki/index.php/Berryman_Hicks; Find A Grave.
3. Ancestry Tree.
4. Ancestry Tree; http://www1.cpdl.org/wiki/index.php/Berryman_Hicks; Find A Grave.
5. Larry Elmore, Ancestry, July 23, 2003.
6. http://www1.cpdl.org/wiki/index.php/Berryman_Hicks; George Pullen Jackson, *White Spirituals in the Southern Uplands* (Chapel Hill: University of North Carolina, 1933), reprinted (New York: Dover, 1965).
7. Find A Grave.
8. Larry Elmore, Ancestry, July 23, 2003.
9. http://mtruhama.com/history/.
10. Larry Elmore, Ancestry, July 23, 2003; George Pullen Jackson, *White Spirituals in the Southern Uplands* (Chapel Hill: University of North Carolina, 1933), reprinted (New York: Dover, 1965), p. 203.
11. George Pullen Jackson, *White Spirituals in the Southern Uplands* (Chapel Hill: University of North Carolina, 1933), reprinted (New York: Dover, 1965), p. 204.
12. John R. Logan, *Sketches of the Broad River and King's Mountain Baptist Associations* (Shelby, NC, 1887), 400 ff, quoted in George Pullen Jackson, *White Spirituals in the Southern Uplands* (Chapel Hill: University of North Carolina, 1933), reprinted (New York: Dover, 1965), p. 203.
13. Doc Watson and Clarence Ashley, "Hick's [sic] Farewell," 1994, disc 2/track 10 on *Original Folkways Recordings, 1960–1962*, Smithsonian-Folkways Recordings, compact disc.
14. https://en.wikipedia.org/wiki/The_Christian_Harmony.
15. Larry Elmore, Ancestry, July 23, 2003.
16. Find A Grave.
17. Find A Grave.
18. Marriage Records.
19. Myra Helen Hicks Ezell and Helen Martin, *Stories of Our People*, p. 7, Ancestry.
20. Larry Elmore, Ancestry, July 23, 2003.
21. Find A Grave.
22. July 20, 1870, Census.
23. Larry Elmore, Ancestry, July 23, 2003; Myra Helen Hicks Ezell and Helen Martin, *Stories of Our People*, p. 7, Ancestry.
24. Myra Helen Hicks Ezell and Helen Martin, *Stories of Our People*, p. 7, Ancestry.

Notes—Chapter One

25. Find A Grave.
26. Military records show as a private in North Carolina Confederate Calvary, enlisted Wake County, September 21, 1864; Myra Helen Hicks Ezell and Helen Martin, *Stories of Our People*, p. 7, Ancestry; Larry Elmore, Ancestry, July 23, 2003; "Dr. Romeo Hicks Taken by Death," *Asheville Citizen-Times*, February 4, 1930.
27. 1880–1920 Census.
28. "Dr. Romeo Hicks Taken by Death," *Asheville Citizen-Times*, February 4, 1930.
29. Death Certificate; "Dr. Romeo Hicks Taken by Death," *Asheville Citizen-Times*, February 4, 1930.
30. *Charlotte Observer*, January 15, 1910.
31. *Charlotte Observer*, January 15, 1910.
32. Find A Grave; *Charlotte Observer*, January 15, 1910.
33. Find A Grave.
34. *Rutherford Banner*, November 24, 1882.
35. Receipt, Ancestry.
36. Find A Grave; *Yorkville Enquirer*, May 20, 1891.
37. *Yorkville Enquirer*, March 17, 1897.
38. *Yorkville Enquirer*, December 19, 1900; *Yorkville Enquirer*, November 28, 1900.
39. Death Certificate.
40. Death Certificate; June 6, 1900, Census; 1903, 1905, 1908, 1910–1911, 1913, 1916 Spartanburg City Directory; April 19, 1910, Census.
41. Find A Grave.
42. Find A Grave; June 8, 1900, Census; "Mrs. H. Z. Hicks Is Buried at Arrowood," *Gaffney Ledger*, January 15, 1935.
43. Joe L. Hughes II, "Crowds will convene this weekend," *Gaffney Ledger*, November 4, 2011.
44. https://www.scpictureproject.org/cherokee-county/zeno-hicks-house.html.
45. Death Certificate.
46. Find A Grave; "Zeno Hicks, of Chesnee, Died Monday Afternoon," *Gaffney Ledger*, March 30, 1922.
47. Find A Grave.
48. Find A Grave; June 15, 1900, Census.
49. January 31, 1920, Census; Find A Grave; Ancestry Family Tree.
50. "Hicks Orchestra Here March 18th," Forest City newspaper, March 1921, reproduced in Myra Helen Hicks Ezell and Helen Martin, *Stories of Our People*, p. 7, Ancestry.
51. "Hicks Orchestra Here March 18th," Forest City newspaper, March 1921, reproduced in Myra Helen Hicks Ezell and Helen Martin, *Stories of Our People*, p. 7, Ancestry.
52. *Gaffney Ledger*, April 19, 1895; *Sun*, April 13, 1905; *Gaffney Ledger*, January 3, 1906.
53. *Gaffney Ledger*, June 7, 1910.
54. *Gaffney Ledger*, May 16, 1911.
55. July 19, 1860, Census.
56. Death Certificate; Find A Grave; Hubert Hendrix, *Herald*, clipping, Ancestry; "Chesnee Man Remembers Civil War," *Chesnee Times*, June 4, 1954; "D.P.L. Martin Gets Greetings from President," *Gaffney Ledger*, June 9, 1955; April 3, 1930, Census.
57. *Gaffney Ledger*, April 21, 1898.
58. June 16, 1900, Census; 1903, 1905 Spartanburg City Directory.
59. April 15, 1910, Census; *Watchman and Southron*, September 23, 1916.
60. *Gaffney Ledger*, March 29, 1912.
61. *Greenville News*, August 14, 1914.
62. *Greenville News*, March 6, 1957.
63. https://en.wikipedia.org/wiki/The_Christian_Harmony; *Spartanburg Herald*, June 6, 1942, quoted in James D. Martin, *The Family Lines*.
64. *Gaffney Ledger*, August 12, 1897.
65. *Gaffney Ledger*, December 29, 1934.
66. Death Certificate; February 9, 1920, Census; Death Certificate.
67. North Carolina Birth Index.
68. "Hicks Orchestra Here March 18th," Forest City newspaper, March 1921, reproduced in Myra Helen Hicks Ezell and Helen Martin, *Stories of Our People*, p. 7, Ancestry.
69. "Hicks Orchestra Gives a Concert," *Gaffney Ledger*, November 1, 1921.
70. Guthrie T. Meade, Jr., et al., *Country Music Sources* (Chapel Hill: University of North Carolina Press, 2002), p. 410.
71. Guthrie T. Meade, Jr., et al., *Country Music Sources* (Chapel Hill: University of North Carolina Press, 2002), p. 751.
72. Guthrie T. Meade, Jr., et al.,

Notes—Chapter Two

Country Music Sources (Chapel Hill: UNC Press, 2002), p. 344.
73. Guthrie T. Meade, Jr., et al, *Country Music Sources* (Chapel Hill University of North Carolina Press, 2002), p. 341.
74. https://babel.hathitrust.org/cgi/pt?id=mdp.39015096538346&view=1up&seq=1.
75. https://levysheetmusic.mse.jhu.edu/collection/061/033.
76. http://www.joemorley.co.uk/pages/cover.htm.
77. Guthrie T. Meade, Jr., et al., *Country Music Sources* (Chapel Hill: University of North Carolina Press, 2002), p. 287.
78. Death Certificate; "Dr. W. R. Hicks Dies in Columbia," *Greenville News*, April 3, 1951.
79. *Sun*, April 13, 1905.
80. *Gaffney Ledger*, June 3, 1910; June 5, 1917, Draft Registration.
81. "Dr. W. R. Hicks Dies in Columbia," *Greenville News*, April 3, 1951.
82. June 5, 1917, Draft Registration; January 31, 1920, Census; May 7, 1930, Census.
83. "New Music Club," *Gaffney Ledger*, January 7, 1922.
84. *Cherokee Times*, May 11, 1928.
85. For example: "Musical Program Is Offered on Tomorrow," *Cherokee Times*, April 9, 1925.
86. Find A Grave; Headstone Applications for Military Veterans; Death Certificate; "Dr. W. R. Hicks Dies in Columbia," *Greenville News*, April 3, 1951.
87. Death Certificate; "Dr. W. R. Hicks Dies In Columbia," *Greenville News*, April 3, 1951.

Chapter Two

1. "Old Fiddlers at Cliffside," *Highlander*, April 1905 or 1908, Cleveland County Historical Museum, from Tommy Forney.
2. *Gaffney Ledger*, February 26, 1918.
3. Gail Gillespie and Wayne Martin, *Raleigh Fiddlers' Convention* (Raleigh: Pinecone, 1990), p. 7.
4. Find A Grave.
5. https://en.wikipedia.org/wiki/Carolina_Power_%26_Light_Company; Bob Carlin, *String Bands in the North Carolina Piedmont* (Jefferson, NC: McFarland, 2004), pp. 106–108.
6. Bob Carlin, *String Bands in the North Carolina Piedmont* (Jefferson, NC: McFarland, 2004), pp. 108–118.
7. For example: "Best Ever Held," *Gaffney Ledger*, March 24, 1916.
8. "Fiddler's Convention at Theatre Tuesday," *Gaffney Ledger*, March 17, 1916.
9. "Ye Old Fiddlers Tomorrow Night," *Gaffney Ledger*, February 28, 1918; "Ye Old Fiddlers Loudly Applauded," *Gaffney Ledger*, March 5, 1918.
10. "Old Fiddlers Convention Will Have New Feature," *Gaffney Ledger*, May 3, 1921.
11. Death Certificate; March 2, 1920, Census; Find A Grave.
12. Ancestry Family Tree.
13. "Mrs. Rebecca D'Staffino Passes to Great Beyond," *Gaffney Ledger*, June 1, 1929; Death Certificate.
14. Ancestry Family Tree; June 18, 1900, Census; 1888, 1891, 1894 Tax Rolls, Fannin County, TX.
15. June 13, 1900, Census.
16. Ancestry Family Tree; March 2, 1920, Census.
17. "Fred Destaffino [sic] Goes to Reward," *Gaffney Ledger*, July 1, 1922; Death Certificate, Melrose DeStaffino; April 28, 1930, Census; "Entertaining Program Will Be Given Tonight," *Gaffney Ledger*, June 16, 1921; *Gaffney Ledger*, May 29, 1968; March 2, 1920, Census.
18. *Gaffney Ledger*, June 23, 1905; March 2, 1920, Census; 1921 Gaffney City Directory; "Fred Destaffino [sic] Goes to Reward," *Gaffney Ledger*, July 1, 1922.
19. *Gaffney Ledger*, March 7, 1916.
20. *Gaffney Ledger*, May 19, 1921; *Gaffney Ledger*, June 23, 1921.
21. Wikipedia.
22. "Entertaining Program Will Be Given Tonight," *Gaffney Ledger*, June 16, 1921.
23. "Fred Destaffino [sic] Goes to Reward," *Gaffney Ledger*, July 1, 1922; Death Certificate.
24. "Old Fiddlers' Convention," *Gaffney Ledger*, March 10, 1916.
25. "Interest Grows Among Fiddlers," *Gaffney Ledger*, June 12, 1920.

Notes—Chapter Two

26. *Yorkville Enquirer*, June 9, 1908.

27. *Gaffney Ledger*, October 2, 1911.

28. "Old Fiddlers' Convention," *Gaffney Ledger*, March 10, 1916; *Gaffney Ledger*, January 24, 1908; *Gaffney Ledger*, February 14, 1908; *Gaffney Ledger*, April 15, 1910; "Old Fiddlers at Cliffside," *Highlander*, April 1905 or 1908, Cleveland County Historical Museum, from Tommy Forney; *Gaffney Ledger*, August 10, 1915; *Gaffney Ledger*, March 24, 1916; "Entrants in Fiddlers Convention," *Gaffney Ledger*, March 14, 1916; "Fiddler's Convention at Theatre Tuesday," *Gaffney Ledger*, March 17, 1916; *Gaffney Ledger*, July 28, 1916; "Fiddler's Convention," *Gaffney Ledger*, September 11, 1919; *Yorkville Enquirer*, September 16, 1919; "Fiddlers' Convention Is Enjoyed by Many People," *Gaffney Ledger*, June 22, 1920; *Yorkville Enquirer*, May 12, 1908; *Yorkville Enquirer*, June 9, 1908; *Yorkville Enquirer*, March 21, 1911; *Yorkville Enquirer*, March 23, 1911; *Yorkville Enquirer*, September 5, 1911; *Yorkville Enquirer*, September 26, 1911; *Yorkville Enquirer*, October 17, 1911; *Gaffney Ledger*, October 27, 1911; *Yorkville Enquirer*, November 7, 1911; *Gaffney Ledger*, December 8, 1911; *Gaffney Ledger*, January 16, 1912; *Yorkville Enquirer*, February 23, 1912; *Yorkville Enquirer*, April 9, 1912; *Gaffney Ledger*, October 8, 1912; *Gaffney Ledger*, February 18, 1913; "Fiddlers in Convention," *Yorkville Enquirer*, February 8, 1921; *Yorkville Enquirer*, August 9, 1921; *Yorkville Enquirer*, August 16, 1921; *Yorkville Enquirer*, April 11, 1922; *Cheraw Chronicle*, April 20, 1922; *Cherokee Times*, April 6, 1925; "Prizes Awarded at Fiddlers Convention," *Cherokee Times*, May 18, 1925; "Urge York Champion Fiddlers to Contest," *Greenville News*, November 21, 1929; "Unusual Music Event Planned," *Greenville News*, August 18, 1927; "Old Time Music Meet Pleasing," *Charlotte Observer*, November 24, 1929; *Greenville News*, November 21, 1929; *Gaffney Ledger*, February 26, 1918; *Gaffney Ledger*, March 28, 1918, quoting *Rock Hill Evening Herald*, March 16, 1918; *Gaffney Ledger*, April 19, 1919; "Fiddler's Prize to Sam Gaffney," *Gaffney Ledger*, November 17, 1921; "'Ye Ole Tyme Fiddlers' Convention' October 6," *Gaffney Ledger*, September 26, 1922; *Cherokee Times*, November 29, 1923; *Gaffney Ledger*, October 21, 1924; "Old Time Fiddlers Meet in Blacksburg," *Cherokee Times*, November 10, 1924; *Gaffney Ledger*, December 13, 1924; "Fiddlers to Convene at Blacksburg Friday," *Gaffney Ledger*, October 29, 1925; *Gaffney Ledger*, October 27, 1927; "Old Fiddlers Convention," *Gaffney Ledger*, October 9, 1930; "Old Fiddlers to Play at Blacksburg Friday," *Gaffney Ledger*, November 6, 1930; "Fiddlers Convention Here on Friday Night," *Gaffney Ledger*, June 16, 1931; "Only One-Armed Fiddler," *Gaffney Ledger*, February 26, 1915; "Fiddlers' Convention Here," *Gaffney Ledger*, March 9, 1917; "Be Good Music at Convention Here," *Gaffney Ledger*, June 14, 1919; *Gaffney Ledger*, July 24, 1919; *Gaffney Ledger*, July 31, 1919; *Charlotte Observer*, August 3, 1919; "Interest Grows Among Fiddlers," *Gaffney Ledger*, June 12, 1920; "Old Fiddlers Convention Will Have New Feature," *Gaffney Ledger*, May 3, 1921; *Cleveland Star*, October 21, 1921; "Old Fiddlers' Convention at the Strand Theatre," *Gaffney Ledger*, November 10, 1921; "The Old Fiddlers' Convention," *Gaffney Ledger*, March 30, 1922; "Fiddlers' Convention for Rutherfordton," *Asheville Citizen-Times*, October 16, 1922; "Glorious Fourth Quiet in Shelby," *Cleveland Star*, July 6, 1923; "Fiddlers' Convention for Rutherfordton," *Asheville Citizen-Times*, October 16, 1922; *Gaffney Ledger*, October 13, 1923; *Cherokee Times*, October 15, 1923; *Gaffney Ledger*, January 29, 1925; *Cherokee Times*, April 6, 1925; *Gaffney Ledger*, October 12, 1926; *Gaffney Ledger*, April 9, 21, 1927; "Old Fiddlers' Meeting," *Gaffney Ledger*, November 7, 1929; "Fiddlers Convention to Be Held Jan. 25th," *Gaffney Ledger*, January 11, 1930; "Fiddlers Convention," *Cherokee Times*, December 31, 1925; *Gaffney Ledger*, August 10, 1915; *Gaffney Ledger*, November 10, 1927; Rex Long, "Fiddlers' Convention Is Successful Affair," *Gaffney Ledger*, November 22, 1927; *Gaffney Ledger*, May 3, 1928; "Woolbright's Outfit Wins Contest Prize," *Gaffney Ledger*, September 23, 1930; *Gaffney Ledger*, November 29, 1930; "All in Readiness for Old Fiddlers," *Gaffney Ledger*, May 12, 1921.

29. Marriage Certificate.

Notes—Chapter Two

30. *Sun*, April 9, 1903.
31. "Patron Saint of Hollis," *Charlotte Observer*, December 14, 1907.
32. "The Rock School House," *Cleveland Star*, October 7, 1903.
33. "The Hollis Picnic," *Cleveland Star*, July 9, 1902.
34. Ancestry, posted by Robin Withrow.
35. "Mrs. J.P.D. Withrow Answers Summons," *News and Observer*, August 27, 1925.
36. Death Certificate.
37. *Charlotte Observer*, October 21, 1974; Find A Grave.
38. Find A Grave; Ancestry Family Tree; Pat Borden, "Memories Linger at End of Road," *Charlotte Observer*, March 12, 1972.
39. Marriage Records; Find A Grave.
40. September 12, 1918, Draft Registration; January 24, 1920, Census; February 18 1920, Census; May 5, 1930, Census; April 18, 1940, Census.
41. June 1900 Census; April 20, 1910, Census; May 5, 1930, Census; NC Death Collection; Ancestry.
42. Birth Indexes; NC Death Collection; Social Security Death Index; April 21, 1930, Census; Ancestry.
43. Unknown, "Speech" (made at meeting honoring Smith Hammett, Forest City, NC, November 20, 1980), from Larry Hammett.
44. Joe DePriest, "Country music roots reach into Cleveland, Rutherford," *Shelby Star*, October 25, 1985, from Larry Hammett.
45. *Gaffney Ledger*, September 28, 1900.
46. *Gaffney Ledger*, October 3, 1902.
47. Find A Grave.
48. Find A Grave.
49. *Yorkville Enquirer*, March 22, 1893.
50. *Gaffney Ledger*.
51. *Yorkville Enquirer*, February 20, 1897.
52. June 5, 1900, Census.
53. April 28, 1910, Census; March 4, 1920, Census; April 8, 1930, Census.
54. Find A Grave.
55. Find A Grave.
56. *Gaffney Ledger*, November 22, 1912; *Gaffney Ledger*, November 29, 1912.
57. *Yorkville Enquirer*, March 21, 1913.
58. Find A Grave; Ancestry Family Tree.
59. Ancestry Family Tree.
60. Find A Grave.
61. *Yorkville Enquirer*, January 10, 1867.
62. Find A Grave; *Yorkville Enquirer*, May 19, 1870.
63. Find A Grave; September 12, 1918, Draft Registration; *Gaffney Ledger*, September 22, 1899; *Gaffney Ledger*, September 19, 1899.
64. Find A Grave.
65. *Gaffney Ledger*, November 27, 1900.
66. Family Tree.
67. May 6, 1910, Census; January 14–15, 1920, Census.
68. September 12, 1918, Draft Registration.
69. Death Certificate; *Gaffney Ledger*, August 31, 1954; *Greenville News*, September 1, 1954.
70. Death Certificate.
71. *Gaffney Ledger*, September 16, 1897.
72. *Gaffney Ledger*, December 22, 1899.
73. Find A Grave; *Greenville News*, January 11, 1948.
74. Find A Grave; *Gaffney Ledger*, December 7, 1943.
75. April 15, 1910, Census; September 12, 1918, Draft Registration; January 14, 1920, Census.
76. Find A Grave.
77. June 1, 1900, Census.
78. May 3–4, 1910, Census.
79. September 12, 1918, Draft Registration; March 4, 1920, Census.
80. *Greenville News*, January 24, 1959.
81. Find A Grave.
82. Ancestry Family Tree.
83. Find A Grave; June 1, 1900, Census.
84. June 1, 1900, Census.
85. *Gaffney Ledger*, June 15, 1900.
86. *Gaffney Ledger*, December 4, 1900; *Gaffney Ledger*, February 28, 1905.
87. *Gaffney Ledger*, February 20, 1903; *Gaffney Ledger*, February 24, 1903.
88. *Gaffney Ledger*, November 30, 1909; *Yorkville Enquirer*, February 14, 1911; *Gaffney Ledger*, March 17, 1911; *Gaffney*

Notes—Chapter Three

Ledger, March 1, 1912; *Gaffney Ledger*, March 7, 1913; *Yorkville Enquirer*, August 15, 1913; *Gaffney Ledger*, August 29, 1913; *Gaffney Ledger*, July 10, 1914; *Yorkville Enquirer*; May 3, 1912, *Gaffney Ledger*, May 3, 1912; *Gaffney Ledger*, August 16, 1912.

89. Find A Grave; Death Certificate.
90. Find A Grave; Death Record; *Yorkville Enquirer*, January 23, 1906.
91. Ancestry Family Tree.
92. Death Record; *Yorkville Enquirer*, December 9, 1921.
93. June 9, 1900, Census; May 3–4, 1910, Census; January 13, 192,0 Census.
94. Wikipedia; "Aged Fiddler Dies at York," *Charlotte Observer*, May 10, 1933.
95. "Famous Fiddler Heard at Charlotte Reunion," *Gaffney Ledger*, June 11, 1929.
96. Find A Grave; Death Certificate.
97. Find A Grave.
98. *Yorkville Enquirer*, December 8, 1881.
99. *Gastonia Gazette*, April 28, 1905.
100. *Yorkville Enquirer*, November 13, 1908.
101. *Yorkville Enquirer*, February 26, 1909; April 13, 1910, Census; January 2, 1920, Census; *Gaffney Ledger*, January 8, 1929.
102. *Yorkville Enquirer*, October 17, 1913.
103. *Yorkville Enquirer*, August 3, 1915.

Chapter Three

1. Find A Grave.
2. August 16, 1860, Census; July 187,0 Census; June 30, 1880, Census.
3. "Mrs. John W. Ross Dead," *Gaffney Ledger*, June 20, 1899.
4. June 14, 1900, Census.
5. *Newberry Weekly Herald*, February 16, 1909; "New Trial Refused!" *Dispatch-News*, March 16, 1910; May 4, 1910 Census.
6. "Only One-Armed Fiddler," *Gaffney Ledger*, February 26, 1915.
7. *Gaffney Ledger*, January 24, 1908; *Gaffney Ledger*, February 18, 1908; "The Fiddlers Last Night," *Gaffney Ledger*, February 25, 1908; *Gaffney Ledger*, February 28, 1908.
8. "Old Fiddlers' Convention," *Gaffney Ledger*, March 10, 1916; "Entrants in Fiddlers Convention," *Gaffney Ledger*, March 14, 1916.
9. Ancestry Family Tree; Find A Grave; *Greenville News*, August 17, 1927.
10. "Ye Old Fiddlers Tomorrow Night," *Gaffney Ledger*, February 28, 1918; "Old-Time Fiddlers Meet," *Gaffney Ledger*, March 27, 1917.
11. Death Certificate.
12. Historic Marker.
13. "Death Takes S.S. Gaffney, Rites Held," *Gaffney Ledger*, January 30, 1945; "Mrs. Louisa H. Gaffney," *Greenville News*, June 5, 1938; Find A Grave; "Cherokee Couple Married 50 Years," *Gaffney Ledger*, March 9, 1929.
14. June 1900, Census; "Cherokee Couple Married 50 Years," *Gaffney Ledger*, March 9, 1929.
15. April 28, 1930, Census; "Death Takes S.S. Gaffney, Rites Held," *Gaffney Ledger*, January 30, 1945.
16. "Mrs. Louisa Gaffney Is Claimed by Death," *Gaffney Ledger*, June 7, 1938.
17. Death Certificate; "Death Takes S.S. Gaffney, Rites Held," *Gaffney Ledger*, January 30, 1945.
18. Ancestry Family Tree; McDaniel Research.
19. Ancestry Family Tree; McDaniel Research; Draft Registration; 1930 census; Death Certificate; Find A Grave.
20. June 14, 1900, Census.
21. Ancestry Family tree; McDaniel research.
22. *Gaffney Ledger*, November 18, 1910.
23. *Gaffney Ledger*, August 10, 1915.
24. Ancestry Family Tree; Find A Grave.
25. "Entrants in Fiddlers Convention," *Gaffney Ledger*, March 14, 1916.
26. "Fiddler's Convention at Theatre Tuesday," *Gaffney Ledger*, March 17, 1916.
27. Discogs.com.
28. "Best Ever Held," *Gaffney Ledger*, March 24, 1916.
29. Ancestry Family Tree; 1930 Census; June 5, 1917, Draft Registration.
30. Delayed Birth; Death Certificate.
31. "Old-Time Fiddlers Meet," *Gaffney Ledger*, March 27, 1917.

Notes—Chapter Three

32. June 5, 1917, Draft Registration.
33. Family Tree.
34. *Gaffney Ledger*, February 26, 1918; *Gaffney Ledger*, March 28, 1918, quoting *Rock Hill Evening Herald*, March 16, 1918.
35. https://musicpolitics.as.ua.edu/projects/primary-source-projects/werecoming-fodder-abraham-were-coming-in-a-horn-a-civil-war-song-parody/.
36. "Ye Old Fiddlers Tomorrow Night," *Gaffney Ledger*, February 28, 1918.
37. https://lyricsplayground.com/alpha/songs/h/hedhavetogetundergetoutandgetunder.html.
38. "Ye Old Fiddlers Loudly Applauded," *Gaffney Ledger*, March 5, 1918.
39. *Gaffney Ledger*, March 21, 1918.
40. May 24, 1918, Order to Report; U.S. Army Transport List; Military Service.
41. September 12, 1918, Draft registration.
42. *Gaffney Ledger*, May 1, 1919.
43. "Be Good Music at Convention Here," *Gaffney Ledger*, June 14, 1919; "Fiddlers' Convention Here," *Gaffney Ledger*, June 17, 1919.
44. "Fiddlers' Convention Here," *Gaffney Ledger*, June 17, 1919; "Fiddlers to Gather at Gaffney Saturday," *Greenville News*, June 7, 1919.
45. February 1920, Census.
46. April 30, 1930, Census.
47. "Old Fiddlers Convention Will Have New Feature," *Gaffney Ledger*, May 3, 1921; "All in Readiness for Old Fiddlers," *Gaffney Ledger*, May 12, 1921; *Gaffney Ledger*, May 17, 1921.
48. Ancestry Family Tree; Death Record.
49. "Prize Winners at the Old Fiddlers Convention," *Cleveland Star*, August 15, 1919.
50. *Gaffney Ledger*, September 6, 1919; *Gaffney Ledger*, October 11, 1919.
51. Ancestry Family Tree.
52. February 26, 1920, Census; 1921 Gaffney City Directory.
53. "Musicale at Butlers," *Gaffney Ledger*, March 2, 1920.
54. "Interest Grows Among Fiddlers," *Gaffney Ledger*, June 12, 1920; "Fiddlers' Convention," *Charlotte Observer*, June 15, 1920; "Fiddlers' Convention Is Enjoyed by Many People," *Gaffney Ledger*, June 22, 1920.
55. "Old Fiddlers Convention Will Have New Feature," *Gaffney Ledger*, May 3, 1921; "All in Readiness for Old Fiddlers," *Gaffney Ledger*, May 12, 1921; *Gaffney Ledger*, May 17, 1921.
56. *Gaffney Ledger*, May 19, 1921; *Gaffney Ledger*, May 24, 1921; *Gaffney Ledger*, May 31, 1921.
57. "Rotarians Enjoy Ladies Night with Health Talks," *Gaffney Ledger*, December 8, 1921.
58. "'Ye Ole Tyme Fiddlers' Convention' October 6," *Gaffney Ledger*, September 26, 1922.
59. "Musical Entertainment Tuesday," *Gaffney Ledger*, January 16, 1923.
60. *Gaffney Ledger*, February 22, 1907.
61. June 11, 1900, Census; Ancestry; June 5, 1917, Draft Registration.
62. *Gaffney Ledger*, July 23, 1901; *Gaffney Ledger*, November 12, 1901.
63. *Gaffney Ledger*, February 22, 1907; April 22, 1910, Census; Ancestry.
64. April 22, 1910, Census; June 5, 1917, Draft Registration.
65. South Carolina Death Index; Death Record.
66. June 5, 1917, Draft Registration.
67. "Entertaining Program Will Be Given Tonight," *Gaffney Ledger*, June 16, 1921; *Gaffney Ledger*, June 23, 1921.
68. "Old Fiddlers' Convention at the Strand Theatre," *Gaffney Ledger*, November 10, 1921; "Arange [sic] Varied Program for Old Fiddlers Meet," *Gaffney Ledger*, November 12, 1921; "Old Fiddlers to Convene Tonight," *Gaffney Ledger*, November 15, 1921.
69. *Gaffney Ledger*, October 13, 1923; *Cherokee Times*, October 15, 1923; "Convention Successful," *Gaffney Ledger*, October 23, 1923.
70. *Gaffney Ledger*, October 13, 1923.
71. "Mrs. Charles Parker Dies at Home Here on Thursday," *Gaffney Ledger*, December 20, 1924.
72. "Musical Program at Holly Grove School," *Cherokee Times*, June 15, 1925; *Gaffney Ledger*, June 16, 1925.
73. *Gaffney Ledger*, October 12, 1926.
74. *Gastonia Gazette*, August 27, 1926.

Notes—Chapter Four

75. June 1917, Draft registration.
76. Census, March 2, 1920.
77. Census, April 2, 1930.
78. *Gaffney Ledger*, March 9, 1926; Tony Russell, *Country Music Records: A Discography, 1921–1942* (New York: Oxford University Press, 2004), p. 675.
79. *Gaffney Ledger*, April 9, 1927; Tony Russell, *Country Music Records: A Discography, 1921–1942* (New York: Oxford University Press, 2004), p. 676; Guthrie T. Meade, Jr., et al., *Country Music Sources* (Chapel Hill: University of North Carolina Press, 2002), pp. 15, 149, 440, 451; "Local Musicians Produce Record," *Gaffney Ledger*, July 16, 1927.
80. *Gaffney Ledger*, April 9, 1927.
81. *Gaffney Ledger*, April 9, 1927.
82. "Local Musicians Produce Record," *Gaffney Ledger*, July 16, 1927.
83. *Gaffney Ledger*, August 4, 1927.
84. *Gaffney Ledger*, October 27, 1927.
85. *Gaffney Ledger*, November 1, 1927; *Gaffney Ledger*, November 2, 1927; C.S. Moeller, *Gaffney Ledger*, November 10, 1927; "Kings Creek Entertainment," *Gaffney Ledger*, November 3, 1927.
86. https://www.americanantiquarian.org/thomasballads/items/show/252.
87. Tony Russell, *Country Music Records: A Discography, 1921–1942* (New York: Oxford University Press, 2004), p. 676; Guthrie T. Meade, Jr., et al., *Country Music Sources* (Chapel Hill: University of North Carolina Press, 2002), pp. 15, 149, 440, 451.
88. Tony Russell, *Country Music Records: A Discography, 1921–1942* (New York: Oxford University Press, 2004), p. 676.
89. Earl Scruggs, *Earl Scruggs and the 5-String Banjo* (Milwaukee: Hal Leonard, 2005), pp. 9, 158–9.
90. "Earl Scruggs Makes a Visit Home," *Foothills View*, January 13, 1984.
91. *Gaffney Ledger*, October 13, 1923.
92. "Musical Entertainment Tuesday," *Gaffney Ledger*, January 16, 1923.
93. "Entertaining Program Will Be Given Tonight," *Gaffney Ledger*, June 16, 1921.
94. *Gaffney Ledger*, October 13, 1923.
95. *Gaffney Ledger*, November 10, 1927; Rex Long, "Fiddlers' Convention Is Successful Affair," *Gaffney Ledger*, November 22, 1927.
96. *Gaffney Ledger*, November 10, 1927; Rex Long, "Fiddlers' Convention Is Successful Affair," *Gaffney Ledger*, November 22, 1927.
97. *Gaffney Ledger*, February 11, 1928.
98. *Gaffney Ledger*, May 3, 1928.
99. "Parker Reunion Will Be Held Aug. 3," *The Landmark*, July 29, 1929.
100. "Musical Ntertainment [sic]," *Cherokee Times*, December 14, 1928.
101. "Old Fiddlers' Meeting," *Gaffney Ledger*, November 7, 1929.
102. "Fiddlers Convention to Be Held Jan. 25th," *Gaffney Ledger*, January 11, 1930; *Gaffney Ledger*, January 18, 1930; "Fiddling Tonight," *Gaffney Ledger*, January 25, 1930.
103. "John W. Ross Is Taken by Death," *Gaffney Ledger*, April 1, 1930; Death Certificate; Find A Grave.
104. April 2, 1930, Census.
105. "Old Fiddlers Convention," *Gaffney Ledger*, October 9, 1930; "Old Fiddlers to Play at Blacksburg Friday," *Gaffney Ledger*, November 6, 1930.
106. "Charles Parker Taken by Death," *Gaffney Ledger*, June 11, 1931.
107. Death Certificate.

Chapter Four

1. *Gaffney Ledger*, March 7, 1929.
2. Draft Registration, February 16, 1942.
3. *Gaffney Ledger*, October 6, 1971.
4. Find A Grave.
5. April 23, 1910, Census; January 5, 1920, Census.
6. January 5, 1920, Census.
7. April 25, 1930, Census.
8. *Gaffney Ledger*, October 6, 1971.
9. January 21, 1920, Census; April 17, 1930, Census.
10. October 16, 1940, Draft Registration.
11. September 12, 1918, Draft Registration; Find A Grave.
12. April 17, 1930, Census; Find A Grave; *Index-Journal*, December 31, 1984.
13. Find A Grave; *Index-Journal*, December 31, 1984.

Notes—Chapter Four

14. January 21, 1920, Census; April 17, 1930, Census; October 16, 1940, Draft Registration; Find A Grave.
15. April 17, 1930, Census; October 16, 1940, Draft Registration; *Greenville News*, June 15, 1933.
16. Find A Grave.
17. *Gaffney Ledger*, April 25, 1929.
18. "Woolbright's W.O.W. Serenaders at Meet," *Gaffney Ledger*, August 31, 1929; "Ladies Night to Be Featured by W.O.W.," *Gaffney Ledger*, September 21, 1929; "Ladies Night Event of Woodmen Enjoyed," *Gaffney Ledger*, September 28, 1929; "Woodman Circle to Celebrate Tonight," *Gaffney Ledger*, September 26, 1929; *Gaffney Ledger*, September 25, 1930.
19. "Several Planning to Attend Convention," *Gaffney Ledger*, August 8, 1929.
20. "Music and Dancing for Friday Evening," *Gaffney Ledger*, August 22, 1929.
21. *Gaffney Ledger*, August 29, 1929.
22. "Woolbright's W.O.W. Serenaders at Meet," *Gaffney Ledger*, August 31, 1929.
23. "Chicken Stew Enjoyed on Banks of the River," *Gaffney Ledger*, September 3, 10, 1929.
24. "Holly Grove Summer School Ends," *Gaffney Ledger*, September 19, 1929.
25. "Woodman Circle to Celebrate Tonight," *Gaffney Ledger*, September 26, 1929.
26. "Ladies Night Event of Woodmen Enjoyed," *Gaffney Ledger*, September 28, 1929.
27. "Old Wayside Tells of Gaffney Meeting," *Gaffney Ledger*, November 21, 1929, quoting *Charlotte Observer*, November 19, 1929.
28. April 11, 1940, Census; October 16, 1940, Draft Registration; *Gaffney Ledger*, October 16, 18, 1945; Family Tree; Find A Grave; Death Certificate.
29. "Fiddlers Convention to Be Held Jan. 25th," *Gaffney Ledger*, January 11, 1930.
30. "Woolbright Group to Broadcast Over WSPA," *Gaffney Ledger*, February 22, 1930; "Martin Musicians to Broadcast Over WSPA," *Gaffney Ledger*, February 25, 1930.
31. "To Broadcast Friday Night," *Gaffney Ledger*, May 27, 1930.
32. *Gaffney Ledger*, January 10, 1931.
33. *Gaffney Ledger*, May 1, 1930; *Gaffney Ledger*, August 9, 1930; "Pacolet Mills Post Sponsoring Movie," *Greenville News*, October 17, 1930; "Auxiliary Sponsor Party at Theatre," *Greenville News*, December 19, 1930.
34. "Woolbright's Outfit Wins Contest Prize," *Gaffney Ledger*, September 23, 1930.
35. "Anniversary Dinner Given D. J. Wilson," *Gaffney Ledger*, November 1, 1930.
36. *Gaffney Ledger*, February 5, 1931.
37. "Martin Musicians to Broadcast Over WSPA," *Gaffney Ledger*, February 25, 1930.
38. Ancestry Family Tree; June 26, 1900, Census.
39. *Gaffney Ledger*, February 4, 1910; Ancestry Family Tree; June 26, 1900, Census.
40. April 15, 1930, Census; Find A Grave.
41. June 5, 1917, Draft Registration.
42. "Martin Musicians to Broadcast Over WSPA," *Gaffney Ledger*, February 25, 1930.
43. "Martin Returns to His Former Business," *Gaffney Ledger*, June 27, 1936.
44. *Gaffney Ledger*, January 1, 1929.
45. *Gaffney Ledger*, August 4, 1962.
46. January 13, 1920, Census; April 2, 1930, Census.
47. *Gaffney Ledger*, May 10, 1971; Death Certificate.
48. Find A Grave.
49. *Gaffney Ledger*, June 22, 1966; Draft Registration.
50. April 2, 1930, Census; *Gaffney Ledger*, June 26, 1928.
51. Find A Grave.
52. May 23, 1910, Census; February 27, 1920, Census; Find A Grave.
53. April 7, 1930, Census.
54. 1931 Anderson, SC, City Directory; April 12, 1940, Census.
55. *Gaffney Ledger*, September 17, 1932.
56. "New Pleasant School Presentation Scene," *Gaffney Ledger*, September 2, 1933.

Notes—Chapter Four

57. April 22, 1933, Marriage Record.
58. *Gaffney Ledger*, January 8, 1929; *Gaffney Ledger*, February 26, 1929; "Chicken Stew Enjoyed on Banks of the River," *Gaffney Ledger*, September 3, 10, 1929; *Gaffney Ledger*, September 10, 1929; *Gaffney Ledger*, December 10, 1929; "Kangaroo Court to Be Staged Tonight," *Gaffney Ledger*, March 18, 1930; "Cherry Camp Plans Mock Trial Tonight," *Gaffney Ledger*, September 30, 1930; *Gaffney Ledger*, June 25, 1931; "Home Coming for Cherry Woodmen," *Gaffney Ledger*, November 28, 1931; "Open Meet Declared a Genuine Success," *Gaffney Ledger*, July 28, 1932; "Woodmen Meeting Is an Enjoyable Affair," *Gaffney Ledger*, May 27, 1933; *Gaffney Ledger*, September 29, 1934; *Gaffney Ledger*, January 5, 1935; *Gaffney Ledger*, April 27, 1935; *Gaffney Ledger*, April 17, 1937.
59. "Cream of Talent in Woodmen Show Here," *Gaffney Ledger*, July 30, 1931; *Gaffney Ledger*, June 8, 1935; "DeCamp and Dobson Address Local WOW," *Gaffney Ledger*, November 1, 1938.
60. "Palmetto Camp to Install Officers," *Gaffney Ledger*, January 15, 1929; *Gaffney Ledger*, January 17, 1929; *Gaffney Ledger*, February 26, 1929; "Grove to Celebrate Date of Anniversary," *Gaffney Ledger*, September 24, 1929; "Woodmen Circle to Celebrate Tonight," *Gaffney Ledger*, September 26, 1929; *Gaffney Ledger*, January 16, 1934; "Wenonah Council Has Delightful Meeting," *Gaffney Ledger*, December 14, 1929; "Granberry and Fort State Line Speakers," *Gaffney Ledger*, April 4, 1929.
61. "Shealy Is Speaker at Chicken Banquet," *Gaffney Ledger*, December 13, 1928; "Gaffney Musicians Ellenboro Visitors," *Gaffney Ledger*, January 31, 1929; *Gaffney Ledger*, February 28, 1929; *Gaffney Ledger*, May 28, 1929; "String Band Concert at Elm Street School," *Gaffney Ledger*, June 13, 1929; *Gaffney Ledger*, June 15, 1929; "Music and Dancing for Friday Evening," *Gaffney Ledger*, August 22, 1929; "Martin's Melody Boys to Present Program," *Gaffney Ledger*, October 8, 1929; "Mrs. Joel Atkin to Give Program," *Gaffney Ledger*, November 2, 1929; "Dobbins to Conduct Tent Meeting Here," *Gaffney Ledger*, April 10, 1930; "McKown's Mountain Session Is Closed," *Gaffney Ledger*, May 1, 1930; "Melody Boys Play at Dobbins Meeting," *Gaffney Ledger*, June 10, 1930; *Gaffney Ledger*, December 18, 1930; *Gaffney Ledger*, January 6, 1931; *Gaffney Ledger*, May 26, 1931; *Gaffney Ledger*, October 31, 1931; *Greenville News*, November 6, 1931.
62. *Gaffney Ledger*, January 1, 1929; "Hit Made Over Radio by Gaffney Musicians," *Gaffney Ledger*, January 5, 1929; "Anniversary Dinner Given D.J. Wilson," *Gaffney Ledger*, November 1, 1930.
63. *Gaffney Ledger*, January 8, 1929; "Gaffney Musicians Score Second Hit Over Radio; Third Engagement Made," *Gaffney Ledger*, January 12, 1929; "Third Program Given by Local Musicians," *Gaffney Ledger*, February 2, 1929; *Gaffney Ledger*, February 19, 1929.
64. "Martin Musicians to Broadcast Over WSPA," *Gaffney Ledger*, February 25, 1930; "Invite Melody Boys to Broadcast Again," *Gaffney Ledger*, February 27, 1930; *Gaffney Ledger*, November 26, 1931.
65. "Band Concert at Harris Tonight," *Charlotte News*, June 15, 1929.
66. "Old Fiddlers' Meeting," *Gaffney Ledger*, November 7, 1929; "Fiddlers Convention to Be Held Jan. 25th," *Gaffney Ledger*, January 11, 1930; "Old Fiddlers Convention," *Gaffney Ledger*, October 9, 1930; *Gaffney Ledger*, November 29, 1930; "Fiddlers Convention Here on Friday Night," *Gaffney Ledger*, June 16, 1931.
67. "Record By Martin's Melody Boys Selling," *Gaffney Ledger*, July 11, 1929.
68. *Gaffney Ledger*, March 9, 1926; Tony Russell, *Country Music Records: A Discography, 1921–1942* (New York: Oxford University Press, 2004); Guthrie T. Meade, Jr., et al., *Country Music Sources* (Chapel Hill: University of North Carolina Press, 2002), pp. 205, 246, 866–7.
69. "Martin's Melody Boys to Present Program," *Gaffney Ledger*, October 8, 1929.
70. Find A Grave.
71. Draft Record; April 3, 1930, Census.
72. Wikipedia.
73. "Wenonah Council Has Delightful Meeting," *Gaffney Ledger*, December 14, 1929.

Notes—Chapter Four

74. "New Pleasant School Presentation Scene," *Gaffney Ledger*, September 2, 1933.
75. *Gaffney Ledger*, October 26, 1981; Find A Grave.
76. April 30, 1930, Census; Find A Grave.
77. "New Pleasant School Presentation Scene," *Gaffney Ledger*, September 2, 1933.
78. Find A Grave; *Pensacola News Journal*, October 27, 1992.
79. *Gaffney Ledger*, June 25, 1931; *Gaffney Ledger*, July 16, 1931; "Home Coming for Red Men Enjoyed," *Gaffney Ledger*, November 14, 1931; *Gaffney Ledger*, November 26, 1931; "Home Coming for Cherry Woodmen," *Gaffney Ledger*, November 28, 1931; "Open Meet Declared a Genuine Success," *Gaffney Ledger*, July 28, 1932; *Gaffney Ledger*, October 25, 1932; *Gaffney Ledger*, November 1, 1932; "Cherry Camp Organized Thirty-Three Years Ago," *Gaffney Ledger*, March 25, 1933; "Woodmen Meeting Is an Enjoyable Affair," *Gaffney Ledger*, May 27, 1933; *Gaffney Ledger*, September 23, 1933; *Gaffney Ledger*, October 3, 1933; *Gaffney Ledger*, December 3, 1933; *Gaffney Ledger*, January 16, 1934; *Gaffney Ledger*, January 25, 1934; "Modoc Tribe Notes," *Gaffney Ledger*, February 1, 1934; *Gaffney Ledger*, March 22, 1934; "Martin On Job," *Gaffney Ledger*, August 4, 1934; *Gaffney Ledger*, September 29, 1934; *Gaffney Ledger*, October 27, 1934; *Gaffney Ledger*, November 15, 1934; *Gaffney Ledger*, January 5, 1935; *Gaffney Ledger*, April 27, 1935; *Gaffney Ledger*, June 8, 1935; *Gaffney Ledger*, April 17, 1937; *Gaffney Ledger*, December 10, 17, 1938.
80. *Gaffney Ledger*, December 10, 17, 1938.
81. "Convention Set in Gaffney for Order Red Men," *Greenville News*, April 12, 1940; *Gaffney Ledger*, November 9, 1946; "News in Brief Woodmen-Red Men," *Gaffney Ledger*, February 15, 1947.
82. Find A Grave.
83. Death Record.
84. April 16, 1930, Census; April 3, 1940, Census.
85. Ancestry Family Tree.
86. "King D. Garner Taken by Death; Rites Set Today," *Gaffney Ledger*, March 29, 1958.
87. *Gaffney Ledger*, January 9, 1932; "Holly Grove Summer School Ends Friday," *Gaffney Ledger*, September 19, 1929; *Gaffney Ledger*, February 28, 1931.
88. "Anniversary Dinner Given D.J. Wilson," *Gaffney Ledger*, November 1, 1930.
89. *Gaffney Ledger*, April 20, 1929; *Gaffney Ledger*, May 4, 1929; *Gaffney Ledger*, August 29, 1929; *Gaffney Ledger*, April 3, 1930; "Happenings Around Star Farm Section," *Gaffney Ledger*, August 2, 1930.
90. Death Record; September 12, 1918, Draft Registration.
91. *Gaffney Ledger*, September 20, 1923; "Musicale at Gallman Home Enjoyed Event," *Gaffney Ledger*, October 10, 1931.
92. Ancestry Family Tree.
93. "Picnic Ends Session at Star Farm School," *Gaffney Ledger*, April 11, 1929; "Commencement Held at Star Farm School," *Gaffney Ledger*, April 19, 1930.
94. *Gaffney Ledger*, April 14, 1928.
95. "Auxiliary Sponsor Party at Theatre," *Greenville News*, December 19, 1930.
96. "To Play for Supper," *Gaffney Ledger*, November 3, 1934.
97. "Concert at Macedonia," *Gaffney Ledger*, March 28, 1935.
98. "2 Rural Routes' Patrons Picnic," *Gaffney Ledger*, August 29, 1931.
99. *Gaffney Ledger*, July 27, 1935.
100. *Gaffney Ledger*, December 5, 1935.
101. "Music School Opened at Thickety Mountain," *Gaffney Ledger*, January 30, 1936.
102. *Gaffney Ledger*, January 9, 1936.
103. *Gaffney Ledger*, March 7, 1936.
104. *Gaffney Ledger*, May 26, 1936.
105. "Musical Entertainment," *Gaffney Ledger*, November 11, 1937.
106. "Honor Mrs. Fred Peek with Birthday Party," *Gaffney Ledger*, February 17, 1940.
107. "Whelchel Family Reunion Planned," *Gaffney Ledger*, August 6, 1940.
108. "Special Music," *Gaffney Ledger*, August 7, 1943.

Notes—Chapter Five

109. "Speer Addresses Local Woodmen at Home-Coming," *Gaffney Ledger*, November 9, 1943.
110. Ancestry Family Tree.
111. Social Security Death Index.
112. *Gaffney Ledger*, January 12, 2004.
113. "More Than Just Meals," *Gaffney Ledger*, May 18, 1984.
114. 1958 Gaffney City Directory, p. 223; *Gaffney Ledger*, October 4, 2006.
115. *Gaffney Ledger*, March 30, 1944; *Gaffney Ledger*, February 6, 1945.
116. "Blaze Destroys Frame Dwelling on 13th Street," *Gaffney Ledger*, September 22, 1956.
117. *Spartanburg Herald and Journal*, June 3, 1960; *Gaffney Ledger*, June 4, 1960; December 6, 2006, interview, George Hutchins.

Chapter Five

1. 1908–1996, North Carolina Death Collection; January 28, 1920, Census; Ancestry.
2. Michael Hofer, *History of Banjos*, 2001, http://banjobasics.julieferris.com/BANJOPLAYERS/2.html; Folkstreams.net/content, p. 125.
3. http://www.rfci.net/wdfloyd/cemb11.html; http://www.gencircles.com/users/latham-hendrix/1/data/193; http://www.gencircles.com/users/latham-hendrix/1/data/181; Cleveland County Marriage Records; May 1910 Census; January 7–8, 1920, Census; North Carolina Death Index; Social Security Death Index; Ancestry; "Mrs. Matt Brooks Dies at Bostic," *Shelby Star*, July 5, 1945; Roy Brooks, "Madison Monroe Brooks," *Heritage of Rutherford County North Carolina, Volume I* (Winston-Salem, NC: Hunter, 1984), p. 133; September 12, 1918, Draft Registration.
4. 1910 Census; January 7–8, 1920, Census; Ancestry; http://www.gencircles.com/users/latham-hendrix/1/data/21; Cleveland County Register Of Deeds, Birth Records, 8/323.
5. Cleveland County Birth Records, 9/769, p. 770; April 5, 1930, Census; Ancestry.
6. Michael Hofer, *History of Banjos*, 2001, http://banjobasics.julieferris.com/BANJOPLAYERS/2.html; Folkstreams.net/content, p. 125.
7. http://www.rfci.net/wdfloyd/cemb11.html; Cleveland County Vital Statistics, 18/313; "Four Violent Deaths in County During Weekend—Three in Auto Wrecks," *Shelby Star*, October 21, 1935.
8. November 15, 1980, from Larry Hammett.
9. Earl Scruggs, *Earl Scruggs and the 5-String Banjo* (Milwaukee: Hal Leonard, 2005), pp. 9, 158–9.
10. "Smith Hammett Dedication Tribute Set Thursday Night," *Spartanburg Herald-Journal*, November 12, 1980; "Banjo 'Legend' Honored," *Shelby Daily Star*, November 20, 1980; "3-fingered picker to be honored here," *Shelby Star*, November 20, 1980, from Larry Hammett.
11. January 6, 2007, email, Johnny L. Williams; Ancestry.com/cgi-bin/igm.cgi?op=GET&db=bigwills&id=I37918; July 1870 Census; June 9, 1880, Census; June 4, 1900, Census; June 21, 1900, Census; Ancestry.
12. "Smith Hammett Dedication Tribute Set Thursday Night," *Spartanburg Herald-Journal*, November 12, 1980; "Banjo 'Legend' Honored," *Shelby Daily Star*, November 20, 1980; "3-fingered picker to be honored here," *Shelby Star*, November 20, 1980, from Larry Hammett.
13. January 2007, interview, Larry Hammett.
14. March 13, 2007, interview, Jesse Hammett.
15. North Carolina Birth Index; February 10–11, 1920, Census; Ancestry; January 2007, interview, Larry Hammett; Delayed Birth, 8/137; "Martin Hammett Died Oct. 6, 2006," *Shelby Star*; Township No 7, 4/1013, 1818; http://awtc.http://www.http://www.ancestry.com.com/cgi-bin/igm.cgi?op=GET&db=bigwills&id=I37918; "Smith Hammett Dedication Tribute Set Thursday Night," *Spartanburg Herald-Journal*, November 12, 1980; "Banjo 'Legend' Honored," *Shelby Daily Star*, November 20, 1980; "3-fingered picker to be honored here,"

Notes—Chapter Five

Shelby Star, November 20, 1980, from Larry Hammett.
16. For example: *Gaffney Ledger*, March 4, 1910.
17. September 8, 1870, Census.
18. Find A Grave.
19. April 20, 1910, Census.
20. *Greenville News*, May 30, 1949; Find A Grave.
21. January 7, 1920, Census.
22. June 12, 1900, Census; April 20, 1910, Census.
23. *Gaffney Ledger*, March 4, 1910; *Gaffney Ledger*, February 26, 1918; January 7, 1920, Census.
24. *Gaffney Ledger*, October 14, 1924; May 5, 1930, Census; April 25, 1940, Census; "L. D. McCraw Honored," *Gaffney Ledger*, May 2, 1946.
25. *Gaffney Ledger*, March 4, 1910.
26. Find A Grave.
27. *Gaffney Ledger*, February 26, 1918.
28. Death Certificate; Ancestry Family Tree.
29. Strangely, both these pieces have roots in the 18th century. According to http://tunearch.org/wiki/Annotation:Guard_House_(The), "Guard House" is an English/Scottish tune, and "Julia Grover" an Irish stage actress (https://www.encyclopedia.com/women/encyclopedias-almanacs-transcripts-and-maps/glover-julia-1779-1850). "Ye Old Fiddlers Tomorrow Night," *Gaffney Ledger*, February 28, 1918.
30. *Gaffney Ledger*, February 14, 1908.
31. "Fiddlers' Convention Is Enjoyed by Many People," *Gaffney Ledger*, June 22, 1920; "Eight Piece Orchestra to Play at Convention," *Gaffney Ledger*, May 7, 1921.
32. *Gaffney Ledger*, June 5, 1930.
33. *Gaffney Ledger*, January 14, 1930.
34. "L.D. McCraw Is Taken by Death," *Gaffney Ledger*, January 26, 1950.
35. June 5, 1917, Draft registration.
36. March 13, 2007, interview, Jesse Hammett.
37. February 10–11, 1920, Census; Ancestry.
38. *Gaffney Ledger*, June 8, 1929.
39. 1938–1946, World War II Army Enlistment Records; Social Security Death Index; 1908–1996, North Carolina Death Collection; Ancestry.
40. "Smith Hammett Dedication Tribute Set Thursday Night," *Spartanburg Herald-Journal*, November 12, 1980; "Banjo 'Legend' Honored," *Shelby Daily Star*, November 20, 1980; "3-fingered picker to be honored here," *Shelby Star*, November 20, 1980, from Larry Hammett.
41. 1979–82, North Carolina Department of Health, North Carolina Deaths; June 1, 1900, April 20, 1910, Census; January 6–7, 1920, Census; Ancestry.
42. September 12, 1918, Draft registration; April 11, 1930, Census; Ancestry.
43. April 11, 1930, Census; Ancestry.
44. June 11, 1900, Census; April 19, 1910, Census; January 1920 Census; May 2, 1930, Census; September 12, 1918, Draft Registration; North Carolina Birth Index, 12/763; North Carolina Death Collection; ca. 1775–2006, United States Veterans Gravesites; Social Security Death Index; 1908–1996, North Carolina Death Collection; Ancestry.
45. Joe DePriest, "Country music roots reach into Cleveland, Rutherford," *Shelby Star*, October 25, 1985, from Larry Hammett.
46. April 27, 1910, Census; April 10, 1930, Census; North Carolina Birth Index, 26/200; United States Veterans Gravesites; Social Security Death Index; North Carolina Birth Index, 36b/421; Ancestry.
47. Joe DePriest, "Country music roots reach into Cleveland, Rutherford," *Shelby Star*, October 25, 1985, from Larry Hammett.
48. June 30, 1942, Draft Registration.
49. Cleveland County, BC026 66001, 20/875; Shelby, Cleveland County, 22/331; Shelby, Cleveland County, 33/1, 42; June 11, 2007, phone interview, Patricia Camp; Joe DePriest, "Country music roots reach into Cleveland, Rutherford," *Shelby Star*, October 25, 1985, from Larry Hammett; 1908–1996, Cleveland County, NC, Death Collection; 1930 Census; Social Security Death Index; Ancestry.
50. January 14, 2007, phone interview, Hammett, Ronald.
51. North Carolina Death Collection; Ancestry; March 13, 2007, interview, Jesse Hammett.

Notes—Chapter Six

52. Birth index, Rutherford County, NC, 1/635; March 13, 2007, interview, Jesse Hammett; April 2, 2007, phone interview, Tommy Ramsey.
53. Delayed Birth, 8/138; January 2007, interview, Larry Hammett; March 13, 2007, interview, Jesse Hammett.
54. January 12, 2007, phone interview, Jesse Hammett; Delayed Birth, 6/279; Social Security Death Index; Ancestry.
55. *Shelby Star*, April 14, 2003.
56. Cleveland County, 7/405.
57. June 1880 Census; June 5, 1900, Census; April 21, 1910, Census; January 10, 1920, Census; September 12, 1918, Draft Registration; Ancestry.
58. Earl Scruggs, *Earl Scruggs and the 5-String Banjo* (Milwaukee: Hal Leonard, 2005), pp. 9, 158–9; Tony Trischka and Bela Fleck, "Earl Scruggs," *Banjo NewsLetter*, November 2006, p. 15; Tony Trischka and Pete Wernick, *Masters of the 5-String Banjo* (New York: Oak Publications, 1988), p. 16.
59. February 21, 2007, email, James Bollman.
60. April 20, 2007, interview, Doris Hammett Brady.
61. *Gaffney Ledger*, January 14, 1930; *Gaffney Ledger*, March 8, 1930.
62. http://awtc.http://www.http://www.ancestry.com/cgi-bin/igm.cgi?op=GET&db=bigwills&id=I37918.
63. "Smith Hammett Shot to Death," *Gaffney Ledger*, February 4, 1930; Mrs. B. B. Godfrey, "Huge Crowd Attends Slain Man's Funeral," *Gaffney Ledger*, February 6, 1930.

Chapter Six

1. Jim Mills, *Gibson Mastertone* (Anaheim Hills, CA: Centerstream, 2009), pp. 48–59.
2. Various interviews, Hellen Hendley Permar.
3. *Messenger and Intelligencer*, December 21, 1911.
4. NCPedia.
5. https://www.lostcolleges.com/rutherford-college.
6. *Charlotte Observer*, December 15, 1913; *Salisbury Evening Post*, February 26, 1914; *News-Herald*, April 2, 1914; *Salisbury Evening Post*, April 14, 1914.
7. *The Charlotte Observer*, January 29, 1912; *The Charlotte Observer*, February 5, 1912; *The Charlotte Observer*, March 18, 1912.
8. *The Charlotte Observer*, March 20, 1911; *Hickory Democrat*, March 23, 1911; *The Charlotte Observer*, April 3, 1911.
9. *Charlotte News*, March 26, 1906.
10. *News and Observer*, September 16, 1914; *Wilmington Morning Star*, September 16, 1914.
11. *Durham Recorder*, June 9, 1910; *Messenger and Intelligencer*, September 5, 1910; *Messenger and Intelligencer*, May 29, 1911; *News and Observer*, September 23, 1910.
12. *News and Observer*, March 14, 1911; *Messenger and Intelligencer*, April 10, 1911; *Raleigh Times*, April 17, 1911; *Raleigh Times*, June 15, 1911; *Raleigh Times*, June 19, 1911; *Asheville Gazette-News*, July 20, 1911; *Asheville Gazette-News*, July 22, 1911.
13. "Rutherford College Club," *Trinity Chronicle*, October 14, 1914.
14. 1915 Trinity College Yearbook, *The Chanticleer*, pp. 85, 99, 177, 165.
15. "Trinity Ball Team Now Hard at Work," *Trinity Chronicle*, September 23, 1914.
16. "Trinity Overwhelms Ancient Rivals," *Trinity Chronicle*, April 28, 1915; "Trinity Defeats Wake Forest," *Trinity Chronicle*, April 14, 1915; "Second of Series Is Won by Wake Forest," *Trinity Chronicle*, April 21, 1915.
17. "Glee Club Returns From Annual Tour," *Trinity Chronicle*, December 2, 1914; "Glee Club Recital Is Successful Event," *Trinity Chronicle*, November 25, 1914.
18. "Hendley's Advocation Outdistances His Vocation," *Charlotte Observer*, December 11, 1932.
19. https://www.wm.edu/sites/wmcar/research/hopewellarch/history/index.php.
20. June 5, 1917, Draft Registration.
21. "Hendley's Advocation Outdistances His Vocation," *Charlotte Observer*, December 11, 1932.
22. *Messenger and Intelligencer*, April 25, 1918.

Notes—Chapter Six

23. *Messenger and Intelligencer,* August 30, 1917.
24. *Messenger and Intelligencer,* December 19, 1918; https://www.wm.edu/sites/wmcar/research/hopewellarch/history/index.php.
25. "Hendley's Advocation Outdistances His Vocation," *Charlotte Observer,* December 11, 1932.
26. *Messenger and Intelligencer,* September 2, 1920; *Messenger and Intelligencer,* September 23, 1920; *Messenger and Intelligencer,* February 17, 1921.
27. *Messenger and Intelligencer,* April 14, 1921; *Oxford Public Ledger,* July 22, 1921; *Messenger and Intelligencer,* November 24, 1921; *Messenger and Intelligencer,* November 30, 1922; *Messenger and Intelligencer,* June 7, 1923; *Messenger and Intelligencer,* September 20, 1923.
28. *Messenger and Intelligencer,* April 26, 1923.
29. *Albemarle Press,* May 24, 1923.
1. *Albemarle Press,* October 8, 1925.
2. *Albemarle Press,* November 29, 1923.
3. "Hendley's Advocation Outdistances His Vocation," *Charlotte Observer,* December 11, 1932.
4. 1900 census.
5. 1910 census.
6. Draft Registration.
7. *Rowan Record,* February 19, 1918.
8. Marriage Record; *Rowan Record,* February 19, 1918.
9. Death Certificate; *Salisbury Evening Post,* November 15, 1918.
10. Marriage Record.
11. Find A Grave.
12. 1910 Census; 1920 Census; Death Certificate.
13. Death Certificate.
14. 1910 Census.
15. *Enterprise,* June 21, 1917; 1920 Census; Passenger List, U.S. Army.
16. *Enterprise,* August 30, 1917.
17. *Stanly News,* September 3, 1920.
18. *Stanly News-Herald,* January 4, 1921; *Stanly News,* March 12, 1920.
19. *Albemarle Press,* July 30, 1925.
20. "Hendley's Advocation Outdistances His Vocation," *Charlotte Observer,* December 11, 1932.
21. *Albemarle Press,* May 21, 1925; *Albemarle Press,* August 20, 1925.

22. Draft Registration; *Charlotte Observer,* January 27, 1946; Find A Grave; Death Certificate.
23. 1930 Census; 1940 Census.
24. Death Certificate.
25. Death Certificate.
26. *Enterprise,* October 31, 1912; Marriage Certificate.
27. *Charlotte Observer,* June 7, 1971; Find A Grave.
28. *Charlotte Observer,* February 3, 2004; Draft Registration.
29. Draft Registration.
30. Draft Registration.
31. *Charlotte Observer,* September 27, 1925; Draft Registration.
32. *Albemarle Press,* May 24, 1923.
33. *Charlotte Observer,* September 27, 1925.
34. *Charlotte News,* June 23, 1935.
35. *Charlotte News,* June 22, 1937.
36. *Charlotte Observer,* September 17, 1968; Death Certificate.
37. *Charlotte Observer,* September 25, 1984.
38. *Charlotte Observer,* February 3, 2004.
39. *Charlotte Observer,* May 5, 2007.
40. *Charlotte Observer,* March 27, 2012.
41. *Albemarle Press,* December 17, 1925.
42. *Albemarle Press,* December 31, 1925.
43. *Charlotte News,* February 26, 1926; *Charlotte News,* March 5, 1926.
44. Find A Grave.
45. Find A Grave; Marriage Records.
46. Find A Grave.
47. 1910 Census; 1920 Census; Draft Registration.
48. 1930 Census.
49. 1940 Census.
50. May 23, 2020, Ancestry message, Marc Howell.
51. Death Certificate.
52. *News and Observer,* April 27, 1989.
53. Find A Grave.
54. "Hendley's Advocation Outdistances His Vocation," *Charlotte Observer,* December 11, 1932.
55. *Enterprise,* October 25, 1906; *Charlotte Observer,* September 10, 1923.
56. Howell Family Tree, Ancestry.

Notes—Chapter Seven

57. Death Certificate.
58. 1900 Census.
59. 1910 Census.
60. Draft Card.
61. Order to Report; Application for Military Headstone.
62. Death Certificate; 1920 Census; 1930 Census.
63. Find A Grave.
64. 1940 Census.
65. 1930 Census.
66. Death Certificate.
67. Draft Registration; Social Security Death Index.
68. *Statesville Record and Landmark*, April 22, 1929.
69. 1930 Census.
70. Draft Registration.
71. *Statesville Record*, October 28, 1950; *The Daily Tar Heel*, November 6, 1952.
72. *Statesville Record and Landmark*, December 13, 1961.
73. Find A Grave.
74. 1900 Census.
75. 1940 Census.
76. *Enterprise*, October 12, 1911; *Enterprise*, June 14, 1917; Marriage License.
77. *Albemarle Press*, January 29, 1925; Marriage Certificate; Find A Grave.
78. *Charlotte Observer*, January 25, 2000; Social Security Applications Index.
79. Della Coulter and John Rumble, "The Piedmont Tradition" and "Charlotte Country Music Story: A Sixty-Year Tradition," *The Charlotte Country Music Story* (Charlotte: NCAC Spirit Square Arts Center, 1985), p. 7; WBT website.
80. "Gaffney Musicians to Play on WBT Again," *Charlotte Observer*, January 9, 1929.
81. Various, *Charlotte Observer*.
82. *Charlotte Observer*, weekly radio listings for 1929.
83. *Charlotte Observer*, December 23, 1928–March 9, 1929.
84. Barry Mazor, *Ralph Peer and the Making of Popular Roots Music* (Chicago: Chicago Review Press, 2015), pp. 133, 152.
85. "Stanly County Men to Record for Victor Co," *Charlotte Observer*, October 9, 1930.
86. *Charlotte Observer*, March 7, 21, 1931.
87. "Entertainment Tonight at School in Albemarle," *Charlotte News*, March 7, 1930; *Asheville Citizen-Times*, April 21, 1931; *Miami News*, June 26, 1931; *Charlotte News*, July 10, 1931; *Charlotte Observer*, September 16, 1931; "Fiddlers Convention at Mathews Friday," *Charlotte News*, February 10, 1932; *Charlotte News*, April 4, 1932; *Charlotte News*, May 5, 1933; *Charlotte Observer*, May 12, 1935; *Charlotte Observer*, May 19, 1935.
88. *Statesville Record*, November 12, 1931.
89. *Times Union*, October 23, 1933; *St. Louis Post-Dispatch*, October 23, 1933; *Akron Beacon Journal*, October 23, 1933.

Chapter Seven

1. *Charlotte Observer*.
2. *News and Observer*, October 29, 1933; *Asheville Citizen-Times*, November 23, 1933.
3. *Charlotte Observer*, February 6, 1934.
4. "Crazy Water Crystals Show Colossal Gain," *Charlotte Observer*, May 20, 1934.
5. Della Coulter and John Rumble, "The Piedmont Tradition" and "Charlotte Country Music Story: A Sixty-Year Tradition," *The Charlotte Country Music Story* (Charlotte: NCAC Spirit Square Arts Center, 1985), p. 10.
6. *Courier-Journal*, March 28, 1936; *Asheville Citizen-Times*, August 22, 1934.
7. Pat J. Ahrens, "Crazy Water Crystals and Its Union With Pioneer String Band Performers," *Bluegrass Unlimited*, August 2001, pp. 56–60; Della Coulter and John Rumble, "The Piedmont Tradition" and "Charlotte Country Music Story: A Sixty-Year Tradition," *The Charlotte Country Music Story* (Charlotte: NCAC Spirit Square Arts Center, 1985), p. 7; Pamela Grundy, "We Always Tried to Be Good People: Respectability, Crazy Water Crystals, and Hillbilly Music on the Air, 1933–1935," *The Journal of American History*, March 1995, pp. 1591–1620.
8. *Asheville Citizen-Times*, April 24, 1934; *Asheville Citizen-Times*, May 5, 1935.

Notes—Chapter Seven

9. Della Coulter and John Rumble, "The Piedmont Tradition" and "Charlotte Country Music Story: A Sixty-Year Tradition," *The Charlotte Country Music Story* (Charlotte: NCAC Spirit Square Arts Center, 1985), pp. 4–5.
10. https://www.imdb.com/name/nm0366940/bio?ref_=nm_ov_bio_sm.
11. Draft Registration.
12. Find A Grave.
13. "Tennessee Rambler Cecil Campbell Dies," *Charlotte Observer*, June 20, 1989.
14. 1930 Census.
15. Della Coulter and John Rumble, "The Piedmont Tradition" and "Charlotte Country Music Story: A Sixty-Year Tradition," *The Charlotte Country Music Story* (Charlotte: NCAC Spirit Square Arts Center, 1985), p. 30.
16. Ivan M. Tribe and Barry McCloud, ed., "Tennessee Ramblers," *Definitive Country: The Ultimate Encyclopedia of Country Music and Its Performers* (New York: Berkley, 1995), pp. 797–798.
17. John Bush, https://itunes.apple.com/us/artist/cecil-campbell-his-tennessee-ramblers/id269255920.
18. *Charlotte News, Charlotte Observer*, various, starting January 27, 1934.
19. For example, *Charlotte Observer*, May 6, 1934; *Charlotte News*, June 9, 1934.
20. For example, *Charlotte Observer*, August 29, 1934; *Statesville Daily Record*, September 18, 1934; *Charlotte News*, October 2, 1934; *Robesonian*, October 4, 1934; *Burlington Times-News*, October 23, 1934.
21. Tony Russell, *Country Music Records: A Discography, 1921–1942* (New York: Oxford University Press, 2004), p. 407.
22. http://www.hillbilly-music.com/groups/story/index.php?groupid=10921.
23. Tony Russell, *Country Music Records: A Discography, 1921–1942* (New York: Oxford University Press, 2004), p. 407.
24. Find A Grave.
25. Draft Registration; 1920 Census; 1930 Census; 1940 Census.
26. Find A Grave.
27. *Charlotte Observer*, August 25, 1977; Draft Registration; Find A Grave; 1945 City Directory.
28. Draft Registration; 1940 Census; *Charlotte Observer*.
29. Draft Registration; Find A Grave.
30. Draft Registration; Social Security Death Index.
31. Draft Registration; Social Security Death Index.
32. 1940 Census; Draft Registration.
33. Draft Registration; Virginia Divorce Decree.
34. *Times-Dispatch*, December 20, 1940; *Times-Dispatch*, December 26, 1940.
35. *Newport News Daily Press*, February 19, 1941; *Bee*, May 1, 1941; "Entertainers to Appear at the Natural Chimneys," *Staunton News-Leader*, June 29, 1941.
36. *Times-Dispatch*, February 27, 1942.
37. *Salisbury Daily Times*, April 16, 1942; *News*, May 15, 1942.
38. Enlistment Records.
39. Draft Registration; https://petermoruzzi.com/2011/05/22/nucky-and-skinnys-atlantic-city/.
40. IMDB.Com.
41. https://www.youtube.com/watch?v=gsY4sHeEVKw; https://www.youtube.com/watch?v=SWAVd2CYU5I; https://www.youtube.com/watch?v=fnAl2mUDalc.
42. http://www.45worlds.com/78rpm/record/nc114370us.
43. https://books.google.com/books?id=RAEEAAAAMBAJ&pg=PA33&lpg=PA33&dq=broome+bros%2Bcrystal+records&source=bl&ots=vU8_YogCK0&sig=ACfU3U0GUPh2oxZT8KEg4IXDIvsJS5cU-w&hl=en&sa=X&ved=2ahUKEwi3n5-psdfpAhVPSN8KHb54Dz0Q6AEwA3oECAYQAQ#v=onepage&q=broome%20bros%2Bcrystal%20records&f=false.
44. http://www.45worlds.com/78rpm/record/nc214265us.
45. *Desert Sun*, November 20, 1993.
46. *Charlotte Observer*, December 2, 1993.
47. Draft Registration.
48. North Carolina Death Index.
49. 1900 Census; 1910 Census.
50. 1910 Census; Draft Registration.

Notes—Chapter Seven

51. Veterans Affairs Death File.
52. Marriage Certificate.
53. 1930 Census; Draft Registration; 1951, 1956, 1959 Kannapolis City Directories.
54. *Concord Daily Tribune*, January 1, 1916.
55. Find A Grave.
56. 1900 Census; 1910 Census.
57. Find A Grave; Marriage Certificate; Marriage Record.
58. Draft Registration.
59. 1920 Census; 1930 Census; 1940 Census; 1950–1, 1953, 1956–7 Kannapolis City Directory.
60. Draft Registration; Find A Grave; 1930 Census.
61. *Charlotte Observer*, March 22, 1961; Draft Registration; Find A Grave.
62. *Concord Daily Tribune*, May 18, 1916; Find A Grave.
63. *Concord Times*, August 26, 1912.
64. *Charlotte Observer*, April 7, 1929; *Charlotte News*, April 13, 1929; *Charlotte News*, May 11, 1929; *Charlotte News*, May 18, 1929; "WOW Band Signs Radio Contract," *Charlotte News*, June 21, 1929; *Charlotte Observer*, February 24, 1929; *Charlotte Observer*, April 20, 1929; "Charlotte Radio Station Starts Charity Drive," *Charlotte Observer*, November 3, 1929.
65. Find A Grave; Draft Registration.
66. Find A Grave.
67. 1910 Census.
68. 1920 Census.
69. Find A Grave; 1930 Census.
70. 1950, 1953, 1956 Kannapolis City Directory.
71. *Charlotte Observer*, July 12, 1989; North Carolina Death Index.
72. Find A Grave; North Carolina Death Index; Death Certificate.
73. North Carolina Death Index.
74. 1910 Census; 1920 Census; 1940 Census; *Charlotte News*, June 8, 1929.
75. Death Certificate.
76. Find A Grave.
77. 2005 interview.
78. Headstone Application.
79. Marriage Certificate.
80. Draft Registration.
81. 2005 interview.
82. October 16, 1940, Draft Card; *Charlotte Observer*, August 13, 1986.
83. Find A Grave.
84. 1920 Census; 1930 Census; 1940 Census.
85. Draft Card; 1930 Census; Find A Grave.
86. Find A Grave.
87. Enlistment Records.
88. Draft Card; *Charlotte Observer*, November 21, 2005; 1920 Census; 1930 Census; 1940 Census.
89. Draft Registration.
90. 1920 Census; 1940 Census; Draft Registration; Enlistment Records.
91. Draft Registration; *Charlotte Observer*, March 7, 2007.
92. 1930 Census; 1940 Census; Draft Registration; *Charlotte Observer*, March 7, 2007; *Charlotte News*, November 24, 1940.
93. 2005 interview.
94. Death Certificate.
95. *Charlotte Observer*, March 28, 1932; *Charlotte Observer*, March 24, 1932.
96. *Charlotte Observer*, December 18, 1930; *Charlotte Observer*, February 21, 1931.
97. *Charlotte Observer*, March 28, 1932; *Charlotte Observer*, March 24, 1932.
98. *Charlotte Observer*, March 28, 1932; *Charlotte Observer*, March 24, 1932.
99. *Charlotte Observer*, December 11, 1928.
100. "Wayside Entertainers at Rowland Fri. Eve," *Robesonian*, February 9, 1931; "Waysiders Give Fine Entertainment at Flora MacDonald," *Robesonian*, November 26, 1931; *Statesville Record and Landmark*, November 4, 1932; *Charlotte News*, July 11, 1933; "Old Wayside Program Here Friday Evening," *Gaffney Ledger*, March 15, 1934.
101. "Ten Amateurs on Strand Program," *Charlotte News*, February 7, 1926; "Music Contest at York Is Event of Much Interest," *Greenville News*, October 22, 1929; "Old Time Music Meet Pleasing," *Charlotte Observer*, November 24, 1929; *Greenville News*, November 21, 1929.
102. "Waysiders Give Fine Entertainment at Flora MacDonald," *Robesonian*, November 26, 1931.
103. Find A Grave.
104. Find A Grave.
105. *Charlotte News*, October 19, 1932.

Notes—Chapter Eight

106. Della Coulter and John Rumble, "The Piedmont Tradition" and "Charlotte Country Music Story: A Sixty-Year Tradition," *The Charlotte Country Music Story* (Charlotte: NCAC Spirit Square Arts Center, 1985), pp. 26–7; Dick Spottswood, "Happy Birthday, Wade!," *Bluegrass Unlimited*, January 1998, pp. 20, 53–55; Dick Spottswood, *Banjo on the Mountain: Wade Mainer's First Hundred Years* (Jackson: University Press of Mississippi, 2010); Wesley Wallace, "Development of Broadcasting in North Carolina, 1922–1928" (Dissertation, University of North Carolina-Chapel Hill, 1962), summary available online: http://www.unc.edu/~bsemonch/radio.html.

107. *Asheville Citizen Times*, September 12, 1934; *Asheville Citizen-Times*, September 17, 1934; *Asheville Citizen-Times*, October 4, 1934; *Charlotte Observer*, October 7, 21, 28, 1934; *Asheville Citizen-Times*, October 7, 1934; *Asheville Citizen Times*, December 7, 1934; *Charlotte Observer*, October 21, 1934.

108. *Charlotte News*, February 3, 1935.

109. *Asheville Citizen-Times*, April 12, 19, 1930; *Asheville Citizen-Times*, August 5, 1932.

110. Pat Ahrens, *The Legacy of Two Legends: Snuffy Jenkins and Pappy Sherrill* (self-pub., 2013).

111. *News and Observer*, February 8, 1930; *News and Observer*, June 15, 1930.

112. Della Coulter and John Rumble, "The Piedmont Tradition" and "Charlotte Country Music Story: A Sixty-Year Tradition," *The Charlotte Country Music Story* (Charlotte: NCAC Spirit Square Arts Center, 1985), pp. 7, 21–22; *Crazy Barn Dance and Crazy Bands* (Charlotte: WBT, ca. 1934), from Rachel Wiles.

113. *Charlotte Observer*, December 16, 1934.

114. "Letter to National Sunshine Club from Blanche Rivenbark, Marion, SC," *Charlotte Observer*, August 18, 1935.

115. *Charlotte Observer*, August 20, 1935.

116. *Charlotte Observer*, August 31, 1935.

117. 1935 Charlotte, NC City Directory; "Crazy Crystals Company Is Sued by Entertainer," *Charlotte Observer*, November 26, 1935; *Charlotte News*, January 20, 1938.

118. *Charlotte News*, November 3, 1935; *Charlotte News*, March 15, 1936.

119. *Charlotte News*, May 9, 1937.

Chapter Eight

1. "Greenville Radio Station to Go on Air Next Month," *Greenville News*, April 30, 1933.

2. "Station WFBC to Celebrate Second Anniversary May 20," *Greenville News*, March 31, 1935.

3. *Greenville News*, November 10, 1935.

4. https://upstatebusinessjournal.com/events/balentine-packing-company/.

5. "New Broadcast to Start Today on Station WFBC," *Greenville News*, October 9, 1935.

6. *Towawanda News*, November 15, 1941.

7. "New Broadcast to Start Today on Station WFBC," *Greenville News*, October 9, 1935.

8. https://www.youtube.com/watch?v=As_84Cd3T6I.

9. *Kingston Daily Freeman*, March 14, 1934.

10. Death Certificate.

11. 1930 Census.

12. *Greenville News*, January 26, 1936.

13. *Crazy Barn Dance and the Crazy Bands* (Charlotte: WBT, ca. 1934).

14. "Move Two Broadcasts," *Greenville News*, January 19, 1936.

15. *Greenville News*, January 26, 1936; *Greenville News*, March 29, 1936.

16. *Greenville News*, March 1, 1936.

17. 1936 Charlotte City Directory; *Greenville News*, March 1, 1936.

18. *Courier-Journal*, August 2–3, 1936.

19. *Greenville News*, September 18, 1936.

20. *Charlotte Observer*, January 26, 1975; Death Certificate.

21. 1910 Census; 1920 Census; 1930 Census.

22. *Charlotte Observer*, January 26, 1975.

23. Draft Registration.

Notes—Chapter Eight

24. Birth Index; Social Security Death Index.
25. 1920 Census; 1930 Census; 1936 Gastonia, NC City Directory.
26. *Greenville News*, December 5, 1936.
27. Draft Registration.
28. *Greenville News*, December 3, 1971.
29. Draft Registration.
30. *Greenville News*, December 31, 1936.
31. *Greenville News*, April 23, 1937.
32. *Greenville News*, February 14, 1937; *Index-Journal*, March 7, 1937; *Greenville News*, April 11, 1937; *Greenville News*, March 7, 1937.
33. *Greenville News*, February 14, 1937.
34. *Greenville News*, April 25, 1937.
35. Draft Registration.
36. *Greenville News*, June 27, 1980.
37. Draft Registration; *Greenville News*, June 27, 1980.
38. 1920 Census
39. Find A Grave.
40. *Greenville News*, April 10, 1935; *Greenville News*, April 19, 1935; *Greenville News*, March 27, 1936.
41. Enlistment Records.
42. *Greenville News*, May 22, 1937.
43. *Greenville News*, May 30, 1937.
44. "Pigs to Leave Air for Summer Vacation," *Greenville News*, June 30, 1937.
45. *Greenville News*, March 21, 1937.
46. *Greenville News*, August 29, 1937; *Greenville News*, September 1, 1937.
47. *Greenville News*, September 5, 1937.
48. *Greenville News*, September 11, 1937; *Greenville News*, September 21, 1937; *Greenville News*, September 23, 1937; *Aiken Standard*, October 15, 1937; *Greenville News*, October 17, 1937; *Greenville News*, October 29, 1937; *Greenville News*, November 4, 1937; *Greenville News*, November 5, 1937; *Greenville News*, December 4, 1937; *Greenville News*, December 14, 1937.
49. *Greenville News*, December 16, 1937; *Greenville News*, December 20, 1937; *Greenville News*, December 21, 1937.
50. *Greenville News*, December 17, 1937.
51. *Greenville News*, January 23, 1938.
52. *Greenville News*, January 16, 1938.
53. *Greenville News*, January 30, 1938.
54. *Greenville News*, January 30, 1938; *Greenville News*, February 4, 1938; *Greenville News*, February 10, 1938; *Greenville News*, February 19, 1938; *Greenville News*, February 19, 1938; *Greenville News*, March 6, 1938; *Greenville News*, March 13, 1938; *Greenville News*, March 20, 1938; *Greenville News*, March 28, 1938; *Greenville News*, April 4, 1938; *Greenville News*, April 7, 1938; *Greenville News*, April 3, 1938; *Greenville News*, April 25, 1938; *Greenville News*, April 26, 1938; *Greenville News*, May 1, 1938; *Greenville News*, May 10, 1938; *Greenville News*, May 11, 1938; *Greenville News*, May 17, 1938; *Greenville News*, May 19, 1938; *Greenville News*, May 24, 1938; *Index-Journal*, May 19, 1938; *Greenville News*, May 27, 1938; *Greenville News*, May 29, 1938; *Greenville News*, June 5, 1938; *Index-Journal*, June 6, 1938; *Greenville News*, June 16, 1938; *Index-Journal*, June 16, 1938; *Greenville News*, June 19, 1938; *Greenville News*, June 24, 1938; *Greenville News*, June 27, 1938.
55. *Greenville News*, June 29, 1938.
56. *Index-Journal*, December 15, 1938.
57. Tony Russell, *Country Music Records: A Discography, 1921–1942* (Oxford University Press, 2004).
58. *Times and Democrat*, September 20, 1938; *Times and Democrat*, September 24, 1938; *Times and Democrat*, September 27, 1938; *Aiken Standard*, October 21, 1938; *Index-Journal*, October 23, 1938; *Greenville News*, November 4, 1938; *Times and Democrat*, November 9, 1938; *Times and Democrat*, November 15, 1938; *Aiken Standard*, November 11, 1938; *Aiken Standard*, November 23, 1938; *Times and Democrat*, November 18, 1938; *Times and Democrat*, December 6, 1938; *Aiken Standard*, December 9, 1938; *Index-Journal*, December 15, 1938; *Times and Democrat*, December 23, 1938; *Greenville News*, December 28, 1938; *Aiken Standard*, December 30, 1938; *Times and Democrat*, January 6, 1939; *Times and Democrat*, January 10, 1939; *Aiken Standard*, January 27, 1939; *Times and Democrat*, January 20, 1939; *Times and Democrat*, January 21, 1939; *Times*

Notes—Chapter Eight

and Democrat, February 10, 1939; *Times and Democrat*, February 23, 1939; *Greenville News*, March 4, 1939; *Times and Democrat*, March 21, 1939; *Times and Democrat*, April 6, 1939; *Aiken Standard*, April 5, 1939; *Times and Democrat*, April 12, 1939; *Aiken Standard*, May 5, 1939; *Aiken Standard*, May 10, 1939; *Times and Democrat*, May 5, 1939; *Times and Democrat*, May 6, 1939; *Index-Journal*, May 20, 1939; *Times and Democrat*, June 1, 1939.

59. Find A Grave.
60. *Greenville News*, September 25, 2000; *Greenville News*, November 12, 1939.
61. *Times and Democrat*, February 7, 23, 1940.
62. 1940 Census.
63. Draft Registration; 1941 Greenville, SC City Directory.
64. *Greenville News*, February 14, 1943; *Greenville News*, October 24, 1943.
65. *Index-Journal*, October 2, 1944; *Greenville News*, October 15, 1943; *Greenville News*, October 24, 1943.
66. 1954 Greenville, SC, City Directory.
67. *Greenville News*, December 5, 1971.
68. *Greenville News*, March 12, 1978.
69. *Times and Democrat*, February 7, 23, 1940.
70. Draft Registration.
71. Find A Grave; 1920 Census; 1930 Census.
72. *Gaffney Ledger*, June 13, 1935; *Charlotte Observer*, July 2, 1939.
73. Henry Gaston, "Music gives richness to our lives," *Charlotte Observer*, October 4, 2001.
74. Google.
75. *Times and Democrat*, May 18, 1940; *Aiken Standard*, June 21, 1940.
76. *Greenville News*, January 29, 1942.
77. *Index-Journal*, July 27, 1946.
78. Draft Registration.
79. Find A Grave.
80. 1920 Census; 1930 Census.
81. *Aiken Standard*, April 8, 1949.
82. 1952–1954, 1957–1958 Columbia, SC, City Directory.
83. *Greenville News*, July 7, 1940.
84. *Greenville News*, September 2, 1940.
85. Draft Registration.
86. *Charlotte Observer*, June 20, 1987.
87. 1930 Census.
88. Find A Grave.
89. Marriage Records.
90. 1943, 1945 Columbia, SC, City Directory.
91. *Index-Journal*, May 9, 1941.
92. Draft Registration.
93. Social Security Claims.
94. 1930 Census.
95. *Greenville News*, April 28, 1933.
96. 1940 Census.
97. Draft Registration.
98. *Greenville News*, May 27, 1941.
99. *Greenville News*, April 21, 1942.
100. Enlistment Records.
101. *Times and Democrat*, March 21, 1942.
102. Enlistment Records.
103. "Program of Aristocratic Pigs Sponsored by Senior Class of O.H.S. Saturday Night," *Times and Democrat*, November 14, 1940; *Index-Journal*, November 29, 1940.
104. *Charlotte News*, October 4, 1943; *Greenville News*, July 31, 1945.
105. "Spartanburg Choir Personnel Listed," *Greenville News*, November 16, 1945.
106. *Gastonia Gazette*, June 11–12, 1947; *Gastonia Gazette*, June 19, 1947; *Gastonia Gazette*, December 27, 1947; *Gastonia Gazette*, February 12, 1948; *Gastonia Gazette*, April 27, 1948; *Gastonia Gazette*, December 18, 1948; *Gastonia Gazette*, December 20, 1948; *Gastonia Gazette*, November 10, 1951; *Gastonia Gazette*, December 24, 1954; *Gastonia Gazette*, February 7, 1955; *Gastonia Gazette*, February 23, 1955; *Gastonia Gazette*, March 19, 1955; *Gastonia Gazette*, March 29, 1955; *Gastonia Gazette*, April 8, 1955; *Gastonia Gazette*, September 2, 1955; *Gastonia Gazette*, November 17, 1955; *Gastonia Gazette*, May 23, 1956; *Gaffney Ledger*, September 4, 1956; *Statesville Record and Landmark*, April 21, 1962.
107. *Gastonia Gazette*, July 25, 1959.
108. *Gastonia Gazette*, August 18, 1968; *Asheville Citizen-Times*, June 19, 1983.
109. *Asheville Citizen-Times*, June 22,

Notes—Chapter Eight

1980; *Rocky Mount Telegram*, June 17, 1983.
110. Joe DePriest, "A Valentine so sweet, tender," *Charlotte Observer*, February 13, 2008.
111. *Greenville News*, September 10, 1942.
112. https://www.ncbi.nlm.nih.gov/pmc/articles/PMC6047296/; *Greenville News*, June 20–21, 1943; *Greenville News*, June 23-October 11, 1943; *Greenville News*, October 14-November 18, 1943; *Greenville News*, November 20, 27, 1943.
113. *Greenville News*, November 30, 1943, December 9, 1943, December 11, 1943-February 1, 1944.
114. *Index-Journal*, November 25, 1943; *Index-Journal*, December 2, 1943; *Index-Journal*, January 20, 1944; *Index-Journal*, February 17, 1944.
115. *Times and Democrat*, October 26, 1945; *Times and Democrat*, November 28, 1945.
116. Find A Grave.
117. 1930 Census.
118. Find A Grave.
119. Enlistment Records; *Greenville News*, March 6, 1942; Prisoners of War; *Aiken Standard*, May 25, 1945; Muster rolls.
120. 1957–8 Columbia, SC, City Directory.
121. Find A Grave.
122. Ahrens, 2013, p. 19.
123. 1930 Census; Draft Registration.
124. Pat Ahrens, *The Legacy of Two Legends: Snuffy Jenkins and Pappy Sherrill* (self-pub., 2013), p. 19.
125. Social Security Death Index.
126. 1940 Census; Draft Registration.
127. Della Coulter and John Rumble, "The Piedmont Tradition" and "Charlotte Country Music Story: A Sixty-Year Tradition," *The Charlotte Country Music Story* (Charlotte: NCAC Spirit Square Arts Center, 1985), pp. 20–21; Draft Registration; 1948–50 Columbia, SC, City Directory.
128. *Index-Journal*, December 4, 1945; *Greenville News*, January 24, 1946.
129. *Index-Journal*, July 27, 1946.
130. *Times and Democrat*, October 4, 1946.
131. Find A Grave; 1930 Census.
132. Draft Registration; *Times and Democrat*, March 14, 1946; *Times and Democrat*, April 5, 1946.
133. March 2000, interview, Al Wall.
134. *Times and Democrat*, January 6, 1947.
135. https://www.scstatehouse.gov/sess108_1989-1990/hj90/19900116.htm.
136. 1930 Census; 1940 Census.
137. https://www.scstatehouse.gov/sess108_1989-1990/hj90/19900116.htm.
138. *Times and Democrat*, March 13, 1947.
139. *Aiken Standard*, September 16, 1949; *Index-Journal*, January 18, 1950; *Index-Journal*, April 14, 1950; *Times and Democrat*, December 7, 1950; 1949–1950 Columbia, SC, City Directory; *Aiken Standard*, April 8, 1949.
140. 1950–1952, 1954, 1957–1958 Columbia, SC, City Directory; Florida Death Records.
141. 1951 Columbia, SC, City Directory; *Charlotte Observer*, June 20, 1987.
142. *Times and Democrat*, March 26, 28, 1947.
143. *Times and Democrat*, March 21, 1947.
144. *Times and Democrat*, January 15, 1948.
145. *Times and Democrat*, May 27–28, 1949; *Times and Democrat*, June 9–11, 1949.
146. *Times and Democrat*, March 26, 28, 1947.
147. *Florence News*, May 9, 1948.
148. *Florence News*, July 26, 1949; *Robesonian*, May 24, 1950.
149. https://www.scstatehouse.gov/sess106_1985-1986/hj86/19860312.htm; https://www.scstatehouse.gov/sess108_1989-1990/hj90/19900116.htm.
150. *Times and Democrat*, September 1, 1948; *Times and Democrat*, September 18, 1948; 1949 Columbia, SC, City Directory.
151. *Times and Democrat*, September 1, 1948; *Times and Democrat*, September 16, 1948.
152. 1948 Columbia, SC, City Directory.
153. 1951 Sarasota, FL, City Directory; *Tampa Tribune*, February 2–8, 1952.
154. *Tampa Tribune*, May 2, 1954.

Notes—Chapter Nine

155. *Orlando Evening Star*, February 28, 1963.
156. *Orlando Sentinel*, April 17, 1977.
157. 1951, Medical College, VCU, Yearbook; *Tampa Tribune*, September 22, 1952.
158. *Orlando Sentinel*, June 16, 1957.
159. Social Security Death Index.
160. *Orlando Sentinel*, July 27, 1951; *Tampa Tribune*, July 30, 1951; *Orlando Sentinel*, August 5, 1951.
161. *Orlando Sentinel*, August 17, 2017.

Chapter Nine

1. Gordon Castelnero and David L. Russell, *Earl Scruggs: Banjo Icon* (Lanham, MD: Rowman & Littlefield, 2017), pp. 13–15; Tom Ewing, *Bill Monroe* (Urbana: University of Illinois Press, 2018), pp. 129–131.
2. Neil V. Rosenberg, *Flatt & Scruggs: 1948–1959* (Bear Family Records, 1991).

Bibliography

Articles and Papers

Ahrens, Pat J. "Crazy Water Crystals and Its Union with Pioneer String Band Performers." *Bluegrass Unlimited*, August 2001, pp. 56–60.
Carlin, Bob. "Al Wall: One of Fisher Hendley's Boys." *The Old Time Herald* 10/12, August-September 2007, pp. 26–28.
Carlin, Bob. "High on the Hog: Fisher Hendley and the Aristocratic Pigs." *The Old Time Herald* 10/6, August-September 2006, pp. 16–33.
Carlin, Bob. "Roots of Earl and Snuffy." *Bluegrass Unlimited* 43/11, May 2009, pp. 54–60.
Grundy, Pamela. "We Always Tried to Be Good People: Respectability, Crazy Water Crystals, and Hillbilly Music on the Air, 1933–1935." *The Journal of American History*, March 1995, pp. 1591–1620.
Spottswood, Dick. "Happy Birthday, Wade!" *Bluegrass Unlimited*, January 1998, pp. 20, 53–55.
Trischka, Tony, and Bela Fleck. "Earl Scruggs." *Banjo NewsLetter*, November 2006, p. 15.
Unknown. "Speech" (made at meeting honoring Smith Hammett, Forest City, NC, November 20, 1980), courtesy Larry Hammett.

Books and Dissertations

Ahrens, Pat. *The Legacy of Two Legends: Snuffy Jenkins and Pappy Sherrill.* Self-published, 2013.
Bastin, Bruce. *Crying for the Carolinas.* London: Studio Vista, 1971.
Bastin, Bruce. *Red River Blues.* Urbana: University of Illinois Press, 1986.
Brooks, Roy. "Madison Monroe Brooks." *Heritage of Rutherford County North Carolina, Volume I.* Winston-Salem, NC: Hunter, 1984.
Carlin, Bob. *String Bands in the North Carolina Piedmont.* Jefferson, NC: McFarland, 2004.
Castelnero, Gordon, and David L. Russell. *Earl Scruggs: Banjo Icon.* Lanham, MD: Rowman & Littlefield, 2017.
The Chanticleer. Durham, NC: Trinity College, 1915.
Coulter, Della, and John Rumble. "The Piedmont Tradition" and "Charlotte Country Music Story: A Sixty-Year Tradition." *The Charlotte Country Music Story.* Charlotte: NCAC Spirit Square Arts Center, 1985.
Crazy Barn Dance and Crazy Bands. Charlotte: WBT, ca. 1934.
Ewing, Tom. *Bill Monroe.* Urbana: University of Illinois Press, 2018.
Ezell, Helen Hicks, and Helen Martin. *Stories of Our People.* Self-published, 1971.
Fowler, John Thomas. *Trotting Sally.* Spartanburg, SC: Kennedy Free Press, 2014.

Bibliography

Gillespie, Gail, and Wayne Martin. *Raleigh Fiddlers' Convention*. Raleigh, NC: Pinecone, 1990.
Jackson, George Pullen. *White Spirituals in the Southern Uplands*. Chapel Hill: University of North Carolina, 1933. Reprinted New York: Dover, 1965.
Logan, John R. *Sketches of the Broad River and King's Mountain Baptist Associations*. Shelby, NC: 1887. Quoted in Jackson, George Pullen. *White Spirituals in the Southern Uplands*. Chapel Hill: University of North Carolina, 1933. Reprinted New York: Dover, 1965.
Mazor, Barry. *Ralph Peer and The Making of Popular Roots Music*. Chicago: Chicago Review Press, 2015.
Meade, Guthrie T., Jr., et al. *Country Music Sources*. Chapel Hill: University of North Carolina Press, 2002.
Medical College Yearbook. Richmond: Virginia Commonwealth University, 1951.
Mills, Jim. *Gibson Mastertone*. Anaheim Hills, CA: Centerstream, 2009.
Rosenberg, Neil V. *Flatt & Scruggs: 1948–1959*. Bear Family Records, 1991.
Russell, Tony. *Country Music Records: A Discography, 1921–1942*. New York: Oxford University Press, 2004.
Scruggs, Earl. *Earl Scruggs and the 5-String Banjo*. Milwaukee: Hal Leonard, 2005.
Spottswood, Dick. *Banjo on the Mountain: Wade Mainer's First Hundred Years*. Jackson: University Press of Mississippi, 2010.
Tribe, Ivan M., and Barry McCloud, eds. "Tennessee Ramblers." *Definitive Country: The Ultimate Encyclopedia of Country Music and its Performers*. New York: Berkley, 1995.
Trischka, Tony, and Pete Wernick. *Masters of the 5-String Banjo*. New York: Oak Publications, 1988.
Wallace, Wesley. "Development of Broadcasting in North Carolina, 1922–1928." Dissertation, University of North Carolina–Chapel Hill, 1962. Summary available online: http://www.unc.edu/~bsemonch/radio.html.

Birth and Death Records, City Directories and Other Public Records

Birth and Death Records

Cleveland County, NC, Birth Records, 9/769 and 9/770
Cleveland County, NC Death Collection, 1908–1996
Florida Death Records
North Carolina Birth Index
North Carolina Death Collection, 1908–1996
Rutherford County, NC, Birth index, 1/635
Social Security Applications and Death Indexes

City Directories

Anderson, SC: 1931
Charlotte, NC: 1935–1936, 1945
Columbia, SC: 1943, 1945, 1948–1954, 1957–1958
Gaffney, SC: 1921, 1958
Gastonia, NC: 1936
Greenville, SC: 1941, 1954
Kannapolis, NC: 1950–1951, 1953, 1956–1957
Sarasota, FL: 1951
Spartanburg, SC: 1903, 1905, 1908, 1910–1911, 1913, 1916

Bibliography

Other Public Records

Appointments of Postmasters, October 16, 1893; July 1, 1895
Cleveland County, NC Marriage Records
Cleveland County, NC Vital Statistics, 18/313
Draft Registration
Passenger List, U.S. Army
Tax Rolls, Fannin County, TX, 1888, 1891, 1894
U.S. Census, 1860–1940.
U.S. Veterans Gravesites, ca. 1775–2006
World War II Army Enlistment Records, 1938–1946

Interviews

All interviews conducted by the author.
Brady, Doris Hammett, April 20, 2007.
Camp, Patricia, phone, April 29, 2007, June 11, 2007.
Deaton, Mrs., phone, April 27, 2007.
Hammett, Jesse, phone, January 12, 2007; in person, March 13, 2007.
Hammett, Larry, January 2007.
Hammett, Ronald, phone, January 14, 2007.
Harrington, Jack, 2005.
Hutchins, George, December 6, 2006.
McKee, Charles Robert, phone, April 21, 2007.
Permar, Hellen, various, 2006–2007.
Ramsey, Tommy, phone, April 2, 2007.
Smith, Lois Melton, phone, April 20, 2007.
Wall, Al, March 2000.
Wheless family, 2005.
Withrow, Jenna, June 12, 2007.

Newspapers

Aiken Standard, 1937–1940, 1945, 1949
Akron Beacon Journal, 1933
Albemarle Press, 1923, 1925
Asheville Citizen-Times, 1922, 1930–1935, 1980, 1983
Asheville Gazette-News, 1911
Bee, 1941
Burlington Times-News, 1934
Charlotte News, 1906, 1926, 1929–1938, 1940, 1943
Charlotte Observer, 1905, 1907, 1909, 1911–1913, 1919–1920, 1923, 1925, 1928–1935, 1939, 1946, 1961, 1968, 1971–1972, 1974–1975, 1977, 1984, 1986–1987, 1989, 1993, 2000–2001, 2003–2005, 2007–2008, 2012
Cheraw Chronicle, 1922
Cherokee Times, 1923–1925, 1928
Chesnee Times, 1954
Cleveland Star, 1902–1903, 1919, 1921, 1923
Concord Times, 1912
Concord Tribune, 1916
Courier-Journal, 1936
Daily Phoenix, 1873
Daily Tar Heel, 1952

Bibliography

Desert Sun, 1993
digitalnc.org/collections/newspapers/
Dispatch-News, 1910
Durham Recorder, 1910
Enterprise, 1906, 1911–1912, 1917
Florence News, 1948–1949
Foothills View, 1984
Gaffney Ledger, 1895, 1897–1903, 1905–1938, 1940, 1943–1947, 1950, 1954–1956, 1958, 1960, 1962, 1966, 1968, 1971, 1981, 1984, 2004, 2006, 2011
Gastonia Gazette, 1905, 1926, 1947–1948, 1951, 1954–1956, 1959, 1968
Greenville News, 1914, 1919, 1927, 1929–1931, 1933, 1935–1946, 1948–1949, 1951, 1954, 1957, 1959, 1971, 1978, 1980, 2000
Hickory Democrat, 1911
Highlander, 1905 or 1908
Index-Journal, 1937–1941, 1943–1946, 1950
Kingston Daily Freeman, 1934
Messenger and Intelligencer, 1910–1911, 1917–1918, 1920–1923
Miami News, 1931
Newberry Weekly Herald, 1909
News, 1942
News and Observer, 1910–1911, 1914, 1925, 1930, 1933, 1989
News-Herald, 1914
Newspapers.com
Orlando Evening Star, 1963
Orlando Sentinel, 1951, 1957, 1977, 2017
Oxford Public Ledger, 1921
Pensacola News Journal, 1992
Raleigh Times, 1911
Robesonian, 1931, 1934, 1950
Rocky Mount Telegram, 1983
Rowan Record, 1918
Rutherford Banner, 1882
Rutherfordton Tribune, 1901
St. Louis Post-Dispatch, 1933
Salisbury Daily Times, 1942
Salisbury Evening Post, 1914, 1918
Shelby Star, 1935, 1945, 1980, 1985, 2003, 2006
Spartanburg Herald, 1942
Spartanburg Herald-Journal, 1960, 1980
Stanly News, 1920
Stanly News-Herald, 1921
Statesville Record and Landmark, 1929, 1931–1932, 1934, 1950, 1961–1962
Staunton News-Leader, 1941
Sun, 1905
Tampa Tribune, 1951–1952, 1954
Times and Democrat, 1930, 1938–1940, 1942, 1945–1950, 1947
Times Union, 1933
Times-Dispatch, 1940–1941
Towawanda News, 1941
Trinity Chronicle, 1914–1915
Watchman and Southron, 1916
Wilmington Morning Star, 1914
Yorkville Enquirer, 1867, 1870, 1873, 1876, 1881, 1891, 1893, 1896–1897, 1900–1901, 1906, 1908–1909, 1911–1913, 1915, 1919, 1921–1922

Bibliography

Recordings

Hartford, John. "The Boys From North Carolina." 1992. John Hartford Music, BMI. Track 8 on *Goin' Back to Dixie*. Small Dog A-Barkin,' compact disc.

Watson, Doc, and Clarence Ashley. "Hick's [sic] Farewell." 1994. Disc 2/track 10 on *Original Folkways Recordings, 1960–1962*. Smithsonian-Folkways Recordings, compact disc.

Websites

45worlds.com, including:
http://www.45worlds.com/78rpm/artist/the-broome-brothers
http://www.45worlds.com/78rpm/record/nc114370us
http://www.45worlds.com/78rpm/record/nc214265us
Ancestry.com, including:
Ancestry.com/cgi-bin/igm.cgi?op=GET&db=bigwills&id=I37918
http://awtc.http://www.http://www.ancestry.com/cgi-bin/igm.cgi?op=GET&db=bigwills&id=I37918
http://awtc.http://www.http://www.ancestry.com/cgi-bin/igm.cgi?op=GET&db=bigwills&id=I37918
Hendrix, Hubert, *Herald*, clipping
Howell Family Tree, Marc Howell
Howell, Marc, message, May 23, 2020, Ancestry
Nancy-Summer Ezell, Larry Elmore, July 23, 2003
Gencircles.com, including:
http://www.gencircles.com/users/latham-hendrix/1/data/181
http://www.gencircles.com/users/latham-hendrix/1/data/193
http://www.gencircles.com/users/latham-hendrix/1/data/21
IMDB.com, including:
https://www.imdb.com/name/nm0366940/bio?ref_=nm_ov_bio_sm
Rfci.net, including:
http://www.rfci.net/wdfloyd/cemb11.html
http://www.rfci.net/wdfloyd/cemb11.html
Scstatehouse.gov, including:
https://www.scstatehouse.gov/sess106_1985-1986/hj86/19860312.htm
https://www.scstatehouse.gov/sess108_1989-1990/hj90/19900116.htm
Wikipedia, including:
http://www1.cpdl.org/wiki/index.php/Berryman_Hicks
https://en.wikipedia.org/wiki/Carolina_Power_%26_Light_Company
https://en.wikipedia.org/wiki/The_Christian_Harmony
http://tunearch.org/wiki/Annotation:Guard_House_(The)
YouTube, including:
https://www.youtube.com/watch?v=As_84Cd3T6I
https://www.youtube.com/watch?v=gsY4sHeEVKw
https://www.youtube.com/watch?v=SWAVd2CYU5I
https://www.youtube.com/watch?v=fnAl2mUDalc

Other Websites

Discogs.com
Find A Grave.com
Folkstreams.net
NCPedia.org

Bibliography

http://banjobasics.julieferris.com/BANJOPLAYERS/2.html
http://mtruhama.com/history/
http://www.hillbilly-music.com/groups/story/index.php?groupid=10921
https://books.google.com/books?id=RAEEAAAAMBAJ&pg=PA33&lpg=PA33&dq=broome+bros%2Bcrystal+records&source=bl&ots=vU8_YogCK0&sig=ACfU3U0GUPh2oxZT8KEg4IXDIvsJS5cU-w&hl=en&sa=X&ved=2ahUKEwi3n5-psdfpAhVPSN8KHb54Dz0Q6AEwA3oECAYQAQ#v=onepage&q=broome%20bros%2Bcrystal%20records&f=false
https://lyricsplayground.com/alpha/songs/h/hedhavetogetundergetoutandgetunder.html
https://musicpolitics.as.ua.edu/projects/primary-source-projects/were-coming-fodder-abraham-were-coming-in-a-horn-a-civil-war-song-parody/
https://petermoruzzi.com/2011/05/22/nucky-and-skinnys-atlantic-city/
https://upstatebusinessjournal.com/events/balentine-packing-company/
https://www.encyclopedia.com/women/encyclopedias-almanacs-transcripts-and-maps/glover-julia-1779–1850
https://www.lostcolleges.com/rutherford-college
https://www.ncbi.nlm.nih.gov/pmc/articles/PMC6047296/
https://www.scpictureproject.org/cherokee-county/zeno-hicks-house.html
https://www.wm.edu/sites/wmcar/research/hopewellarch/history/index.php
https://itunes.apple.com/us/artist/cecil-campbell-his-tennessee-ramblers/id269255920
https://babel.hathitrust.org/cgi/pt?id=mdp.39015096538346&view=1up&seq=1
https://levysheetmusic.mse.jhu.edu/collection/061/033
http://www.joemorley.co.uk/pages/cover.htm
https://www.americanantiquarian.org/thomasballads/items/show/252

Index

Numbers in ***bold italics*** indicate pages with illustrations

Allen, Shelley Kaylor "Shell" *107*, 115–*117*, *118–119*
Allen, Worth T. 89–90
Andrews, William Johnston "Buck" 19, 32

Ballard, C.S. 62
Ballard, Ray Ezra 90
Barrier, Hugh 90
Baucom, Luther "Luke" 127
Bennett, "Handsome" Bill 132–133
Bennett, Olive Edna McDaniel 27–28
Bennett, "Red" 151
Berry, George 151, *152*
Bishop, Johnnie 156
Blackwell, Charlie Acey "Asa" Harris 30
Blackwell, Coy Fletcher 57, 62
Blackwell, Ethel Isabella Strain 27, 30
Blackwell, Noble Jackson 27, 29
Blair, William John "Horse Thief Harry" *107*, 109–*110*, *111*
Bowers, Cecil Augustine 151–*152*, 153, 156–*157*, 158–*159*
Bradley, Hampton Lorance "Little Boy Blue" *132*–133, 137, 139–140, 142, *144*, 157–*158*
Brooks, Madison Monroe "Matt" 65–67
Brooks, Rex 65–*66*, 67, *70*, 73–74, 163
Broome, Joe Neal *107*, 112, 114–115
Broome, Joseph Henry *107*, 112
Broome, Joseph Homer *107*, 112
Broome, Leroy "Lee Roy" *107*, 112–*113*, 114–115
Broome, Marshall Ray *107*, 112–*113*, *114*–115
Broome, Robert Henry *107*, 112
Butler, Dennis 27
Butler, Solon Beam 27

Campbell, Cecil Robert "Curley" *107*, 109–*110*, *111*
Carpenter, Hildreth Boyden 130
Carver, Willie *155*–156

Casey, Claude 114
Chandler, Hosea Clarence *150*–152
Chapman, Buddy 141
Cole, Gowan Wesley 89–90
Colvard, James J. "Jimmie" *144*
Comer, Sylvanus C. "Vaney" 27, 29–30
Compton, Harold 133
Crawford, Ed *12*, *14*, *17*
Crawford, Robert *12*, *14*, *17*
Crotts, Porter 27
Crow, Mack 41, 102–103
Crowell, John 91
Crowell, T.F. 91

Dayvault, Adolphus Wilson "Dolph" 115–116, *118–119*
Dayvault, Carl Henderson *107*, 116–*117*, *118–119*
DeStaffino, Eugene 23
DeStaffino, Frederick Lewis 22–23
DeStaffino, Hattie Belle Floyd 23
DeStaffino, Melrose 23
Dixon, Dorsey *107*, 127
Dixon, Howard *107*, 127

Edminister, V.C. *94*–96
Eidson, James William 145–146
Eudy, Claude 97–*98*

Fincher, H.T. *107*
Fincher, James Wesley 105, *107*, 125, 127–128
Fisher, Coley *70*–71
Flatt, Lester 1–2, 158, 163
Fox, Daniel Leroy 55
Fox, John Richard 53–56, 61–62
Furr, Marvin Deamus *91*, *92*–93
Furr, Prince Alexander 90–*91*, *92*–93
Furr, Rayvon Elbert *91*, *92*–93
Furr, Thaddeus Alexander *91*, *92*–93
Furr, William Belvin "Pee Wee" 90–*91*, *92*–93

Index

Gaffney, Carl Leonard 39
Gaffney, Samuel Shelton 20, 36–*37*, *38*–39, 44, 47, 52, 58
Gallman, Arthur Vanderbilt "Vannie" 62
Gallman, Joseph Wallace 62
Gaston, Henry Lewis 143–*144*, *147*–148
Gillette, "Montana" Jack 112
Goforth, Euphra Frodie McCraw 69
Goodman, Arthur *107*, *117*–118
Goodwin, Gene Randolph *152*–153, *154*, 156, 158
Gordon, Welford
Grady, Jim *70*–71
Grady, Will *70*–71
Greene, George *26*
Griffith, Dr. S.H. 11
Guthrie, Joseph Buren 56–58, 60

Hall, Jay Hugh 153
Hammett, Howard Luke 73
Hammett, James Nathan 73
Hammett, Jessie Smith 25, 65, 67–*68*, 69–*70*, 71–74, 163
Hammett, John Martin "Mart" 68
Hammett, Ruby 73
Hammett, Tommy Thirston 3, 73
Hamrick, Coy *71*–72
Harrington, Edwin Jackson "Jack" 120, 122–*123*, 124
Harris, Daniel Jefferson 96–*97*, *98*
Hartman, Dick *107*, 109–*110*, *111*
Harvey, Rast 153
Hatley, Earl Alonzo 90, 97–*98*, 104, *107*
Hatley, Spencer Bruin 97–*98*
Haynes, Luther Gordon *26*, 65
Hendley, Graham Fisher *94*, 96, *135*, 137, 140, *144*, *147*–149, 153, 160–161
Hendley, James W. "Squire Jim" 77
Hendley, Walter Fisher 65, 75–*79*, 80–*81*, 82–*88*, 89–*94*, 95–*98*, 99–*100*, 101–*103*, 104, *107*–108, 112, 116, 120, 125–*126*, 127–*130*, *131*–*132*, *133*–*134*, 136–*138*, *139*, *141*–*144*, 145–*147*, 148–149, *150*–151, *152*–153, 156–*157*, 159–*160*, 161, 163
Hendley, William Eugene 77
Hensley, Reese 55, 62
Hicks, Berriman Theodore 10–*12*, 13–*14*
Hicks, the Rev. Berryman Theodore 6–8
Hicks, Duke Wellington 9, 11
Hicks, Dr. Henry Zeno *6*, *10*–12, 13–*14*, 15
Hicks, Lola 13, 16–17
Hicks, Mary Elizabeth *12*–13
Hicks, Myra Leanora "Nora" 13–*14*,
Hicks, Nancy Elizabeth McKinney *10*, 13
Hicks, Richard Henry 8
Hicks, Romeo 8–9
Hicks, Volney Charles *9*, 11
Hicks, Dr. William Richard 11, *12*–14, 15–*17*

Hildreth, Blake Eason 120–*121*, 122–123
Hildreth, James Dunlap 122–123
Hildreth, Joseph Leroy 123
Hileman, John Franklin 116
Howell, Conrad Therian *94*–96
Howell, James (Mc)Coy *94*–*96*, 97
Hudson, DeWitt 91

Ingold, Helen "Miss Honey" Burgess 145, *150*, *158*
Ingold, "Hillbilly" John Martin 144–145, *147*, *150*–151, 157–*158*
Irvin, Smith "Smitty" 73
Ivydale, Colin 141

Jackson, Ode *71*–72
Jackson, Paul *71*–72
Janssen, "Zeb" 129–*130*
Jenkins, Dennis E. *107*, 127
Jenkins, DeWitt "Snuffy" 3, 58, 65, 67, 70, 74, *107*, 127, 152
Jenkins, Verl *66*, *107*, 127
Johnson, Clifford 156
Johnson, John 70

Kirby, Fred 114
Krimminger, Wade Hampton 116

LaFrance, Franklin 158
Lear, David 120–*121*
Lenzer, Joseph "Elmer" 129–*130*
Lindsey, Charles 153
Love, "Daddy" John 125, *127*
Lowder, Hoyle 90

Mabry, Frank 90
Mainer, Faye 153
Mainer, Joseph Emmett *107*, 124–*126*, 127, 153
Mainer, Wade Eckhart *107*, 124–*126*, 127, 139, 153
Martin, Alfred David 56–*58*, *60*–*61*, 62, 99
Martin, Archie Durham 62
Martin, Dillard Perry Lemon *12*–*13*, *14*–15
Martin, Elmer 158
Mayberry, Preston Lee "Press" 89–90
McCaskill, Jenny *122*
McCraw, John C. 69
McCraw, Lawson Davis 68–69, 74
McCraw, Rector Roland "Rex" 71
McDaniel, Bernard Clement "Big Mac" *70*–*71*
McDaniel, Dewey 24–25, *70*–*71*
McDaniel, Estelle Strain *27*–*28*
McDaniel, Floyd 158
McDaniel, Henry Brooks *27*–*28*, 32

Index

McDaniel, Martha Wilma 27
McDaniel, Otho "Otis" A. 27–*28*
McKee, "Big" George A. *26*
McKee, Charlie Andrew *26*
McKee, George William *26*
McKee, Samuel Lee *26*
McKinney, Grady 27
Medford, M.P. 127
Medlin, Julian Leonard "Greasy" 151–152, 158–*159*
Melton, Charles 27
Melton, Claudius 27
Miller, Lost John 162
Monroe, Bill 1–2, 129–130, 153, 162–163
Moody, Clyde 153
Moore, Herman 61
Morris, Claude Edward "Zeke" 125, *127*, 139
Morris, Fred "Happy" *111*–112
Morris, Lee 120–*121*
Mullins, George "Trotting Sally" 4

Newton, Clete 27

Parker, Charles Monroe "Charlie" 35–36, 38–*39*, 41–42, 44–53, 55, 58, 74, 163
Parker, Oris B. 42, 60–61
Parker, Robert Otto 36, 39–*40*, 41–43,
Patrick, Ralph Edward 53–54, 57, 61–62
Patterson, "Curley" 147, *150*
Peer, Ralph 101–102
Permar, Margaret Hellen Hendley Rogers 76, 82, 95, 108, *135*, 137, *140*, *144*, *147*–149, 153, 161
Plexico, Alan Feemster 31–32
Poplin, Sam Wesley 97, *107*, *132*, *136*–137, *139*, 142–143
Price, Dewey 151, 153

Rednour, Emerson Orley "Black Sheep" 133
Richardson, Don 34
Rinzler, Ralph 2
Robinson, John Joseph Jefferson 30–32
Robinson, "Uncle" Joe 124
Robinson, Zeke *107*, 124
Roper, "Cousin" Ezra Leroy *132*–133, 135–137, 140–*141*, *142*–143, *144*, *147*, 157–*158*
Ross, John Wyles, Jr. 22, 32–*34*, 35–36, 39, 42–47, 50, 52, 55, 58, *68*–69
Ruff, Larry 156
Ruppe, Donnie Clifton 70
Russell, Fred Tyler 97–*98*, *107*, 127
Russell, George 90
Russell, James 97–*98*, *107*, 127

Sauceman, Carl *155*–156
Sauceman, J.P. *155*–156
Scruggs, Earl Eugene 1–5, 25, 44, 48, 50, 65, 67, 70, 72–75, 127, 156, 162–163

Scruggs, George Elam 73
Scruggs, Junius Emmett "Junie" 49, 73–74
Scruggs, Louise 2
Sherrill, Homer Lee "Pappy" 127, 153
Shields, Phillip 74
Shippers, "Zeke" 129–*130*
Shumate, Jim 162
Simpson, Richard Clyde 90
Sims, Benny *155*–156
Skiles, Blackie 114
Small, Marshall Albert 96–97, 102
Smart, Solon David *71*
Smith, Arthur "Guitar Boogie" 141, 153
Smith, Cordell *107*
Smith, Eddie *130*
Smith, Frank 90
Smith, Mr. and Mrs. Leroy *107*, 127
Smith, Robert Lee "Bob" 143–*144*, *147*, 151, 157–*158*
Sowers, Ken 153
Sprouse, Erston 53–54, 61
Stacy, Edgar Lionel 41
Stewart, George Dixon "Baby Ray" *132*–133, *136*, 140–*143*, 146
Stewart, Sybil Imogene "Sue" Moore 140
Strain, James Newton Butler "Jimmy" 27–*29*, 32
Strain, Mamie "Nora" Oceola Comer 29
Strain, Samuel Jefferson 27, *29*–30
Summey, Reid 127
Suther, Harue Franklin *107*, *117*–118, *119*

Thompson, Claude 56–57, 61–62
Thompson, Glenn Elbert 56–57, 61
Thompson, Grover "Doodly Squat" 90
Thornburg, Raymond L. *107*, *118*–119

Waddill/Waddell, Adolphus A. "Dolph" 120
Waddill/Waddell, John Birdson 120
Wade, George 127
Walker, William "Singing Billy" 7–8, 13
Wall, Alvin Jerome "Slim" 151–*152*, 153, *155*–157
Watson, Doc 7
Watts, Arthur "Sandy" 151–152
Weaver, Lawrence Eular 46–47, 58, 60
Westrope, Gordon 23–*24*
Wheless, Arthur Benjamin 120
Wheless, Dewitt Talmadge 119–*121*, 123–124
Wheless, John Washington 120
Whisnant, Johnny 27
Whitaker, Charles Zack 19, 32
White, Milton Thompson 120–*121*, 122
Whitter, Henry 101–102
Wilkie, Grady [Lee] *71*–72

Index

Williams, Hayes *94*–96
Withrow, Grady 24
Withrow, Julius Plato Durham 23–24, 26
Whitley, Tom G. 91
Wolfe, Kenneth "Pappy" *107*, 109–*110*, *111*

Woolbright, George Mack 36, 39, 44–56, 58, 61–*64*, 65, 74, 163
Wooten, Art 153

Young, Erskine 53–54, 61

www.ingramcontent.com/pod-product-compliance
Ingram Content Group UK Ltd.
Pitfield, Milton Keynes, MK11 3LW, UK
UKHW021845140426
5217IPUK00022B/1605